Unrecognized States and Secession in the 21st Century

Martin Riegl · Bohumil Doboš
Editors

Unrecognized States and Secession in the 21st Century

Springer

Editors
Martin Riegl
Institute of Political Studies
Charles University
Prague
Czech Republic

Bohumil Doboš
Institute of Political Studies
Charles University
Prague
Czech Republic

ISBN 978-3-319-56912-3   ISBN 978-3-319-56913-0   (eBook)
DOI 10.1007/978-3-319-56913-0

Library of Congress Control Number: 2017939086

© Springer International Publishing AG 2017
This work is subject to copyright. All rights are reserved by the Publisher, whether the whole or part of the material is concerned, specifically the rights of translation, reprinting, reuse of illustrations, recitation, broadcasting, reproduction on microfilms or in any other physical way, and transmission or information storage and retrieval, electronic adaptation, computer software, or by similar or dissimilar methodology now known or hereafter developed.
The use of general descriptive names, registered names, trademarks, service marks, etc. in this publication does not imply, even in the absence of a specific statement, that such names are exempt from the relevant protective laws and regulations and therefore free for general use.
The publisher, the authors and the editors are safe to assume that the advice and information in this book are believed to be true and accurate at the date of publication. Neither the publisher nor the authors or the editors give a warranty, express or implied, with respect to the material contained herein or for any errors or omissions that may have been made. The publisher remains neutral with regard to jurisdictional claims in published maps and institutional affiliations.

Printed on acid-free paper

This Springer imprint is published by Springer Nature
The registered company is Springer International Publishing AG
The registered company address is: Gewerbestrasse 11, 6330 Cham, Switzerland

Preface

The issue of international recognition and secession is one of the key topics within the framework of the contemporary geopolitical research. As such, it was also one of the key topics studied by us and the colleagues at our institute since the beginning of our geopolitical research. In November 2015, we decided that it would be definitely worth the time and effort to dedicate a scholarly monograph to the various facets and aspects of this issue; thus, we decided to bring experts from around the world together to share their research with us and with the wider academic community. We were and still are very happy with the response this call for papers has generated. Based on these contributions of our colleagues and some additional research added later, we are finally able to bring you this volume presenting the contemporary topics of research on the unrecognized states and secession in general. We were lucky enough not only to get contribution from the foremost experts in the field such as Nina Caspersen or Mikulas Fabry but also to get contribution from experts dealing with some of the less known but still very interesting topics like the Bougainville issue presented by Vladimír Baar.

The selection of the topic is important for one other reason. Since the end of the Cold War and the diminishing likelihood of the global nuclear annihilation, the focus of the international community and, subsequently, the academia turned to other issues. One of the most prominent of these is the tension between the principle of territorial integrity and the right of self-determination in the context of the post-Second World War delegitimization of war as a means of political conduct. This topic has been brought up repeatedly, as evident from cases like the dissolution of Yugoslavia, recognition of East Timor and South Sudan, or more recently in the attempts to utilize the self-determination principle in places such as Eastern Ukraine and Kurdistan. Clearly, the topic is not going away, and the proper understanding of the issue is crucial for better grasp on these important issues. This is one of the main aims not only of this book but also of the whole geopolitical research as exemplified by the Geopolitical Studies Research Centre at the Institute of Political Studies, Faculty of Social Sciences, Charles University, from which the Editors of this volume originate.

We would also like use the opportunity to thank all the people that helped make this book happen. First of all, we thank the authors that took the time to share with us their top research, without which this work as we present it to you would not exist. Second, it is necessary to thank the Institute of Political Studies not only for institutional support as the book was financed by the Charles University Research Development Schemes, programme PROGRES Q18—Social sciences: from multidisciplinary to interdisciplinary, but also to Annual of Language & Politics and Politics of Identity journal that allowed us to share part of the papers published by the institution in this book. Third, we thank our colleague Jan Bečka for language consultations that helped us in a big way. Next, we would like to thank all those who support the geopolitical research at our institute, be it people from the Faculty in general, our students, or our colleagues that did not publish in this volume but provide stimulating research that helps the entire department to move forward. Last but not least, we cannot omit the readers of this volume without whom the whole publishing process would be pointless. We hope that this volume will provide you with a stimulating look at the contemporary research regarding the two main issues raised in the title—unrecognized states and secession.

Prague, Czech Republic
Martin Riegl
Bohumil Doboš

Contents

Introduction: Secession and Recognition
in the Twenty-first Century 1
Eiki Berg, Martin Riegl and Bohumil Doboš

Part I Theoretical Perspectives

Making Peace with De Facto States............................. 11
Nina Caspersen

Unrecognized States and National Identity 23
Mikulas Fabry

Ontological Security of the Post-Soviet de Facto States 35
Urban Jakša

Contemporary Referendum on Independence (RI) and Linguistic
Aspects of an Intelligible Referendum Question (RQ) 53
Přemysl Rosůlek

(Super)Power Rule: Comparative Analysis of Parent States 85
Martin Riegl and Bohumil Doboš

Part II Case Studies

Political Institutions in the Post-Soviet De Facto States
in Comparison: Abkhazia and Nagorno-Karabakh 111
Vincenc Kopeček

Iran's Problems with Territorial Non-state Actors: A Case
Study of Sistan and Balochistan................................ 137
Robert Czulda

Kurdistan Region's Quest for Independent Statehood: Trapped
in Internal and Geopolitical Rivalries 153
Martin Riegl, Bohumil Doboš, Jakub Landovský and Shmuel Bar

Bougainville: From Conflict to Independence Under the Law? 169
Vladimír Baar

The Right to Self-determination or Inviolability of Borders in the Horn of Africa? The African Union Approach 187
Kateřina Rudincová

Long Way to Recognition: Challenges Facing the European "Newborn" from the 2015 Perspective 205
Jan Bečka

Conclusion: Future of International Recognition? 223
Martin Riegl and Bohumil Doboš

Editors and Contributors

About the Editors

Martin Riegl was born in 1980. He currently lectures at the Institute of Political Studies of Faculty of Social Sciences, Charles University. He graduated in 2010 at Faculty of Social Sciences, Charles University (programme Political Science), where he successfully finished doctoral studies in the field of political geography. Since 2008, he has been lecturing at the Department of Political Science (FSS, UK). His academic research is focused on the institution of the sovereign state, geopolitics of political disintegration, secession, unrecognized states, and state failure. He actively participated at scientific conferences and workshops in the Czech Republic, Slovakia, Germany, Belgium, Poland, UK, Taiwan etc.

Bohumil Doboš is a Ph.D. student at the Institute of Political Studies, Faculty of Social Sciences, Charles University. His research interest lies in areas of post-Westphalian geopolitics, New Middle Age theory, geopolitical anomalies, geopolitics of violent non-state actors, and astropolitics. He is also a coordinator of the Geopolitical Studies Research Centre at the same institute and employee at the Ministry of Defence of the Czech republic—Defence Policy and Strategy Division.

Contributors

Shmuel Bar Institute of Policy and Strategy, Herzliya, Israel

Vladimír Baar University of Ostrava, Ostrava, Czechia

Jan Bečka Faculty of Social Sciences, Institute of International Studies, Charles University, Prague, Czech Republic

Eiki Berg University of Tartu, Tartu, Estonia

Nina Caspersen University of York, York, UK

Robert Czulda University of Lodz, Lodz, Poland

Bohumil Doboš Faculty of Social Sciences, Institute of Political Studies, Charles University, Prague, Czech Republic

Mikulas Fabry Sam Nunn School of International Affairs, Georgia Institute of Technology, Atlanta, USA

Urban Jakša University of York, York, UK

Vincenc Kopeček University of Ostrava, Ostrava, Czech Republic

Jakub Landovský Faculty of Social Sciences, Institute of Political Studies, Charles University, Prague, Czech Republic

Martin Riegl Faculty of Social Sciences, Institute of Political Studies, Charles University, Prague, Czech Republic

Přemysl Rosůlek Department of Political Science and International Relations, Faculty of Arts and Humanities, University of West Bohemia, Pilsen, Czech Republic

Kateřina Rudincová Department of Geography, Faculty of Science, Humanities and Education, Technical University of Liberec, Liberec, Czech Republic

Introduction: Secession and Recognition in the Twenty-first Century

Eiki Berg, Martin Riegl and Bohumil Doboš

Questions of identity, secession and (international) recognition are inherently interconnected. This is relevant especially nowadays, when the number of independent recognized states has grown to over one hundred and ninety and many other territories are striving for entering the club. Most of them have been created through decolonization and devolution processes, yet secessionism as an instrumental way to independent statehood has recently gained more prominence because of incompatibility of facts and norms that had led to increased fragmentation of world political structures.

Fragmentation has subverted the nation-state from within, raising complicated questions about conditions under which groups with different identities can peacefully coexist as well as the criteria for rightful secession (Coppieters and Sakwa 2003). In many secessionist cases, it would be too short-sighted to advocate self-determination of a people within the existing state. Indeed, there is no legal

---

The shortened version of this chapter appeared in The Annual of Language & Language of Politics and Identity (2016), 10, 3–5. This article is updated and reprinted with permission from the copyright holders.

This chapter is dedicated to the Charles University Research Development Schemes, programme PROGRES Q18—Social sciences: from multidisciplinary to interdisciplinary.

E. Berg
University of Tartu, Tartu, Estonia
e-mail: eiki.berg@ut.ee

M. Riegl · B. Doboš (✉)
Faculty of Social Sciences, Institute of Political Studies,
Charles University, Prague, Czech Republic
e-mail: bohumil.dobos@gmail.com

M. Riegl
e-mail: martinriegl@email.cz

basis for a right to self-determination outside the colonial context (Kirchner 2015; Marxsen 2015), but attempted secessions are not illegal either since sub-state entities are not subjects of international law. As a result, international community remains simply hostile to it while demonstrating this by non-recognition.

There is no agreement as to the status of the emerged state-like entities and the most appropriate way to deal with them (Grant 1999; Crawford 2007; Zaum 2007). De facto state is a manifestation of this kind of legal ambiguity, a collision of internal and external aspects of sovereignty which has produced "empty spaces" that legally do not exist. Due to widespread non-recognition, it is a non-qualifying sovereignty aspirant which has been left behind the door of the most privileged club of international society. If this is so, however, then what explains their continuous struggle for extended version of self-government? How have these pathological irregularities been exploited as tools of the international politics? Is strong self-awareness a necessary precondition for successful secessionist mobilization and break-up of the parent state? How do these entities respond to the needs of their population? These and other questions stand at the forefront of any serious discussion of any of the above-mentioned topics.

The issue of de facto states (see more in Pegg 1998) [also known as unrecognized, separatist, or contested states (Lynch 2004; Geldenhuys 2009; Caspersen 2011; Stansfield and Harvey 2011)] is a part of larger research focus approximately since the end of 1990s. In the post-Cold War world that is lacking the immediate threat of potentially apocalyptic bipolar nuclear clash questions of intrastate conflicts, secession, self-determination, recognition, and identity capture the spotlights. Challenged binary nature of geopolitics and recognition (state/no state) (Walter et al. 2014: 18) is especially well exemplified by these, in the Westphalian system irregular, entities. Together with the emerging territorial non-state actors and failed states, the de facto states present the new face of geopolitics—more complex and arguably establishing new kind of world order. Understanding the nature of these entities thus enables us to better comprehend the nature of the contemporary international relations and geopolitics.

The issue of the de facto states is, however, not only part of a closed academic debate but is of major importance for the practice of international politics as well. One case in point is the heated and never-ending debate over the Kosovo issue. Despite the fact that the entity achieved de facto separation from Serbia and quasi-independence accompanied by partial international recognition, it remains outside the framework of the United Nations and is a source of heated debates between its Western backers and Russia. Kosovo issue returned to the media headlines in relation to the recent fighting in Ukraine as Russian foreign policy attempted to justify its annexation of Crimea by utilizing the Kosovo precedent as *sui generis* case. Similar justification is also to be found in other post-Soviet so-called frozen conflicts (despite these being warmed up occasionally as seen in short April armed clash of 2016 over Nagorno-Karabakh)—2008 recognition of Abkhazia and South Ossetia, or unconditional support for secessionist bids in Donetsk and Lugansk People's Republics in eastern Ukraine.

But the topics of the international recognition, secessionism, and de facto statehood are not only related to the post-Soviet region. Strong secessionist movements spread through the Western Europe, be it (after Brexit vote reinvigorated) Scottish movement or long-term Catalonian call for independence. Canada faces long-term secessionist tendencies from Francophone Quebec province. African continent faces many issues related to the topic ranging from the Western Saharan quest for full international recognition, Somaliland's attempt to become a part of the international community, and South Sudan's successful quest for statehood, to secessionist tendencies in places like Azawad. The Middle East faces long-term problem of dealing with the Palestinian issue or future status of the Kurdish territories. East Asian politics is to a large degree influenced by the disagreement over the position of the Republic of China (Taiwan). Bougainville successfully forced through a future independence referendum, while inside the same region, East Timor became the first territory to secede from Indonesia. This is not mentioning movements in places such as India (most prominently Kashmir), Iran, or the Zanzibar issue. The issue, as evident, is widespread ranging from historical crises like the Yugoslavian dissolution to contemporary movements all around the globe.

This volume presents important theoretical perspectives related to the contemporary discussion over de facto states (issues of identity, referendum wording, or role of power politics), as well as an introduction of many important case studies (from Europe and Caucasus, to the Horn of Africa and the Pacific region). Experts from around the world prepared chapters that relate their own research to the topic as to provide readers with informed and well-documented views on the contemporary developments in this field. This book thus consists of both theoretical and empirical part designed to cover as large spectrum of research questions as possible while the structure of the overall picture itself remains coherent and clearly arranged.

The first chapter is written by one of the most appreciated researchers in the field of unrecognized states—Nina Caspersen from the University of York. Dr. Caspersen gives a brief overview of the research of the de facto states and examines whether it matters for the prospect of conflict resolution that these self-proclaimed and largely unrecognized entities are not simply designated as criminalized badlands but often seen as institutionalized and effectively governed territories which enjoy considerable degree of legitimacy in the eyes of the people. She argues that both institution-building and political reforms taking place in de facto states are important conditions that, if taken seriously enough, may pave the way for peace at least in long-term perspective.

After the introduction of the topic of de facto states, Mikulas Fabry from the Georgia Institute of Technology connects the topic of recognition to identity. His work enables us to theorize the role that identity plays in the formation of de facto states while providing empirical evidences about the way these two phenomena interact and strengthen each other. His chapter thus makes another step in our understanding of the connection between identity, secession and non-recognition. If we acknowledge that geopolitics and international politics in general are from a large part defined by identity clashes, understanding of the creation of national identity in the context of the de facto statehood is one of the key topics of research.

In the next chapter, Urban Jakša from the University of York capitalizes on his field research on the Caucasus region and presents an issue of the ontological security of the Caucasian de facto states with a focus on Chechnya. He continues in a similar vein as the previous chapter and connects issues of identity, security, and recognition with focus on the Caucasian region. He answers the question of the relation between physical and ontological security of these states and presents the importance of identity question for the development of the secessionist movements in the region. Based on his theoretical and field research, he provides an explanation of why the ontological security in many instances overcomes the importance of the physical security and even threatens it.

Secession is in many instances closely connected to an independence referendum—especially in a context of secession from a liberal democracy or in situations of arranged secession. The issue of referendum is usually overlooked but, as pointed by Přemysl Rosůlek from University of West Bohemia, the question wording may in many instances largely affect the outcome of the referendum. Based on a research from around the globe, doc. Rosůlek's chapter thus presents many possible variations of the referendum question wording, the mistakes that may appear, and recommendation for the correct phrasing of the problem setting. His recommendations are rooted in a large amount of theoretical literature, as well as analysis of specific examples and opinions presented by institutions all over the world.

Final chapter dedicated to the theoretical part of this book presents a comparative analysis of successful secessions with the focus on characteristics of the parent states. Martin Riegl and Bohumil Doboš from the Institute of Political Studies of the Faculty of Social Sciences, Charles University, present an exhaustive comparison of cases that might be deemed to certain level successful de facto and/or de iure secessions and point to the crucial role of (super)powers in both of the outcomes. By comparing these issues, they stress the role of outside powers in a process of recognition and secession and establish a modified (super)power rule [based on M. Sterio's (2013) ideas] that aims at an explanation of the different outcomes of secessionist attempts. This perspective presents readers with a different outlook on the issue of the international recognition compared to the previous chapters, bringing power politics back into the picture.

The part of this book focused on case studies begins in the Caucasus region. Vincenc Kopeček from the University of Ostrava gives an overview of his research that was conducted on the southern part of the Caucasus mountain range and introduces issues related to the political institutions of Abkhazia and Nagorno-Karabakh. By comparing these two entities and their inner political setting, Kopeček sheds a light on the nature of these entities as representatives of the popular will of its population and the political processes that are taking place inside these entities. He also presents the main political actors of these two de facto states in the south Caucasus region and sketches some possible future developments.

Another region facing challenges of secession is the eastern Iran. Based on his long extensive work on the country, Robert Czulda from the University of Lodz examines the two main secessionist entities in the region—Sistan and Balochistan. He connects the issue of self-determination with the problem of energy security or drug trafficking in order to present a clear overview of the issues related to the region. Despite the fact that the region is usually understudied in the academic literature, it surely presents an important case of the twenty-first century separatism.

Remaining in the region of the Middle East, Martin Riegl, Bohumil Doboš, Jakub Landovský, and Shmuel Bar present the prospect for the international recognition of the Iraqi Kurdistan. Building on a concept of modified (super)power rule as presented in the theoretical part of this book, their article establishes a comprehensive overview of obstacles and opportunities for the independence of the region. Text mainly focuses on attitudes of different actors crucial for the political development of the region toward the possible independence of the Iraqi Kurdistan. The chapter concludes with a rather negative vision for the possibility of an international recognition of possible Kurdish state.

One of the forgotten cases of secessionism is Bougainville. This island in Pacific seeking independence from Papua New Guinea underwent quite turmoil since the decolonization process in the 1970s. The case is not only interesting from a perspective of mitigation strategies utilized by the parent state, but also due to the fact that Bougainville is about to hold an independence referendum that might lead to an establishment of the newest state on the political map of the world. Vladimír Baar from the University of Ostrava presents the history of the region as well as regional dynamics of the case and possible future scenario of development. His analysis is rooted in a long-lasting research interest in the region and many research trips conducted to the area, as well as on the study of large amount of academic literature dealing with the issue.

Kateřina Rudincová from the Technical University of Liberec consequently capitalizes on her experience from her work for the African Union and presents reasons for the diverging attitude of the entity toward the independence bid of South Sudan and Somaliland. She takes a question of different approach of the African Union toward independence bids from Somaliland and South Sudan and attempts to answer it based on the field interviews as well as the utilization of the basic principles of the international politics. The chapter presents reasons for the divergent attitudes of the organization toward different cases of secession in Africa.

Finally, this book cannot omit the case of Kosovo. Jan Bečka from the Ministry of Defence of the Czech Republic and the Institute of International Studies of the Faculty of Social Sciences, Charles University, presents his analysis of the viability of the entity based on his work as a Deputy Political Advisor for KFOR. He presents many issues as well as opportunities for the European "Newborn." The chapter thus gives readers a clear overview of the issues challenging this special case of the European twenty-first century politics with clear implications for the future of the entity and region in general.

As we can clearly surmise, the issue of de facto states and secession in the contemporary world is broad and varied. The aim of this book is to point out the wide range of problems related to the study of these two research fields and not only to highlight the differences among the unrecognized entities but also to present the wide range of both theoretical and practical problems present in the field. The de facto states are clearly not the black holes but interesting political subjects with many viable internal processes as well as a large importance for the international politics making. Secessionism is a multifaceted process with many variables affecting the outcome. It is not only a problem of the past but also a large variable influencing the future outlook of the international politics from Europe (Scotland, Catalonia, Ukraine) to the Middle East (Kurdistan) to Africa (Somaliland) to Pacific (Bougainville) and many more. This book cannot and does not claim to present all the cases and theoretical perspectives regarding the research fields in question, or to cover the full range of the relevant issues, but attempts to present at least the most prominent and novel of them. We hope that the following texts can help spur a discussion on the topic in a new and innovative way. We thus wish the readers a pleasant and stimulating experience while reading the volume.

References

Caspersen, N. (2011). *Unrecognized states: The struggle for sovereignty in the modern international system.* Cambridge: Polity.
Coppieters, B., & Sakwa, R. (Eds.). (2003). *Contextualizing secession: Normative studies in a comparative perspective.* Oxford: Oxford University Press.
Crawford, J. (2007). *The creation of states in international law.* Oxford: Oxford University Press.
Geldenhuys, D. (2009). *Contested states in world politics.* Basingstoke: Palgrave Macmillan.
Grant, T. D. (1999). *The recognition of states: Law and practice in debate and evolution.* Westport: Praeger Publishers.
Harvey, J., & Stansfield, G. (2011). Theorizing unrecognized states: Sovereignty, secessionism and political economy. In N. Caspersen & G. Stansfield (Eds.), *Unrecognized states in the international system* (pp. 11–26). New York: Routledge.
Kirchner, S. (2015). Crimea's declaration of independence and the subsequent annexation by Russia under international law. *Journal of International Law.* https://www.law.gonzaga.edu/gjil/2015/01/crimeas-declaration-of-independence-and-the-subsequent-annexation-by-russia-under-international-law/. Accessed August 15, 2016.
Lynch, D. (2004). *Engaging Eurasia's separatist states: Unresolved conflicts and de facto states.* Washington: USIP Press.

Marxsen, C. (2015). International law in crises—Russia's struggle for recognition. *Max Planck Institute for comparative public law and international law (MPIL) research paper no. 2016-05.* http://ssrn.com/abstract=2771293. Accessed August 18, 2016.

Pegg, S. (1998). *International society and the de facto state*. Aldershot: Ashgate.

Sterio, M. (2013). On the right to external self-determination: "Selfistans", secession, and the great powers' rule. *Minnesota Journal of Int'l Law, 19*(1), 137–176.

Walter, C., von Ungern-Sternberg, A., & Abushov, K. (Eds.). (2014). *Self-determination and secession in international law*. Oxford: Oxford University Press.

Zaum, D. (2007). *The sovereignty paradox: The norms and politics of international statebuilding*. Oxford: Oxford University Press.

Author Biographies

Eiki Berg is a Professor of International Relations at the University of Tartu. Since 1996, he has worked at the Johan Skytte Institute of Political Studies, generally focusing on critical geopolitics and particularly the studies of borders and border regions. Among his recent research activities, most prominent have been studies about territoriality and sovereignty issues in contested states. He has published widely in leading peer-reviewed journals on bordering practices, identity politics, and power sharing in post-conflict settings. He is co-editor of *Routing Borders Between Territories, Discourses and Practices* (Ashgate 2003) and *Identity and Foreign Policy: Baltic-Russian Relations and European Integration* (Ashgate 2009). During the years of 2003–2004, he served as an MP in the Estonian Parliament and observer to the European Parliament in the EPP-ED faction, Committee on Foreign Affairs, Human Rights, Common Security and Defence Policy. In 2012, he received a National Science Award in the field of social sciences for his research on "Identities, Conflicting Self-Determination and De Facto States."

Martin Riegl was born in 1980. He currently lectures at the Institute of Political Studies of Faculty of Social Sciences, Charles University. He graduated in 2010 at Faculty of Social Sciences, Charles University (program Political Science), where he successfully finished doctoral studies in the field of political geography. Since 2008, he has been lecturing at the Department of Political Science (FSS, UK). His academic research is focused on the institution of the sovereign state, geopolitics of political disintegration, secession, unrecognized states, and state failure. Actively, he participated at scientific conferences and workshops in the Czech Republic, Slovakia, Germany, Belgium, Poland, United Kingdom, Taiwan, etc.

Bohumil Doboš is a Ph.D. student at the Institute of Political Studies, Faculty of Social Sciences, Charles University. His research interest lies in areas of post-Westphalian geopolitics, New Middle Age theory, geopolitical anomalies, geopolitics of violent non-state actors, and astropolitics. He is also a Coordinator of the Geopolitical Studies Research Centre at the same institute and Employee at the Ministry of Defence of the Czech Republic—Defence Policy and Strategy Division.

Part I
Theoretical Perspectives

Making Peace with De Facto States

Nina Caspersen

De facto states are typically conceived of as territories that have gained de facto independence, often following warfare, but have failed to achieve (widespread) international recognition. They have demonstrated a certain staying power—two years of territorial control is a common definitional requirement—and display 'strong indigenous roots'; they are not simply 'puppet states' (see, e.g. Pegg 1998; Caspersen 2012). These entities may enjoy many of the attributes of statehood, but they are not members of the exclusive club of (externally) sovereign states. De facto states are not, however, merely esoteric anomalies in the international system, and they also present significant security challenges: the territory to which they lay claim remains contested and the outbreak of renewed warfare is a very distinct possibility.

Nevertheless, when I first started doing research on de facto, or unrecognized, states more than ten years ago, the literature was scarce and there was, in particular, a lack of understanding of the internal dynamics of these entities. The dominant image—in the media, foreign ministries and even some academic literature—was of criminalized badlands that were ruled by infighting warlords and based their survival on extortion and the smuggling of dangerous goods, including drugs and even radioactive material. Models for such an image are not hard to find. Chechnya between 1996 and 1999 was riven by violent infighting and was typically described as 'a hotbed of crime and terror' (Hughes 2007, 93), while inspiration could also be

---

The original version of this chapter appeared in The Annual of Language and Language of Politics and Identity (2016), 10, 7–18. This article is updated and reprinted with permission from the copyright holders.

This chapter is dedicated to the Charles University Research Development Schemes, Programme PROGRES Q18—Social sciences: from multidisciplinary to interdisciplinary.

N. Caspersen (✉)
University of York, York, UK
e-mail: nina.caspersen@york.ac.uk

© Springer International Publishing AG 2017
M. Riegl and B. Doboš (eds.), *Unrecognized States and Secession in the 21st Century*, DOI 10.1007/978-3-319-56913-0_2

taken from the failed states or ungoverned territories that had come to be seen as significant threats to international security. The tribal areas of Pakistan are often described as 'the most dangerous place on earth' (Hussain 2012), and the threats emanating from Yemen and increasingly ungoverned Libya are never far from the news headlines.

What I and other scholars hoped to show was that this image was overplayed (see, e.g. Caspersen 2008; Kolstø and Blakkisrud 2008; Berg and Kuusk 2010). Although control by warlords and a preponderance of organized crime did characterize some de facto states—especially in the early stages of de facto independence—most have in fact taken a decisive step away from this initial disorder, which is in any case not uncommon for a post-conflict context. A lack of external sovereignty does not condemn an entity to disorder and eventual oblivion. De facto states have managed to impose effective control over most of the area to which they lay claim, have built at least rudimentary state institutions, and some have even introduced political reforms. The lack of recognition, in fact, provides a strong incentive to build effective institutions and introduce political reforms: it aids their survival and serves an important legitimating function both internally and externally (Caspersen 2012).

De facto states also tended to be viewed as transitory phenomenon. They existed in a temporary limbo in-between the stable alternatives of de jure independence or, more likely, forceful reintegration into their parent state. Most were consequently expected to soon go the way of Chechnya and Republika Srpska Krajina and become simply a violent footnote in history.

However, it has become clear that de facto states are not simply ephemeral phenomena that will collapse on their own (Broers 2013); they have demonstrated their longevity. The four de facto states in the former Soviet space have all existed for more than two decades, as has Somaliland, while Northern Cyprus has been a de facto state for four decades. Moreover, new contested territories that could be described as de facto states have emerged, most notably the Donetsk People's Republic and the Luhansk People's Republic in Ukraine. These two newest additions to the universe of de facto states have started to create some of the trappings of statehood, although the extent of 'indigenous roots' is still debatable.

In the process of making our peace with the existence of de facto states, our understanding of them has become a lot more nuanced and the research on de facto states has become increasingly sophisticated. From being very much a niche topic, the study of de facto states has gradually moved into the mainstream, not just of conflict studies, which is where my own research originated, but also of area studies and International Relations. De facto states may still be seen as esoteric anomalies, but they are anomalies that can tell us something important about state-building, sovereignty and the international system.

The current state of the research, however, still leaves a number of challenges and areas for further exploration. In this contribution, I will focus on three interrelated issues: related to terminology and the way we conceive of de facto states; the effects of non-recognition; and the way in which our more nuanced understanding of de facto states impact on the prospect for conflict resolution. How can we, literarily, make peace with de facto states? This last question will form the bulk of the contribution, but it is, as I will argue below, affected by the two other issues.

1 Making Peace with—While also Extending: The Concept of De Facto States

As more authors, from different disciplines and with different research foci, have started researching these unrecognized entities, a plethora of terms have been used: de facto states, unrecognized states, contested states, shadow states, para states, phantom states, etc. (see, e.g. Broers et al. 2015). However, there appears to be an emerging consensus on using the term de facto states, and I am happy to bow to this. The term 'unrecognized states', which I initially favoured since I was interested in the effects of non-recognition, worked better as a pre-2008 concept, i.e. before Russia's recognition of Abkhazia and South Ossetia. The term 'de facto states' is better able to encompass such partially recognized states.

Greater terminological consensus would not, however, solve the ongoing discussions over which entities 'qualify' as de facto states. Should we, for example, include territories such as Iraqi Kurdistan, which function as state-like entities but have not formally declared independence, despite strong separatist sentiments? And what about cases such as Palestine and Western Sahara whose right to self-determination is internationally recognized and which exhibit some institutional attributes of statehood, but do not enjoy the territorial control that normally characterizes de facto states? Or what about rebel movements that control pockets of territory and manage to create some form of governance (see Arjona et al. 2015).

I would propose that in order to better uncover the dynamics of de facto statehood and its effects, it is useful to consider de facto states as the end of a spectrum of non-state governance in intra-state conflicts.[1] Territorial control is a question of degree, as is institution-building and even participatory politics. Scholars working on rebel governance have in fact made arguments very similar to the ones made in the de facto state literature: rebels cannot be reduced to warlords and rebel-controlled areas should not be seen as areas where anarchy prevails. Alternative forms of governance often emerge and we may even speak of a rebel political order; institutions may be built and some public services, including health and education, provided (Mampilly 2011; Arjona et al. 2015). Although there is always an element of coercion, citizens are sometimes encouraged to participate in citizens forums or elections for local committees may be held (Kasfir 2015). Rebel forces who develop effective and legitimate governance systems will find themselves strengthened vis-à-vis the state (Arjona et al. 2015).

Kasfir (2015) argues that rebel governments are frequently 'fragile, fluid and short-lived' but also contend that there is a great deal of variation. At the end of the

---

[1]Even if a few of the entities do not emerge from such a context.

rebel governance continuum, we find rebel political order, which is more directly comparable to governance in conventional polities. For this to be possible, a certain duration of territorial control is needed. Now we might assume that de facto states would simply constitute a further extension of this continuum. However, Kasfir argues that with de facto states, we are dealing with a different category, since they are 'no longer governed under the pressure of anticipated violence' and therefore ceases to be cases of rebel governance (2015, 31). But I would argue that this underestimates the continued effect of (potential) violence in the case of de facto states; the type of governance found in de facto states, and in particular its legitimation, is heavily influenced by the unresolved conflict and the persistent threat of a military offensive (Caspersen 2011). Moreover, the definitions of de facto states typically recognize the lack of rigidity, and especially the fact that territorial control is both variable and reversible: rebel governments may increase their territorial control and thereby become de facto states, while some de facto states facing military attacks reverted to being cases of rebel governance (Caspersen 2012). I would therefore argue that it makes sense to see de facto states as the end of a spectrum of rebel governance; their territorial control is more durable and direct violence has largely ceased, thus allowing for greater institution-building. Moreover, the focus of the leaders is no longer on securing a military victory but instead on defending this and pursuing international recognition of the de facto situation. This may make the leaders even more concerned with their international image. But although these entities have passed an important threshold in gaining de facto independence, I would posit that they are not qualitative different.

2 Making Peace with Non-recognition

As I argued above, lack of recognition does not condemn an entity to anarchy, nor to international isolation or to the status of mere puppets. Some de facto states have managed to build surprisingly effective institutions and have introduced political reforms, and some enjoy a reasonably high level of international engagement. Still, I would maintain that the absence of (widespread) recognition matters. The degree of its impact varies, but it is profound. Although some de facto states, such as Taiwan, and to a lesser extent Northern Cyprus and Somaliland, are fairly well integrated into the international system (Berg and Toomla 2009; see also Ker-Lindsay 2012), important doors remain closed, and access still seems to be dependent on the approval of the parent state, or the continued inability of the parent state to function effectively, as in the case of Somaliland (see Caspersen 2015). More research is needed, however, on this aspect, including on the interaction between international engagement, state-building and political reforms. Conceiving of de facto states as the end point of spectrum, and highlighting the differences within the category, could help illuminate some of the key factors, such as the effect of the duration of territorial control, the degree of territorial control, links with patron states, and whether or not independence has been formally declared.

Lack of recognition, moreover, remains an existential threat: the territorial integrity of the parent state is still seen as the overriding international norm, and it is still widely accepted that the parent state is allowed to use force to reintegrate the territory, even if against the will of the population of the de facto state. As the case of Tamil Eelam showed, there may be some international criticism in case of severe human rights violations, but it quickly dies down and the right of the parent state to rule over the territory is not questioned. The narrative of future recognition, moreover, plays an important legitimizing function internally; it helps the leaders excuse current shortcoming and the allows them to keep the entity in a state of exception, for example illustrated by the perpetual martial law in the case of Nagorno Karabakh.

This does not mean that the pursuit of recognition is necessarily the main preoccupation of the leaders of the de facto states. Many of them realize that international recognition is unlikely, at least in the foreseeable future, and instead seek better integration into the international system, as unrecognized or partially recognized entities. They hope that this will improve the status quo and strengthen their de facto independence in the short-to-medium term and possibly make future recognition more likely; or at least make international acceptance of forceful reintegration less likely (Caspersen 2015). However, how sustainable is this and what are the effects on internal dynamics—legitimacy, institution-building—of prolonged experiences of non-recognition? This is another area for future research and one which would again benefit from a more diversified understanding of de facto states: the threat from renewed warfare is, for example, strikingly different for a consolidated entity that enjoys great power support, than for an entity with more insecure territorial control and a lack of external backing. This will also affect the impact of prolonged non-recognition on their internal dynamics.

3 How to Make Peace with De Facto States

There is now a considerably body of research on the internal dynamics of de facto states. This has greatly improved our understanding of them and has helped displace previous simplifications. However, the impact of this more nuanced understanding on conflict resolution has yet to be explored. Regardless of how possible it is to survive, and even thrive, without recognition, the territories remain contested. While the de facto state may be relatively happy with the status quo, the parent state is not and the existence of the de facto state—at least insofar as an explicit demand for independence is made—is seen to violate the principle of territorial integrity.

The question that I will examine for the remainder of this contribution is whether it matters for the prospect of conflict resolution that these entities cannot simply be dismissed as criminalized badlands; that they have managed to create state-like entities, sometimes with surprisingly effective institutions? Does it make it more, or less, likely that a solution can be found? Or does it affect the nature of such a solution?

This has not been systematically analysed in the existing literature. The prevalent view is that the existence of de facto states prolongs a conflict and poses a significant, possibly insurmountable, obstacle to a negotiated solution. The separatists have won the war or at least the first round of conflict. Entities such as Nagorno-Karabakh, Abkhazia, South Ossetia, Somaliland and Northern Cyprus therefore already enjoy the de facto independence and territorial control to which other separatists aspire. A stalemate could be said to exist insofar as the de facto states cannot reach the goal of international recognition through military escalation, and the risk of a catastrophic war is forever present, but it is to a 'soft' stalemate not a hurting one (see, e.g. Hopmann and Zartman 2010, 2). The leaders of these entities therefore have little reason to compromise. As King asks, 'why be a mayor of a small city if you can be president of a country?' 'why be a lieutenant in someone else's army if you can be a general in your own?' (2001, 551).

If we view de facto states as the end of a continuum, as far as territorial control is concerned, then there is little doubt that these entities are negotiating from a relative position of strength and this makes it hard to convince them to accept less than full independence. It is far more common for secessionist movement to control no territory or only a few districts, and often only for a short time, or there may be pockets of contested territories where, for example, the state rules by day, but the rebels by night (Kasfir 2015). In such cases, the secessionist leaders will have far greater incentive to agree to a peace agreement that promises them a degree of self-government or similar; this would in some ways constitute a gain.

The policy implications of this argument are straightforward and readily adopted by central governments: avoid the creation of a de facto state and do your utmost to weaken it if one does emerge. Make sure that incipient rebel governance is not strengthened through international engagement, possibly avoid negotiating directly with rebel leaders as this implies recognition of their status; isolate de facto states, for example through blockades, and fight any links that would legitimize or normalize their existence.

Another version of this argument would point to the involvement of patron states. The secessionist movements strong enough to achieve de facto independence, and in particular maintain it, usually enjoy the support of a patron. Such third party involvement is usually seen as an obstacle to a negotiated solution (Doyle and Sambanis 2000). Although de facto states should not be seen as mere puppets of their patron states, the patron state may enjoy an effective veto in any peace talks which, if nothing else, complicates attempts to find a solution as more players have to come to an agreement.

All else being equal a conflict becomes much harder to resolve once the secessionist forces secure de facto independence and especially if they manage to maintain it for a period of time. However, all else is not equal: the territorial control also makes it possible to build institution and ensure greater internal cohesion

(Kasfir 2015). And this could pull in the opposite direction. One of the factors argued to explain the longevity of civil wars is the number of factions involved: the more factions involved, the longer the war is likely to last (Doyle and Sambanis 2000). This is especially the case if the factions themselves lack cohesion and a clear structure and chain of command. Conflicts with many rebel factions are characterized by both intra- and inter-communal violence, the dynamics are unpredictable, and negotiating a lasting solution is near-impossible: who do you negotiate with; will they be able to deliver their followers? The need for credible commitment in peace talks is widely emphasized in the literature (Walter 2002). Such commitment requires negotiators who are in control of their community[2], and this would suggest that separatist state-building could in fact have a positive effect.

The ability to identify what Zartman (1995) terms a 'valid spokesperson' does not, however, translate into a willingness to accept a compromise solution. In cases where de facto independence has already been achieved, any solution short of independence is unlikely to prove acceptable. The leaders of Nagorno Karabakh are, for example, adamant that independence is non-negotiable, and insist that Azerbaijan has to accept the 'current reality' (i.e. de facto independence).[3] It may, in other words, be possible to negotiate an agreement, but not necessarily one that the parent state would accept. It is possible that there is a threshold beyond which 'rebel control' makes an agreement more difficult to achieve. The Free Aceh Movement (GAM) in Indonesia appears to have been on the 'right' side of this threshold. Between 1998 and 2005, when the Memorandum of Understanding was signed, the Free Aceh Movement had control over a handful of districts and managed to establish certain elements of governance in this area, including the supply of some public services. As part of this strategy, the GAM incorporated different societal forces, which helped ensure a more legitimate and cohesive movement (Barter 2015). However, the territorial control remained confined and GAM suffered significant military setbacks in the years leading up to the agreement. They consequently came to realize that independence was not realistic and eventually settled for extensive autonomy (Merikallio and Ruokanen 2015). But unlike a more fractionalized movement, they were able to make it stick; they avoided a significant split and could use the incipient institutions already created to consolidate their power and implement the agreement (Barter 2015; see also International Crisis Group 2013). In the case of Sudan on the other hand, the Sudanese People's Liberation Movement/Army was in control of most of the southern part of the country and was able to create a partially effective system of governance that provided 'a degree of stability of certain areas of South Sudan' (Mampilly 2011, p. 22). The SPLM/A made clear that they would not settle for autonomy and would only accept an agreement that included an independence referendum following an

---

[2]However, the literature on commitment problems in civil wars has generally treated the conflict parties as unitary actors.
[3]Interview with Hrachya Arzoumanyan, expert in the NKR foreign ministry, Stepanakert, 1 November 2008.

interim period; this would give them a way out, if the central government failed to reform the state sufficiently, and it also satisfied the separatist faction of the SPLM/A. This faction came to be dominant following the signing of the agreement and South Sudan became independent in 2011 (see, e.g. Brosché 2008). Such an agreed secession could provide stability—although it did not in this case, as I will return to shortly—but it will rarely be acceptable to the parent state. A similar framework has been suggested in the case of Nagorno Karabakh: a popular vote following an interim period is to determine the region's future status. Azerbaijan is vehemently opposed to any vote that could lead to independence for Nagorno Karabakh, arguing that the entire country must have a say if the referendum includes the option of independence (see, e.g. Trend Agency 2011). In other conflicts, the insistence on territorial integrity also comes from the international mediators. The 'Basic Principles for the Division of Competencies between Tbilisi and Sukhumi' which the UN proposed in 2001 and which remained the framework for mediation efforts for several years spoke of Abkhazia as a 'sovereign entity, based on the rule of law, within the State of Georgia'. The Abkhaz leadership, however, refused to even receive the document (Francis 2011).

The above arguments have, however, made no distinction between different types of separatist governance: do they, for example, rely on popular support or on coercion? Is their governance focused solely on security or do they also provide other public services such as health and education. Some de facto states have implemented political reforms, and it could be argued that the resulting movement away from military leaders, or warlords, towards civilian politicians would tempter the militaristic rhetoric, increase diversity and open up for alternative solutions. When Abkhazia held multiparty elections in 2004, which resulted in the victory of the non-regime candidate Sergei Bagapsh, there were initially hopes that this transfer of power would make it easier to reach a negotiated solution, especially when combined with the previous year's regime change in Georgia. After all, the new Abkhaz government included people who had taken part in track II dialogue with Georgian counterparts and were said to acknowledge, in private, the need for compromise with Georgia.[4] The problem is, however, that the kind of democratization that we find in de facto states is usually constrained (Caspersen 2011). We may find competing political parties representing diverse views, but on the issue of independence, we tend to observe intra-communal consensus, even if there may be disagreements over how best to achieve international recognition and maintain de facto independence. It is not merely hardliners who regard sovereignty as non-negotiable (see Lynch 2004, 51). Elections are not separate from the overall secessionist project; for example, in both Abkhazia and Nagorno Karabakh, the electoral processes are founded on ethnic exclusion (Ó Beacháin 2015). Moreover, the reasoning for the population can be strikingly similar to the political elites: 'why be a minority in someone else's states when you can be a majority in your own?' Such a question is even easier to answer given the years of propaganda that has

---

[4]Interview with Paata Zakareishvili, Tbilisi, 31 August 2006.

painted the parent state as an enemy bent on their annihilation. Similarly, both institution-building and political reforms will result in stronger and more legitimate entities and both leaders and followers may consequently see even less reason to consider a risky compromise.

On the other hand, in conflicts including de facto states—intra-state conflicts at the extreme end of the rebel governance spectrum—a common state is rarely a realistic solution, at least not in the short term. If the parent state refuses to consider secession, or various forms of shared sovereignty, the best that can be hoped for is for relations to be re-established and mistrust to gradually subside (Caspersen 2012). This will be a lot easier with effective entities that are not ruled by unrepresentative warlords. Over the long term, new dynamics may emerge especially if the security threat subsides. The narrative of future recognition and the persistence of an external threat are powerful instruments for ensuring internal cohesion, but their effectiveness is likely to wane if recognition remains unlikely. This could open the way for a rapprochement with the parent state.

The effect of rebel governance on the prospect of a negotiated settlement is therefore double-sided, but probably tends to make it harder to reach a solution that both sides can agree to, at least at the de facto state end of the spectrum. However, the effect on the post-settlement phase is more likely to be positive. Whether the state is maintained or not, a common cause of instability is a lack of capacity in what now becomes a self-governing region (Caspersen 2017). Without sufficient capacity, the local leaders will be unable to defeat spoilers set on undermining the agreement and will also lack the resources to supply public services and thereby legitimize the agreement in the eyes of the general population. This further adds to the risk of spoiler violence. Such instability is clearly detrimental to human security, but it also risks undermining the agreement as a whole. Following the signing of a peace agreement in 1996, Mindanao in the Philippines, for example, became a byword for anarchy; the autonomous government led by the former rebel movement, the Moro National Liberation Front, did not have the capacity to defeat or marginalize spoiler groups and also struggled to provide public services; as a result the agreement lost backing from the local population and spoiler groups were strengthened (Lara and Champain 2009). The risk of instability is augmented if the former rebels institute a regime that lacks inclusivity. During the war, the rule of the SPLM/A had focused on security; it had failed to build effective institutions and it had also remained dominated by the Dinka ethnic group (Mampilly 2011). This became a problem following the 2005 peace agreement and especially South Sudan's independence. The government was authoritarian and ethnically exclusive and unable to meet the economic expectations of the inhabitants (Sriram 2008; Brosché 2008). It did not take long before internal divisions came to the fore and civil war broke out (Jones and Anderson 2015). This demonstrates that the territories held by rebel forces cannot simply be treated as *terra nullius*. Moreover, not only territorial control matters, institutional capacity and the nature of the separatist regime has an impact on the sustainability of a settlement. It seems that if an agreement is reached—which may be a tall order indeed—then de facto states, or a high degree of rebel political order, could provide a good basis for sustainable peace, especially if they have institutionalized a degree of diversity.

4 Conclusion

This contribution has suggested that the changed understanding of de facto states also has implication for conflict analysis. Reaching a compromise solution when a de facto state is involved will never be easy, but the longer-term prospects, and the conditions for the inhabitants in the meantime, depend on the type of de facto states that has been created; the degree to which effective institutions have been built and political reforms introduced. This, moreover, also matters for the sustainability of any agreement reached. However, these broad hypotheses need to be subjected to systematic research. Conceptually, I have called for viewing de facto states as the end of a continuum of rebel governance, and just like the literature on rebel governance has policy implications, so does the above discussion. Isolating or weakening de facto states is not the only possible response, and it may indeed backfire and simply increase the influence of the patron state. Engagement is an alternative: not just for the sake of civilians during the war (Mampilly 2011), but also to strengthen reform forces within these entities which could gradually create a situation more conducive to compromise and to a sustainable settlement.

Acknowledgements The author would like to thank the two anonymous reviewers for their helpful comments.

References

Arjona, A., Kasfir, N., & Mampilly, Z. (2015). *Rebel governance in civil war*. New York: Cambridge University Press.
Barter, S. J. (2015). The rebel state in society: Governance and accommodation in Aceh, Indonesia. In A. Arjona, N. Kasfir, & Z. Mampilly (Eds.), *Rebel governance in civil war* (pp. 226–245). New York: Cambridge University Press.
Berg, E., & Kuusk, E. (2010). What makes sovereignty a relative concept? Empirical approaches to international society. *Political Geography, 29*(1), 40–49.
Berg, E., & Toomla, R. (2009). Forms of normalisation in the quest for de facto statehood. *International Spectator, 44*(4), 27–45.
Broers, L. (2013). Recognising politics in unrecognized states. *Caucasus Survey, 1*(1), 59–74.
Broers, L., Iskandaryan, A., & Minasyan, S. (2015). Introduction: The unrecognized politics of de facto states in the post-Soviet space. *Caucasus Survey, 3*(3), 187–194.
Brosché, J. (2008). CPA: New Sudan, Old Sudan or Two Sudans? In U. J. Dahre (Ed.), *Post-conflict peace-building in the Horn of Africa* (pp. 231–251). Lund: Department of Social Anthropology and Department of Political Science, Lund University.
Caspersen, N. (2008). Separatism and democracy in the Caucasus. *Survival, 50*(4), 113–136.
Caspersen, N. (2011). Democracy, Nationalism and (lack of) sovereignty: The complex dynamics of democratisation in unrecognized states. *Nations and Nationalism, 17*(2), 337–356.

Caspersen, N. (2012). *Unrecognized states: The struggle for sovereignty in the modern international system*. Cambridge: Polity Press.

Caspersen, N. (2015). The pursuit of international recognition after Kosovo. *Global Governance, 21*(3), 393–412.

Caspersen, N. (2017). *Peace agreements: Finding solutions to intra-state conflicts*. Cambridge: Polity.

Doyle, M. W., & Sambanis, N. (2000). International peacebuilding: A theoretical and quantitative analysis. *The American Political Science Review, 94*(4), 779–801.

Francis, C. (2011). *Conflict resolution and status: The case of Georgia and Abkhazia (1989–2008)*. Brussels: VUB Press.

Hopmann, P. T., & Zartman, I. W. (2010). Overcoming the Nagorno-Karabakh Stalemate. *International Negotiation, 15*(1), 1–6.

Hughes, J. (2007). *Chechnya: From nationalism to jihad*. Philadelphia: University of Pennsylvania Press.

Hussain, Z. (2012). *Pakistan's most dangerous place*. Winter: Wilson Quarterly.

International Crisis Group. (2013). *Indonesia: Tensions over Aceh's Flag* s.l. Asia briefing no. 139.

Jones, S., & Anderson, M. (2015, October). South Sudan civil war inquiry details torture and forced cannibalism. *The Guardian*.

Kasfir, N. (2015). Rebel governance: Constructing a field of inquiry. In A. Arjona, N. Kasfir, & Z. Mapilly (Eds.), *Rebel governance in civil war* (pp. 21–46). New York: Cambridge University Press.

Ker-Lindsay, J. (2012). *The foreign policy of counter secession*. Oxford: Oxford University Press.

King, C. (2001). The benefits of ethnic war: Understanding Eurasia's unrecognized states. *World Politics, 53*(July), 524–552.

Kolstø, P., & Blakkisrud, H. (2008). Living with non-recognition: State- and nation-building in South Caucasian quasi-states. *Europe-Asia Studies, 60*(3), 483–509.

Lara, F. J., Jr., & Champain, P. (2009). *Inclusive peace in muslim Mindanao: Revisiting the dynamics of conflict and exclusion*. London: International Alert.

Lynch, D. (2004). *Engaging Eurasia's separatist states*. Washington, DC: United States Institute of Peace Press.

Mampilly, Z. C. (2011). *Rebel rulers: Insurgent governance and civilian life during war*. Ithaca: Cornell University Press.

Merikallio, K., & Ruokanen, T. (2015). *The mediator: A biography of Martti Ahtisaari*. London: Hurst.

Ó Beacháin, D. (2015). Elections without recognition: Presidential and parliamentary contests in Abkhazia and Nagorny Karabakh. *Caucasus Survey, 3*(3), 239–257.

Pegg, S. (1998). *International society and the De Facto State*. Aldershot: Ashgate.

Sriram, C. L. (2008). *Peace as governance: Power-sharing, armed groups and contemporary peace negotiations*. Houndmills: Palgrave Macmillan.

Trend Agency. (2011, January). Azerbaijani presidential administration: Recognition of illegal 1991 "referendum" in Nagorno-Karabakh is impossible. http://en.trend.az/azerbaijan/karabakh/1818873.html

Walter, B. F. (2002). *Committing to peace: The successful settlement of civil wars*. Princeton: Princeton University Press.

Zartman, I. W. (1995). *Collapsed states: The disintegration and restoration of legitimate authority*. Lynne Rienner: Boulder.

Author Biography

Nina Caspersen is Professor of Politics, at the University of York, UK. She is an internationally recognized expert on separatist conflict and de facto states and the author of Contested Nationalism (Oxford: Berghan, 2010), Unrecognized States (Cambridge: Polity, 2012), Peace Agreements (Cambridge: Polity, 2017), and several articles in leading journals. Some of the research for this article was funded by a Mid-Career Fellowship from the British Academy.

Unrecognized States and National Identity

Mikulas Fabry

What is the effect of being an unrecognized state on the national identity of its population? And how does it compare to the identity effect of having been accorded state recognition? This contribution argues that contrary to socio-psychological theories that make identity dependent on outside recognition (Wendt 2003; Ringmar 2012), refusals of state recognition have, in general, a far stronger affirmative impact on national identity than extensions of it. Recognition may be the central external goal of claimants of statehood, but non-recognition fosters national identity to a much greater degree than recognition. While foreign recognition of statehood may fulfil a deep psychological need, it is its denial that makes a people's collective sense of who they are more robust. Obtaining recognition as a state may, in fact, reveal the fragility of national identity within that state.

These counterintuitive effects can be attributed to two general background conditions operating in the above cases. First, there are multiple identities and levels of identities within the same social setting and these can interact and affect each other. This observation is taken to be a truism in the academic literature, but its theoretical and empirical dimensions are both underexplored (Goff and Dunn 2004, pp. 7–8), not least with respect to identities that are related and pertain to collectivities, not individuals. Although often treated as interchangeable, the corporate identity of an entity as a sovereign, independent state is different from the national identity of its population as a distinct people with political rights and legal claims.

The original version of this chapter appeared in The Annual of Language & Language of Politics and Identity (2016), 10, 19–30. This article is updated and reprinted with permission from the copyright holders.

This chapter is dedicated to the Charles University Research Development Schemes, programme PROGRES Q18—Social sciences: from multidisciplinary to interdisciplinary.

M. Fabry (✉)
Sam Nunn School of International Affairs, Georgia Institute of Technology, Atlanta, USA
e-mail: mfabry@gatech.edu

While the interplay between the two does not necessarily alter either, such an effect is a permanent possibility. Second, there are different forms of identity recognition and some identities do not require any. A basic distinction can be between what Wendt (2003, pp. 511–512) calls "thin" and "thick," or what Agné (2013, p. 96) calls "legal" and "social," recognition. "Thin" or "legal" recognition refers to the external acknowledgment of a subject having a specific formal status or personality within a community of law, whereas "thick" or "social" recognition refers to the outside acknowledgment of particular non-formal character, standing, rank, or position within a larger social setting. Recognition of the corporate identity as a state is a former type of recognition, recognition of the national identity of a people a latter type. However, while the corporate identity of a state cannot exist without external recognition as other states determine through it the fulfillment of the criteria of statehood in international law, the national identity of a people can—it depends exclusively on the self-understanding of the persons composing the group.

1 Collective Identities and Recognition

According to socio-psychological theories that go back to Georg W.F. Hegel, all human beings have a fundamental need to obtain recognition from others (Taylor 1992, p. 26; Greenhill 2008, p. 348; Ringmar 2012, p. 3; Murray 2015, pp. 70–71). This need is existential in the sense that it involves the very constitution of a self and the other in particular identities. According to Wendt (2003, p. 511):

> … [I]t is through recognition by the Other that one is constituted as a Self in the first place. We can see this dependence of Self on Other in our everyday identities – one cannot be a teacher without recognition by students, a husband without recognition by a wife, a citizen without recognition by other citizens. But the point is more general, going all the way down to the constitution of subjectivity itself…Only through recognition can people acquire and maintain a distinct identity. One becomes a Self, in short, via the Other: subjectivity depends on inter-subjectivity. Insofar as people want to be subjects, therefore, they will desire recognition of their difference.

There have been debates as to what acts count as "social" recognition in specific circumstances (Agné 2013, p. 101), but not about this basic general formula. Still, this contribution contends, *contra* Wendt, that there are identities—specifically some collective identities—that do not need recognition by the other to be "acquired and maintained." While indeed requiring the presence of others for defining one's self, their formation and existence depend solely on the mutual understandings of those belonging to the collectivity. This is certainly the case with national identity. The Palestinian national consciousness developed in an interaction with, first, the growing Jewish presence in historical Palestine and, later, the State of Israel, but the Palestinians exist as a distinct people because, and only because, there are individuals who conjointly self-identify as Palestinians. Outside denials that the Palestinians are a separate people persistently voiced by various segments of Israeli society, initially even including highest governmental officials—have not undermined this shared self-understanding.

The national identity of a people, however, differs profoundly from the corporate identity of a sovereign state. The latter is an institutionalized identity which is simultaneously internal and external. It developed to be so gradually. After the post-medieval independent territorial "states" had acknowledged each other in this status and come to conduct their mutual relations on a basis of international law, it was necessary to identify which entities qualified as "states" for the purposes of this law (Warbrick 2006, p. 217). In the cases of new entities claiming the status on the territory of an existing state, this need gave rise to the practice of "recognition." In the absence of central government above them, it would be the existing states themselves that would determine who qualifies as a "state." By extending "recognition," they would cumulatively certify that the new entity possesses in its external interactions all the rights and obligations of a "state" in international relations and law. In its absence, the new entity could not engage in any of the things that "states" are entitled to do internationally, such as acceding to international treaties and conventions, conducting normal diplomatic and economic relations, joining intergovernmental organizations, receiving foreign aid, and enjoying the various protections as a subject of international law. In other words, without it the new entity would not be treated as a "state" by other states and their institutions, however much it may be seen as such by its own citizens. Its claimed identity of a state would exist only for domestic, not international, purposes. Statehood as a corporate identity thus developed from an exclusive domestic category into a simultaneous domestic and international category: It came to pertain both to the state and to the society of states. Domestic society and law delineate the former, international society and law the latter, and recognition links the two.

Still, just because "legal" and "social" forms of recognition/non-recognition apply to different identities does not mean they do not have any effect on one another. State recognition, it is contended here, has not had much of an affirmative effect on national identity, but non-recognition has. Why, and how, has the denial of recognition of statehood tended to strengthen national identity? In answering this question, socio-psychological theories of recognition can be helpful, as long as one acknowledges that recognition/non-recognition may affect a different identity that is being recognized or not. So far, these theories have not explored such a possibility.

2 State Recognition and National Identity

Unrecognized states—often referred to also as de facto states—are entities that have achieved effective independence but not external recognition. They have a government which has managed, substantially by its own efforts, to establish durable rule over the greater bulk of the claimed population and territory to the exclusion of any other claimant of that population and territory. While there are a number of insightful book-length studies of unrecognized states (Pegg 1998; Caspersen and

Stansfield 2011; Caspersen 2012), it is not widely appreciated that they are a phenomenon of a particular historical period: the post-colonial era. Yet this is a crucial historical fact: The great wave of decolonization in the late 1950s and 1960s constitutes the chronological dividing point for both the practice of state recognition and the relationship between state recognition and national identity.

Perhaps the most remarkable thing about de facto statehood is that while, today, it is used as a synonym for unrecognized states, for about 150 years prior to decolonization it, in fact, constituted a basis of state recognition (Fabry 2010, chs. 2–4). The practice of state recognition in this period reveals that de facto statehood *presupposed* a distinct and developed national identity: Its establishment was deemed to have been brought about by the national groups in whose name independence was expressly asserted. Crafted by early nineteenth-century American and British foreign policymakers and normatively grounded in classical liberal thought, the de facto statehood standard was based on the belief that peoples had a natural right to live under independent government of their choosing. As such, they had a right to pursue their choice without interference by third parties and, if successful, have the new state of affairs respected externally (Fabry 2010, Chap. 2). This is how Secretary of State John Quincy Adams justified the US acknowledgment of the first wave of new Latin American states to the parent government in 1822:

> In every question relating to the independence of a nation, two principles are involved; one of *right*, and the other of *fact*; the former exclusively depending upon the determination of the nation itself, and the latter resulting from the successful execution of that determination...The United States...yielded to an obligation of duty of the highest order by recognizing as independent states nations which, after deliberately asserting their right to that character, have maintained and established it against all the resistance which had been or could be brought to oppose it...This recognition...is the mere acknowledgment of existing facts, with the view to the regular establishment, with the nations newly formed, of those relations, political commercial, which it is the moral obligation of civilized and Christian nations to entertain reciprocally with one another.[1] (italics original)

A collectivity that had attained statehood in demonstrable fact was entitled to acknowledgment of that statehood in law due to the decisive normative meaning of the achievement: the formation of a stable, effective entity in which the population habitually obeyed the new rulers was taken as an authoritative expression of the will of the people to constitute an independent state as neither the de facto state's founding nor its continued existence could come to pass without at least tacit approval by its inhabitants. In the absence of an international agreement as to what constitutes a valid method of verifying the popular will, any foreign assessment thereof was necessarily presumptive (Roth 1999, pp. 38–39, 413–414): The de facto state was taken to embody, in Thomas Jefferson's words, "the will of the nation substantially declared."[2] It was this presumption of popular consent—and its normative trumping of the previously dominant idea of dynastic consent—that in

---

[1]Adams to Andagua, April 6, 1822, in Manning (1925, pp. 156–157).
[2]Jefferson to Morris, November 7, 1792, in Wharton (1887, p. 521).

American and British eyes converted the fact of the existence of new independ states into the right to independence and external recognition. The standard of de facto statehood was gradually adopted by other powers, whether they did or did not embrace the Anglo-American normative assumptions behind it. This standard came to inform the practice of state recognition in the Americas, Europe and, in several cases, Africa and the Middle East.

It is vital to underline that as important as it was that new statehood was explicitly asserted in the name of Mexicans, Chileans, Brazilians, Greeks, Belgians, Serbs, Finns, or Latvians, it was in the very process of attaining de facto independence that a group demonstrated conclusively the existence of a genuine body politic and shared national identity. Having no guaranteed outcome and in nearly all cases generating resistance, that process was bound to be arduous. Most commonly taking the form of unilateral secession, it entailed substantial struggle against the parent state—and sometimes other actors—who opposed the secessionist group.[3] Indeed, only rarely did independence bids not involve armed violence. A population could hardly embark on the onerous project of achieving independence if it was either fundamentally uncertain or deeply divided about its national loyalties. Common bonds of identity were a precondition.[4] Indeed, the greater the popular involvement in the struggle—as in many Latin American countries, the nineteenth-century Balkans or Israel—the more robust the national identity tended to be. But even where the struggle was more an elite than grassroots undertaking and national identification with the new state was consequently weaker—as in Yugoslavia or Czechoslovakia after their creation in 1918—there needed to be at least some shared sense of togetherness.

Since national identity solidified prior to, and in the process of, attaining de facto statehood, ensuing acts of external recognition had little impact on it. While undoubtedly having positive psychological effects, the latter normally confirmed rather than altered existing national identification with the new states. The practice of state recognition, however, changed dramatically with the post-1945 decolonization of European empires. In its course, international society largely abandoned the criteria of de facto statehood as a basis for recognizing indigenously founded new states. This does not mean that the countries recognized since then necessarily lacked it, only that it was not a condition of their recognition. Since the late 1950s, the determining recognition criterion has been whether an entity is deemed to have a preexisting international legal right to self-determination, which includes the right

---

[3]In the case of some peoples, such as Uruguayans and Bolivians, the struggle for independence did not involve merely removing the authorities of the parent state but also fending off their neighbors' designs for incorporating them.

[4]This does not mean that there ever was a complete unanimity within a population on this question. There always were minorities who opposed the majority, sometimes by active resistance. As difficult a practical problem as this often became, it never invalidated the concept of national identity. The concept was applied to the bulk of a, not an entire, population and could encompass various ethnic, linguistic, religious and other types of minorities. It is in this sense that national identity is analyzed in this contribution.

to choose independence. The notions that meeting the criteria of de facto statehood qualifies one for foreign acknowledgment as a state—and that falling short of them excludes one from such acknowledgment—have been effectively discarded.

This dramatic shift reflected the global political revolution, which took place in the course of the 1950s, that colonial rule and dependent status were no longer tolerable in international society. Landmark UN General Assembly Resolution 1514 (1960) defined, for the first time, specific peoples a priori entitled to statehood —the populations of the non-self-governing and trust territories—while stipulating both that the entitlement pertains to the territorial populations as a whole and that lack of effectiveness should have no bearing on it. In addition, Resolution 1514 and other documents specified that this right requires colonial powers to withdraw and third states to facilitate the emergence of a new state in their place.

Even though the anti-colonial sentiment across the colonial world had arguably been a mass phenomenon, there were only a few dependencies that disposed of colonial rule by exerting as much effort as had commonly been requisite in the past (Emerson 1969, p. 306). In most cases, colonial powers simply departed, propelled by intense international pressure, and new territories became automatically recognized, both by the departing powers and by the overwhelming majority of other states. Now, the old predecolonization recognition formula had by no means been a guarantee of ironclad and unchangeable national identity. Unilateral secessions of Texas (1836) and Panama (1903) or the centrifugal tendencies consuming interwar Yugoslavia all occurred because of a substantial decline in national identification with the respective parent states. But putting the threshold at the attainment of de facto statehood made the emergence of an authentic political community much more likely than unlikely as it was highly improbable that people who did not see their political future together would join forces and embark on what could be expected to be a taxing quest for a common country. However, as international society embraced the notion that non-sovereign entities are entitled to sovereignty solely because their particular status was no longer admissible, the assumption that the populations previously governed from London, Paris, Brussels, or The Hague would want to continue to live together in independent states governed from the ex-colonial capitals rested on uncertain footing.

As it turned out, national identification with to-be-decolonized territories was often underdeveloped or altogether missing. In contrast to, say, the peoples of the new Latin American states established in the nineteenth century, the loyalty and identification of many people of Sub-Saharan Africa, South Asia, or the South Pacific prone to political mobilization did not surpass their ethnocultural group. The widespread rejection of colonial rule did not necessarily translate into a desire to constitute new states within former colonial confines. On the contrary, accession to independence, promptly recognized by external governments, in numerous cases helped intensify ethnocultural fissures in new states. According to James Mayall (1990, p. 49):

Anti-colonial nationalism was essentially reactive. The nationalist leaders more often than not mobilized diverse groups who shared a hostility to colonial rule rather than a pre-colonial group sentiment or identity of interest. In the aftermath of independence many of the new leaders faced a crisis of legitimacy: political control was now in their hands, yet they were seldom able either to redeem the broad promises they had made to bring about the rapid social and economic transformation of society, or more specifically, to satisfy all the sub-national interests whose competition for state largesse now dominated the political arena.[5]

Many frustrated ethnocultural communities within ex-colonial states became embroiled in conflicts with the group or groups they perceived as unjustly discriminating against them, and these quarrels frequently escalated into open confrontation. The post-colonial world has been a scene of many acts of secession in which ethnocultural groups announced, in some instances not long after the proclamation of independence, that they had a right of self-determination and were entitled to a sovereign state too. There have been many scenes of post-colonial secessionist tensions—and in numerous cases large-scale violence. These as well as non-secessionist ethnic conflicts led Holsti (1992, p. 55) to remark that "it may not be an exaggeration to claim that outside of Latin America only a minority of Third World countries are socially integrated and able to govern effectively over a unified and reasonably disciplined citizenship."[6]

Notwithstanding all these developments, there gradually developed, in response to actual as well as feared potential cases, a global political and legal aversion to unilateral secession. For a number of reasons, the legitimate candidates for recognition were after 1960 restricted to non-self-governing and trust territories whose right to self-determination and independence was blocked, violated, or not yet realized, to constituent units of consensually dissolved states, such as the Mali Federation, and to entities that seceded with the agreement of their parent states, such as Singapore. From the point of view of foreign authorities, each change in the international status of a territory had to be given a blessing by the sovereign government in question.

Withholding state consent has meant almost certain non-recognition and international illegitimacy. Aside from Bangladesh in 1971, no ex-colonial substate entity has been able to create a new state or join some other state without such consent.[7] As Jackson (1990, p. 41) wrote, "Baluchis, Biafrans, Eritreans, Tigreans, Ewes, Gandans, Karens, Katchins, Kurds, Moros, Pathans, Sikhs, Tamils, and many other ethnonationalities are the abandoned peoples of the contemporary

---

[5] Analogous points are made in Jackson (1986, pp. 250–251) and Holsti (1996, Chap. 4).

[6] In 1974 Kamanu (1974, p. 358, n. 1) wrote with respect to independent countries in Sub-Saharan Africa that "perhaps more Africans have lost their lives in the past ten years fighting against tribal or ethnic domination than against European domination during the previous half century. A basic fact of life in Africa is that those outside one's cultural group are regarded as foreigners…".

[7] As in the past, such consent was extremely hard to come by. Between 1945 and 1993 Singapore was the only sub-state unit of a post-colonial country that managed to obtain it when it left Malaysia in 1965 on the initiative of the federal government in Kuala Lumpur.

community of states." This was true even of peoples who managed to create de facto states with effective control over the area they claimed. Under the predecolonization rules, the "Republic of Eritrea," the "Tamil Eelam," the "Free South Sudan," the "Republic of Bouganville," or the "Republic of Somaliland" would have at certain point of their existence likely qualified for foreign recognition, but under the new rules privileging existing states, they were condemned to languish in an international legal and political limbo. Non-recognition meant that they legally remained parts of the states they had broken way from, leaving them permanently exposed to re-absorption by the central government, as "Tamil Eelam" indeed was in 2009. Eritrea and South Sudan did eventually obtain recognition, but this occurred only after their parent state's assent to let the Eritreans and South Sudanese opt for independence in referendums. It was this consent that accomplished what the decades-long control of large swaths of Ethiopian and Sudanese territory could not.

The post-Cold War developments solidified the recognition norms settled in the 1960s and early 1970s. Rather than making any notable dents into the previously established recognition practice, the end of the Cold War in fact extended it beyond the ex-colonial world, effectively precluding secession without the consent of the sovereign government in question as a legitimate way of acquiring statehood. The breakups of the Soviet Union in 1991 and Czechoslovakia in 1993 might have commenced as separatist bids by some of their constituent units, but foreign recognition of the successor states was extended only once the respective central governments had agreed to the dissolution of the unions. For a number of complex reasons, external governments and intergovernmental organizations came to regard the breakup of the Socialist Federal Republic of Yugoslavia (SFRY), despite its non-consensual character, as a case of dissolution legally equivalent to the dissolution of the USSR or Czechoslovakia. Only after this judgment had been made did the individual federal republics become eligible for recognition.

This "neo-decolonization territorial approach" (Hannum 1993, p. 38) again invited the possibility of a mismatch between national identity and new states. Just like in numerous colonial jurisdictions that acceded to independence, the mere fact of living together in the same federal republic did not necessarily indicate either the presence of a shared national identity or the willingness to constitute an independent state within the existing federal borders. Indeed, in both Soviet and Yugoslav cases a number of groups refused to be included in the successor republics and managed to de facto secede from them, thus swelling the ranks of the unrecognized states of the post-colonial world. In Bosnia and Herzegovina, Georgia, Azerbaijan, or Moldova, state recognition itself helped deepen, just as it did, for instance, in the Congo in 1960, the internal divisions stemming from the lack of unified identification with the new states (Lynch 2004, p. 26; Fabry 2010, Chap. 6). Indeed, the pattern seems to have been: The more tenuous the national identity in a territory prior to independence, the more unsettling the aftermath of state recognition.

3 Unrecognized States and National Identity

As seen, the phenomenon of unrecognized states arose in the post-colonial world. It is largely tied to the general international illegitimacy of unilateral secession (McGarry 2004, p. x) that has continued to this day. Prior to decolonization, this illegitimacy did not exist: Unilateral secessionist bids were recognized on a basis of de facto statehood. In the aftermath of decolonization, de facto statehood has been the only way to establish independence on the ground, albeit without general international recognition. The same pattern, however, has been in operation in both cases: Unilateral secessions have entailed a struggle against the parent state that in most instances involved armed violence. And in both cases, this could not happen in the absence of popular identification with the cause of independence that was being pursued. As was the case with predecolonization de facto states, post-colonial unrecognized states, as widely noted (Pegg 1998; Kolstø 2006, pp. 730–731),[8] enjoy considerable popular legitimacy.

If anything, the denial of recognition fosters these sentiments. Unrecognized states subsist in conditions of insecurity and fear. Unable to enjoy the international legal protection of their existence, they are permanently liable to being forcibly reintegrated into the recognized parent state. Even "frozen conflict" and the presence of an external sponsor do not usually attenuate the sense of vulnerability vis-à-vis the parent state. General international isolation only fuels fear and a siege mentality. All these tend to lead to a rallying effect, reinforcing shared national identity among the population of unrecognized states.

Socio-psychological theories of recognition explain well the dynamics of conflict that stems from the denial of recognition, but less well its impact on identity. Wendt (2003, p. 511) is correct in saying that any "recognition is a social act that invests difference with a particular meaning—another actor ('the Other') is constituted as a subject with a legitimate social standing in relation to the Self. This standing implies an acceptance by the Self of normative constraints on how the Other may be treated, and an obligation to give reasons if they must be violated … Actors that are not recognized … do not count and so may be killed or violated as one sees fit." He and other theorists who focus on world politics (Lindemann 2012) are justifiably concerned that if the rebuffed subject nevertheless seeks to gain acceptance of its identity in interaction with others—what is usually referred to as "struggle for recognition"—conflict ensues, with peace and war being at stake. However, recognition must be clearly separated from the existence of an identity. An identity can endure, and even deepen, as others deny it recognition.

---

[8]Pegg (1998, p. 26), in fact, incorporates it into the definition of the de facto state which, he says, "exists where there is an organized political leadership which has risen to power through some degree of indigenous capability; receives popular support; and has achieved sufficient capacity to provide governmental services to a given population in a defined territorial area, over which effective control is maintained for an extended period of time."

The relationship between unrecognized states and national identity is best captured not by socio-psychological theories of recognition, but by writers and theories that emphasize the affirmative impact on a self's collective identity of competitive interactions with a collective other. Psychological theories such as Social Identity Theory and Optimal Distinctiveness Theory investigate collective identity formation and the marked effect on in-group identity of biases against out-groups (Mercer 1995, pp. 237–246; Greenhill 2008, pp. 356–361). Perhaps the most useful is the insight of the political and legal theorist Schmitt (1976), who argued that political identities are strongest in the course of struggles against adversaries. Huntington (1968, p. 123), Tilly (1975), and Herbst (1990) identify this dynamic specifically in the history of state formation—they argue that wars of independence and unification, for all the destruction they brought, helped in the consolidation of national identities. Unrecognized states are a contemporary embodiment of this past phenomenon.

References

Agné, H. (2013). The politics of international recognition: Symposium introduction. *International Theory, 5*(1), 94–107.
Caspersen, N., & Stansfield, G. (Eds.). (2011). *Unrecognized states in the international system*. London: Routledge.
Caspersen, N. (2012). *Unrecognized states: The struggle for sovereignty in the modern international system*. Cambridge: Polity.
Emerson, R. (1969). The problem of identity, selfhood and image in new nations: The situation in Africa. *Comparative Politics, 1*(3), 297–312.
Fabry, M. (2010). *Recognizing states: International society and the establishment of new states since 1776*. Oxford: Oxford University Press.
Goff, P. M., & Dunn, K. C. (2004). Introduction. In defense of identity. In P. M. Goff & K. C. Dunn (Eds.), *Identity and global politics: Theoretical and empirical elaborations* (pp. 1–8). New York: Palgrave McMillan.
Greenhill, B. (2008). Recognition and collective identity formation in international politics. *European Journal of International Relations, 14*(2), 343–368.
Herbst, J. (1990). War and the state in Africa. *International Security, 14*(4), 117–139.
Hannum, H. (1993). Rethinking self-determination. *Virginia Journal of International Law, 34*(1), 1–70.
Holsti, K. J. (1992). International theory and war in the third world. In B. Job (Ed.), *The insecurity dilemma: National security of third world states*. Boulder, CO: Lynne Rienner.
Holsti, K. J. (1996). *The state, war, and the state of war*. Cambridge: Cambridge University Press.
Huntington, S. (1968). *Political order in changing societies*. New Haven, CT: Yale University Press.
Jackson, R. (1986). Negative sovereignty in sub-Saharan Africa. *Review of International Studies, 12*(4), 247–264.
Jackson, R. (1990). *Quasi-states: Sovereignty, international relations and the third world*. Cambridge: Cambridge University Press.
Kamanu, O. S. (1974). Secession and the right to self-determination: An OAU dilemma. *The Journal of Modern African Studies, 12*(3), 355–376.
Kolstø, P. (2006). The sustainability and future of unrecognized quasi-states. *Journal of Peace Research, 43*(6), 723–740.

Lindemann, T. (2012). Concluding remarks on the empirical study of international recognition. In T. Lindemann & E. Ringmar (Eds.), *International politics of recognition* (pp. 209–226). Boulder, CO: Paradigm.

Lynch, D. (2004). *Engaging Eurasia's separatist states: Unresolved conflicts and de facto states.* Washington, DC: United States Institute for Peace.

Manning, W. (Ed.). (1925). *Diplomatic correspondence of the United States concerning the independence of the Latin American nations* (Vol. 1). New York: Oxford University Press.

Mayall, J. (1990). *Nationalism and international society.* Cambridge: Cambridge University Press.

McGarry, J. (2004). Foreword: De facto states and the international order. In T. Bahcheli et al. (Eds.), *De facto states: The quest for sovereignty* (pp. ix–xi). London: Routledge.

Mercer, J. (1995). Anarchy and identity. *International Organization, 49*(2), 229–252.

Murray, M. (2015). Constructing the July crisis: The practices of recognition and the making of the First World War. In C. Daase, A. Geis, C. Fehl & G. Kolliarakis (Eds.), *Recognition in international relations: Rethinking an ambivalent concept in a global context.* London: Palgrave Macmillan.

Pegg, S. (1998). *International society and the de facto state.* Aldershot, UK: Ashgate.

Ringmar, E. (2012). The international politics of recognition. In T. Lindemann & E. Ringmar (Eds.), *International politics of recognition* (pp. 3–24). Boulder, CO: Paradigm.

Roth, B. R. (1999). *Governmental legitimacy in international law.* Oxford: Oxford University Press.

Schmitt, C. (1976). *The concept of the political.* New Brunswick, NJ: Rutgers University Press.

Taylor, C. (1992). The politics of recognition. In A. Gutmann (Ed.), *Multiculturalism and the politics of recognition.* Princeton, NJ: Princeton University Press.

Tilly, C. (1975). Reflections on the history of European state-making. In C. Tilly (Ed.), *The formation of nation-states in Western Europe* (pp. 3–83). Princeton, NJ: Princeton University Press.

Warbrick, C. (2006). States and recognition in international law. In M. D. Evans (Ed.), *International law* (2nd ed., pp. 217–276). Oxford: Oxford University Press.

Wendt, A. (2003). Why a world state is inevitable. *European Journal of International Relations, 9*(4), 491–542.

Wharton, F. (Ed.). (1887). *A digest of the international law of the United States* (Vol. 1). Washington, DC: Government Printing Office.

Author Biography

Mikulas Fabry is Associate Professor in the Sam Nunn School of International Affairs at the Georgia Institute of Technology. He is a political scientist whose research focuses on questions of state, governmental, and territorial legitimacy in international relations and law. He is the author of Recognizing States: International Society and the Establishment of New States since 1776 (Oxford University Press, 2010), multiple chapters in edited volumes, and articles in Ethnopolitics, German Law Journal, International Theory, Nationalities Papers, Diplomacy & Statecraft, Millennium, and Global Society.

Ontological Security of the Post-Soviet de Facto States

Urban Jakša

This contribution begins by recognizing the fact that academic scholarship has hitherto largely neglected the question of identity of de Facto states.[1] We argue that the study of de Facto states would greatly benefit from placing more emphasis on identity by drawing on a growing body of existing literature about state identity and ontological security. The starting premise is that while non-recognition illegalizes de Facto states and threatens their physical security, non-engagement presents no physical threat, but de-legitimizes de Facto states and threatens their ontological security. The argument that we forward on this basis is that de Facto states act to fulfil their self-identity needs and preserve their ontological security, sometimes even to the point of compromising their physical existence.[2] The introduction provides a short overview of the existing scholarship on the identity of de Facto states and introduces three conceptual distinctions crucial to the argument:

The original version of this chapter appeared in The Annual of Language and Language of Politics and Identity (2016), 10, 31–48. This article is updated and reprinted with permission from the copyright holders.

This chapter is dedicated to the Charles University Research Development Schemes, programme PROGRES Q18—Social sciences: from multidisciplinary to interdisciplinary.

---

[1]We use Caspersen and Stansfield's (2011, 337) definition of de facto states as "territories that have achieved de facto independence, often through warfare, and now control most of the area upon which they lay claim. They have demonstrated an aspiration for full de jure independence, but either have not gained international recognition or have, at most, been recognized by a few states".

[2]The argument is based on a similar argument made by Steele (2008, 2) about states in general.

U. Jakša (✉)
University of York, York, UK
e-mail: uj508@york.ac.uk

© Springer International Publishing AG 2017
M. Riegl and B. Doboš (eds.), *Unrecognized States and Secession in the 21st Century*, DOI 10.1007/978-3-319-56913-0_4

recognition-engagement, illegality-illegitimacy, and physical-ontological security. In the first part of the contribution, we proceed to define the concept of ontological security and outline our theoretical framework. In this section we provide arguments why ontological security perspective fits well with our topic and how the adoption of ontological security perspective could enhance thinking about and inform research on de Facto states and—in particular—the post-Soviet de Facto states. In the second part of the contribution we first discuss state identity and ontological security in the Caucasus and shed some light on the relations between honour, identity, and foreign policy. We then apply the ontological security perspective to analyse the decline of the de Facto state Chechen Republic of Ichkeria (CRI) between 1996 and 1999, its eventual defeat and re-incorporation into its parent[3] state—the Russian Federation. In the conclusion we summarize our findings and propose several ways how scholars working on the de Facto states could make use of the ontological security perspective in future research.

The Realist theory of international relations, which has been (implicitly) dominant in the study of de Facto states, emphasizes the physical security of states (Steele 2008, 1). Realists largely view "state motivations as fixed across time and state agents, and myopically connected to the survival drive of states (Steele 2008, 8)." Studies of de Facto states have tended to focus on the de Facto state's relationship to its patron[4] state, parent state or have simply denied any agency to de Facto states (Frear 2014, 83). The support provided by the patron was seen as decisive despite the fact that most de Facto states did not have patrons from the outset and largely won the military conflicts without much external support. When they did secure support of a patron, they began to be seen as pawns in the game of big powers. Claims that Russia is creating a *cordon sanitaire* made of dependent de Facto states were made early on Rywkin (1995) and have increased in volume and intensity following the Ukraine crisis. Overall, there has been little discussion on the identity of de Facto states and when identity was brought up, it was taken as something static and given—as a constant rather than as dynamic and reflexive. Early studies of the 1990s often saw de Facto states as a threat to the international system of sovereign states,[5] as exceptions and temporary anomalies resulting from the dissolution of Soviet Union,[6] as criminalized badlands and black spots (Stanislawski 2008). As Caspersen and Herrberg (2010, 8) have put it: "without sovereignty, anarchy is assumed." With conflicts becoming stable (Rumelili 2015) (rather than frozen)[7] and with the publication of comparative studies[8] (focusing

---

[3]Blakkisrud and Kolstø (2012, 282) define parent state as 'internationally recognized state entity from which the de facto state is trying to break away'.
[4]For a characterization of patron states see Graham and Horne (2012, 10–11).
[5]Hale (2000) used the term 'parade of sovereignties' suggesting the possible domino effect.
[6]See Pegg (1998) and Lynch (2004), for example.
[7]See Rutland (2007) and Broers (2015) for criticism of the concept of frozen conflict.
[8]Pegg (1998, 4–11) was one of the first to make an attempt to theorize engagement with de facto states on a more general level.

mostly on Caucasus)⁹ these views were put into a balance and the de Facto states became somewhat 'normalized' in the academic discourse. In some cases state-building successes and democratic achievements were acknowledged (Abkhazia, Nagorno-Karabakh). Despite these changes in the perception of the de Facto state identity, there was little discussion about identity and its relation to non-recognition, which also remains to be taken for granted as an a priori constraining factor and one that entirely defines the de Facto state's identity.[10]

We will not focus on non-recognition per se, but before proceeding to define the ontological security, we must distinguish between non-recognition and non-engagement, and—related to this—between physical and ontological security. Non-recognition presents a threat to physical security of a de Facto state, since its existence is illegal, and its parent state is legally allowed (within certain limits) to restore its territorial integrity and re-incorporate the entity.[11] Non-engagement presents no physical threat, but makes the entity appear illegitimate and threatens the ontological security of the state.

1 The Perspective of Ontological Security

It would be a mistake to underplay the importance of physical security for de Facto states, especially given the fact that most of them emerged out of violent conflicts. Nevertheless, ontological security is just as important—and as we will see in some cases—more important "because its fulfilment affirms a state's self-identity (i.e. it affirms not only its physical existence but primarily how a state sees itself and secondarily how it wants to be seen by others) (Steele 2008, 3)." Indeed, of what importance is one's physical survival if one is unsure about his own identity and this uncertainty prevents him from defining and pursuing his goals? If this situation lasts long enough, it can even undermine the physical security itself. In the Bible we are asked "For what does it profit a man to gain the whole world, and forfeit his soul? (Marc 8: 36)" and there are several historical examples (from Huns to Mongols) when a nation has conquered other peoples but was in turn conquered by and wholly assimilated into the culture of the conquered. They achieved military

---

[9]De Waal (2003), and Svensson (2009) have compared ethnic-political conflicts and unrecognized entities in the Caucasus, while still focusing primarily on Nagorno-Karabakh. Khintba (2010), Grono (2010) and Popescu (2007) have focused more on Georgia's breakaway republics, but also maintained the regional focus.

[10]For analogous terms see Geldenhuys (2009). Although the term 'unrecognized state' may be more widespread and popular (especially outside academia, in journalistic employ), the majority of scholars studying these entities uses the term 'de facto states' (O'Loughlin et al. 2015, 2), which emphasizes their identity as states over the circumstance of non-recognition.

[11]Non-recognition can also present a threat to ontological security, but this is often of secondary importance. Note that CRI's ontological security only started declining once its physical security has been established and the Russian army forced to leave.

conquest, but lost the ontological war and ceased to exist as a separate people. As we will see, the de Facto states face the same ontological dilemma regarding their relations with parent and patron states: what do they gain if they wrest the territory from the parent state but lose their independence to their patron, if they gain security, but lose their identity in the process?

Ontological security can be defined as a "sense of continuity and order in events (Giddens 1991, 243)" and conversely, ontological insecurity "refers to the deep, incapacitating state of not knowing which dangers to confront and which to ignore, i.e. how to get by in the world (Mitzen 2006, 345)." Ontological secure states are confident about their expectations, aware of their interests and rational when pursuing them. Ontologically insecure states are "consumed meeting immediate needs" and "cannot relate ends systematically to means in the present, much less plan ahead (Mitzen 2006, 345)." But why do states have ontological security, and how can we justify the use of this concept? Steele (2008, 20) convincingly argues that "The reason states have an ontological security is because they have a historical account of themselves that has been 'built up' through the narrative of agents of the past, present, and the future."

The ontological security perspective does not exclude physical security and does not marginalize its importance; it just adds another layer of understanding. In a similar manner, it implies no determination, but simply states that preservation of self-identity matters to states and that failure to fulfil ontological needs of a state can have security consequences that cannot be explained by traditional accounts of security. This perspective sheds light on how states aim to fulfil their self-identity needs and aspires to unpack the 'motives' of state behaviour. While Steele looks at moral, humanitarian, and honour-driven motives (Steele 2008, 2), only the latter will be of immediate interest to us. It is worth mentioning that honour-driven motives may seem "irrational—yet such behaviour must have made sense to the state agents who decided upon that course of action at the time (Steele 2008, 3)." State needs may not be rational (such as to achieve national glory), but their pursuit usually is. In other words: ontological security perspective enables us to see the rationality behind what seems like irrational behaviour on the part of the political elites and decision-makers in (de Facto) states.

There are two versions of the ontological security perspective. The first one is Mitzen's, which focuses on collective aspects, emphasizing identity constitution through interaction. The second version is Steele's and it focuses on individual aspects, looking at how identity arises through the construction of narratives.[12] Steele's version is based on the claim that "actors already constructed some sense of self and some understanding of others prior to contact (Inayatullah and Blaney 1996, 73)." An old philosophical dilemma whether essence precedes existence—which threatens to open up here—is relatively easily resolved when it comes to

---

[12]According to Lebow (2012) there is no identity in the strict sense; we only have a phenomenological identity of the moment. Therefore it is therefore better to speak of identifications rather than of identities.

most de Facto states. It is clear that they only came into existence as de Facto independent in 1990s. While it is in this time period that they have entered into contact and interaction with the outside world, their national identity together with narratives about it has already been established (although it remains to change) as a result of a long historical process.[13] Although providing a convincing account of the internal dynamics of the state, Steele eventually takes a linguistic turn, goes down the postmodernist constructivist path as he becomes increasingly focused on the Self and state narratives that sustain it. Since de Facto states cannot be studied separately from the conflicts and the overall context of the dissolution of the Soviet Union (Tekushev et al. 2013), we are interested primarily in the relation between interaction and the ontological security of de Facto states. We will therefore more closely follow Mitzen's version, which is a better fit, but will incorporate Steele's use of 'routine' and 'critical situation' (concepts taken over from Giddens)—which we proceed to define—into our conceptual framework.

According to Giddens (1984, 171) "[a]gents encounter social structures through the sustained activity of self-identity fulfilment through foreign policy. States consciously reproduce actions that then in turn form a structure through what can be called agency because "human societies, or social systems, would plainly not exist without human agency." Based on this, Steele sees foreign policy as the realisation of self-identity through routines. States construct a notion of Self, they forge their identity out of temporary identifications through *discourse* and *action*: the product of the first are *narratives*, the product of the second are *routines*. The "forging of selves, then, is a path-dependent process, since it has to cram in a number of previously negotiated identities in order to be credible (Neumann 1999, 218–19 in Steele 2008, 32)." If the routines, on which it is based and which sustain it, are disrupted, the ontological security of the state is threatened. Giddens (1984, 61) calls these disruptions 'critical situations' and defines them as "radical disjunctions of an unpredictable kind affecting substantial numbers of individuals." Critical situations need to be interpreted as such by policy makers, they cannot be predicted and normally catch states unprepared (Steele 2008, 12). Ontologically secure states will show more resilience when faced with critical situations, which disrupt routines that sustain a state's self-identity.

Before discussing the relevance of ontological security perspective for analysing the post-Soviet de Facto states, we will briefly look at the 'level of analysis problem' (sometimes referred to as the problem of 'personification' or 'reification' of the state), which however is not unique to the ontological security perspective. In fact "most models of International Relations base the needs of states on some type of individual and human need (Steele and Amoureux 2005, 529)" and then scale it to the collective entity. Realism derives relations between states from Hobbesian relations between individuals and Liberalism from the rational self-interested

---

[13]One could argue that this is not the case of Transnistria. At the time of its emergence as a de facto state it had little in the way of a positive identity, but its negative identity was strong—people did not know what they wanted their state to be, but they knew they did not want to be part of Moldova, which was drawing ever closer to Romania.

homines oeconomici. But this 'everyone else does it' argument is not enough to convince the sceptics of the 'scaling-up' and in addition to Mitzen's three defences, Steele (2008, 18) offers his own defence, which is perhaps the most convincing: "because they represent their state, state agents 'are the state' because they have the moral burden of making policy choices and the capacity to implement those decisions." Here the problem is resolved by conceptualising the state as a socio-political institution based on practices and actions traceable back to individual decision-makers. This is similar to what Isachenko (2012, 7) in her analysis of de Facto states (she calls them 'informal states') calls 'statecraft'—the ways statehood is constructed and maintained as opposed to 'stateness'—the understanding of the state as a fixed territorial entity. She advocates a shift from asking questions about what the state is to how state and sovereignty are produced. This conceptual shift represents the move from Realist ontology of state as a given, objective, territorially fixed and largely unchangeable entity to a Constructivist ontology of state as socially constructed, subjective and ever-changing polity.

These defences notwithstanding, Realists may argue that the concept of ontological security is fuzzy. This accusation can be countered by pointing out that it is the Realist understanding of identity that is fuzzy because it treats identity as a loosely defined 'type' while its behaviourist view of states as 'black boxes' or 'billiard balls' prevents it from exploring intra-state dynamics and providing and account of how identity is shaped by and shapes the (inter)actions of states. This is precisely what the emphasis on ontological security allows us to do. It enables us to structure our understanding of disparate and ever-changing state interests into a more coherent whole: "state interests change all the time, and if this is the case, then identity changes are possible within similar institutional forms. Ontological security helps connect interests to these sudden engagements with identity (Steele 2008, 20)."

2 The Application of Ontological Security to Post-Soviet de Facto States

We now proceed to look at the relevance of ontological security for the study of de Facto states and present the arguments as to why this perspective is appropriate and applies a fortiori to the post-Soviet de Facto states. Two arguments will be provided to support each claim.

The first argument draws on the distinction between domestic and foreign policy that has become blurred in de Facto states. The consequence of this is that turbulences in external relations translate easily into domestic politics, making the ontological security of the de Facto state more vulnerable compared to recognized states. A simple event, such as participation in an international sports competition (Balzani Lööv 2014) can boost confidence and improve ontological security. An equally modest event, such as a high-level meeting of officials from de Facto state's parent and patron states can undermine it. The de Facto states' ontological security is highly dependent on how it perceives other actors in the international community perceive it. Examples include the meaning de Facto states like Nagorno-Karabakh ascribe to their standing according to the Freedom House index (Broers et al. 2015, 4) and the importance which they attribute to visits by foreign officials, such as the one made to Transnistria in 2007 by the then US ambassador in Moldova Michael Kirby (Isachenko 2012, 115). In other words: the interconnectedness of foreign and domestic policies result in the elimination of the border between the inside and outside of de Facto states, 'opening them up' to international politics and making their identity less resilient when faced with external challenges.

The second argument has to do with the distinction between non-recognition and non-engagement mentioned in the introduction. As these two mostly overlap, this distinction is not always evident despite proposals to decouple one from the other.[14] As we have stated before, non-recognition presents a threat to physical security of a de Facto state, while non-engagement presents no physical threat, but threatens ontological security of the state. We argue that due to their isolation, the ontological security of de Facto states is more difficult to preserve (and is therefore more important to them) than is the case with recognized states. The result of non-engagement is isolation and just like an isolated person without a possibility to interact with other people, a de Facto state turns inwards and starts questioning its identity. "Ontological security-seeking behaviour is fulfilled through the reproduction of action that takes the form of routines (Steele 2008, 23)." Non-engagement of the de Facto states prevents the establishment of (foreign policy) routines, undermining the de Facto state's ontological security. As time passes, the ongoing ethno-political conflict has less bearing on the life of the people as they adapt to the situation (however the mindsets, practices and routines related to the conflict stay in place)—during this time the de Facto states realize it is highly unlikely they will ever attain wide recognition and instead focus their efforts on engagement. Since they now prioritize engagement, failure in routinizing interaction with significant others can increase ontological insecurity of a de Facto state. There are de Facto states that have successfully preserved their ontological security and have even strengthened their identity through state-building. A good example is Somaliland, which has achieved remarkable successes in building strong democratic institutions.[15] An opposite example of ontological security breakdown and eventual state collapse is the CRI, which we will look at more closely in the next section.

We now proceed to present the arguments in support of the claim that focusing on ontological security is in particular justified in the case of the post-Soviet de Facto states. First, I argue that this perspective is well suited for analysing de Facto states that have emerged from the violent conflicts following the disintegration of USSR. All the post-Soviet de Facto state have experienced fierce interethnic wars with their parent states and in addition to lost lives and wrecked economies, their

---

[14]Popescu (2007) introduced the concept of 'engagement without recognition', stating that EU should engage with Abkhazia and South Ossetia. This idea was then furthered by Cooley and Mitchell (2010, 80).

[15]See Hansen and Bradbury (2007), Terlinden (2008, 51–67).

identities emerged scarred by siege mentality.[16] Mechanisms for dealing with ontological insecurity exist in society:

> In one sense, society solves its members' ontological security problem for them, since society is a shared cognitive ordering of the environment (Giddens 1991). When trauma happens, the individual's fall is cushioned by the social order, which reproduces a general ontological security until she can pick herself up again. But society is no more than the social practices its members engage in, which means that its continuation depends on the constant reproduction of those practices. Individual-level routines thus constitute society, which in turn stabilizes each individual's sense of self (Mitzen 2006, 348).

However, no such mechanisms exist in the international community, which, far from being an international society, is more like an exclusive club of sovereign states that rigidly and jealously upholds the principle of sovereignty. de Facto states, which emerge out of the trauma of violent conflicts, do not get any cushion as they are considered to be deviant cases challenging the order of sovereignty, and are excluded from the community. Non-recognition prevents the de Facto states from making their voice heard in international fora, while not interacting with them means not hearing what they have to say. In an application of ontological security perspective to conflict resolution, Rumelili (2015) emphasizes that the focus on ontological security can help us explain why some conflicts—she mentions Northern Cyprus, Palestine, and Kurdistan, which are all de Facto states that have emerged from a violent conflict—become protracted. Ontological security becomes especially important when the conflicts become stabilized, where symbolic violence has replaced physical violence and where anxiety about future without recognition has overshadowed security fears of being re-integrated into the parent state. An extreme example of the siege mentality is Abkhazia, where the titular nation—the Abkhaz—represent only 40–50%[17] of the population and fears not only being re-incorporated into Georgia, becoming over-dependent on Russia, but also being 'engulfed'[18] in their own state.[19] As a response to this perceived threat, the Abkhaz have built an ethnocracy[20]—a distinct regime-type based on the control of most governmental positions by the titular nation (Yiftachel and Ghanem 2004).

Second, I argue that the decision of the de Facto states to secede from their parent states and unilaterally declare independence was justified on ontological rather than physical security grounds. Chechens, Abkhaz, Karabakh Armenians, Ossetians and others were not afraid of being physically annihilated or of losing the relative control

---

[16]Siege mentality can be defined as a mental state in which members of a group hold a central belief that the rest of the world has highly negative behavioural intentions toward them (Bar-Tal 1986).

[17]The numbers of the 2011 are likely to be inflated and donot take into account the Georgian refugees/IDPs who were forced to leave Abkhazia during and after the war. Census data is available here: http://www.ethno-kavkaz.narod.ru/rnabkhazia.html (2 November 2015).

[18]Engulfment is the "extreme distress of the person who finds himself under a compulsion to take on the characteristics of a personality/.../ alien to his own" (Laing 1990, 58).

[19]A good account of this is provided by Trier et al. (2010).

[20]See Popescu (2006), O'Loughlin et al. (2011).

over their territory (by centralization and abolishment of the 'autonomous republic' status). They were afraid that in the newly independent parent states, which were embarking on nation-building projects, they will not be able to maintain their national identity and will be discriminated, marginalized, and assimilated. The decision to secede was in itself a product of a looming identity crisis in the final years of the USSR when the people lost faith in their common state and its elites, the communist cause and the value system associated with it. de Facto states had to reinvent and redefine themselves along national lines and nation-building was a way of achieving ontological security despite the fact that this *glasnost*-era outburst of nationalism undermined their physical security. However, despite presenting a danger for physical security, the aggressive behaviour can provide a framework for the sustenance of ontological security. The ontological security perspective allows us to "better understand why states feel compelled to pursue/.../ 'costly' actions and, most importantly, why such action is rational and in a state's self-interest even if it contradicts our prevailing conception of state security (Steele 2008, 5)."

Before applying ontological security to the case study of the CRI, it must be stated that non-recognition does not affect the ontological security of the de Facto states (along with their behaviour) directly. Rather, this happens indirectly as non-recognition is interpreted by the political elites, and it is these elite interpretations of non-recognition and non-engagement that influence the ontological security of de Facto states. All the post-Soviet de Facto states have gone through at least three 'critical situations': (1) collapse of the Soviet Union; (2) war with their parent state for the control over the territory claimed by the de Facto state; and (3) international recognition of territorial integrity of their parent state, ruling out their own recognition of independence. A gradual shift in perception (it sometimes happens at the same time as the third critical situation) occurs when the state is not preoccupied anymore with its own existential questions and tending to its needs, and has the ability and confidence to enter into relations with other states with realistic expectations. Looking at the de Facto states, this usually occurs when the de Facto state stops prioritizing the long-term quest for recognition (accepts its unrecognized status) and focuses instead on short and medium-term goals, such as state-building, attracting aid and investment, and forging cultural links.[21]

3 Ontological Security and Honour in the Caucasus

After justifying the application of ontological security perspective to the post-Soviet de Facto states, we proceed to apply this perspective to identify the role of honour—an important part of culture and identity—in the behaviour of the de Facto

---

[21]De facto states normally do not declare this shift, but the diversification of interests is evident from official statements and foreign policy practices of de facto states. Somaliland, Northern Cyprus and Abkhazia are all good examples, but the best one is probably Taiwan, which has all but abandoned the goal of obtaining recognition for the goal of developing economic relations.

states in the Caucasus in 1990s. The aim of this is to provide cultural and historical context for the case study of the decline and eventual re-incorporation of the CRI into the Russian Federation.

Despite the fact that honour talk today is mostly dismissed as a rhetorical device (O'Neill 1999, 85) and predictably has no role to play in Realist conceptions of international relations, the collapse of Soviet Union and the ensuing transition crisis of 1990 s in most of the post-Soviet space—soaring unemployment, inequality, poverty, crime, interethnic strife—is closely related to the loss of honour. The discourse of national humiliation as a historical trauma is very much present in the post-Soviet space, spearheaded by Russia's rediscovered imperial ambitions and revisionist foreign policy, but also present in other post-Soviet states. "A man who has lost honour is treated as a nonperson in many societies, ignored rather than punished (O'Neill 1999, 87)." In traditional societies (the ones in the Caucasus are among them), the loss of honour is punished by ignoring the offender. We can ask a question here whether this is not exactly how de Facto states are treated by the international community. By ignoring and isolating them, the message of the international community may be that it upholds the principle of state sovereignty and territorial integrity, but this message is interpreted locally[22] as an accusation that the de Facto states have acted dishonourably (for the reasons likely unknown to them).[23] For this reason attaining recognition is for the de Facto states not just a pragmatic political objective, but a moral crusade to regain the honour they have lost.

The function honour performs is the one of physical and ontological protection—it "has a 'Don't Tread on Me' component (O'Neill 1999, 87)," which is especially true for the cultures and societies of the Caucasus, which have been trying to ward off foreign incursions into its ancestral lands for centuries. It has served to protect these communities as "[i]t is the duty of the honourable person to generate common knowledge that he is honourable, to assure everyone that he would be willing to defend the group (O'Neill 1999, 88)." Honour acts as a defence mechanism of small societies—a kind of an automatic commitment to action with which they show the resolve, cohesiveness and determination to answer any provocation and defend themselves. With a strong commitment to action they increase the costs that the potential attacker perceives as tied to his actions and thus attempt to compensate for what they lack in numbers or material.

However, despite protecting the state, honour and its pursuit can undermine the state's physical security. The ontological security perspective "informs a nation-state's conception of honour, and how self-identity needs can completely jeopardize the physical existence of a state (Steele 2008, 23)." This is especially true for the cultural context of the Caucasus where in several moments in history people

---

[22]"The relevant question is not whether the honour of states is challenged, but whether they see it as challenged" (O'Neil 1999, 102).

[23]O'Neill (1999, 91) also states that isolation can be self-induced: "honour is like group membership, in that those who lose honour want to withdraw".

have proven that they rather die than lose honour.[24] This is especially true for the North Caucasus, where informal codes of honour (*adat*) have developed centuries ago. There are historical examples of states choosing to preserve their honour (as a core element of their ontological security) by undermining their physical security, even risking annihilation: from Melians rejecting to join the Athenian alliance to Belgium's rejection of the German ultimatum during the First World War (Steele 2008, 14). "[S]mall states also have an obligation to international society (what I term their 'external honour') (Steele 2008, 14)." In fact, small states often show an inflated sense of moral responsibility that borders on mythical and symbolic narratives. States like Serbia and Georgia have seen themselves as guardians of Christianity and the bulwark against the expansion of Islam. The de Facto states in the Caucasus attempt to regain honour through obtaining recognition, which sometimes involves great risks, including fighting bloody wars, suffering economic hardships or even risking to be defeated militarily and reincorporated into their parent state. However, taking great risks makes sense as it brings valour and increases one's honour.[25] Looking at it from the perspective of ontological security and focusing on its implications for honour, recognition becomes—at least in the regional context of the Caucasus—even more important. It not only brings physical security (sovereignty and territorial integrity), but also has symbolic importance for reaffirming a de Facto state's identity and thus boosts ontological security.

4 Case Study: The Chechen Republic of Ichkeria 1996–1999[26]

Having discussed the applicability of ontological perspective to post-Soviet facto states and the specific cultural and historical context of the Caucasus in which honour is a crucial part, we now turn to our case study in two parts. First we provide justification for the case selection and then present the case itself.

The case of the CRI is a good example that illustrates our main argument and establishes the importance of ontological security perspective for four main reasons. First, the case of CRI shows that ontological security can become compromised even in de Facto states with strong national unity, almost complete ethnic

---

[24]Bullough (2010) recounts a widespread story that during Stalin's 1944 mass deportation of Chechens to Central Asia, the honourable Chechen women were too ashamed to relieve themselves in the railroad cars in front of everyone and they held on until their bladders burst.

[25]"While offering insults was an expected mode of maintaining honour, [a Montenegrin male] also knew that his stronger provocations might get him killed. In the eyes of the tribe, this was exactly what made aggressive behaviour commendable in many contexts. If he offered insults that came close to requiring homicidal retaliation, then no one would doubt his courage" (Boehm 1983, 145 in: O'Neill 1999, 112).

[26]The case study is based on secondary literature, and two visits to CRI in November and December 2014 during which informative interviews with residents of Grozny were conducted.

homogeneity (unlike Abkhazia or Transnistria), and very cohesive society with strong multi-level solidarity based on belonging of each individual to a *teip* (clan), *aul* (village community) and *tukhum* (district; largest social unit uniting dozens of *teips*) (Jaimoukha 2004, 87–93). Second, among the post-Soviet de Facto states, the case of CRI is the most radical example of sacrificing physical security in order to regain lost honour and re-establish ontological security with the most severe consequences.[27] As such it most clearly demonstrates our argument. Third, the case contradicts realist interpretations that place too much emphasis on the (military) relations between the de Facto state and its parent state. The argument that the military imbalance between Russia and CRI was so great that re-incorporation was inevitable is countered by the fact that the ontological security was undermined first and only as a result of that was the physical security undermined. Fourth, the case of Chechnya [which has a rich history and culture and has only come under Russian rule with the surrender of Imam Shamil in 1859 (Souleimanov 2011, 156–157)] is a clear demonstration that identity of the de Facto states precedes interaction, but that interaction (in this case with states spreading radical Wahhabi interpretation of Islam) eventually shapes identity. Here we can agree with Mitzen rather than Steele in the sense that ontological insecurity is the result of interaction rather than a self-induced crisis of the Self or collapse of the state narrative.

After having won the First Chechen War and secured its de Facto independence, Chechnya became increasingly split between nationalists and Islamists. Nationalists, who came mostly from the military, like presidents Dudayev (Soviet major general) and Mashkadov (Soviet officer and the commander in charge of the defence of Grozny during the First Chechen War) were in favour of a secular republic, while presidents Yandarbiyev (writer-poet) and Sadulayev (imam) wanted the creation of an Islamic state based on *sharia law*.[28] While other de Facto states in the post-Soviet space managed to preserve their ontological security and engage in state-building that rallied people around the flag and ensured social cohesion in the face of a common threat (Dembinska 2009, 613), CRI's divided political elites increasingly turned towards each other.[29]

During the period of the de Facto independence CRI became a sort of a 'black hole' (Pegg 1998)—a zone of illegality and organized crime, run by warlords and

---

[27] According to Swirszcz (2009, 61) "The Chechens lived in their tight-knit community, with its complex social layering and clan mentality, tied together by a code of conduct (*nokhchalla*). This code of conduct, finding similar strains among all Caucasian societies (and given the general term of *adat*), has regulated Chechen behavior for centuries".

[28] Schaefer (2010) largely sees the split as internal to religion, as "[b]eing Chechen has always *ipso facto* meant being (Sunni) Muslim" (Gammer 2006, 214). The split that began in the early 1990s and continues to this day is according to Schafer between traditional moderate Sufi orders of Nasqbandi and Qadiri and the new, foreign radicalism of the Saudi-sponsored Wahhabism. Campana (2006, 129) sees it as a struggle for power between four groups: "the separatists, the radical Islamists, the traditionalists and the pro-Russians".

[29] King (2001) has pointed to the benefits these conflicts may bring to the political elites, which have throughout the conflict enriched themselves and occupied the positions of power. This also relates to the problem of conflict-sustaining routines discussed earlier.

riddled with in-fighting and corruption. The Islamists promised to bring security to the local population, eradicate corruption and tackle crime through the implementation of *sharia* law (the Taliban have taken over in Afghanistan with a similar agenda, which is today forwarded by Al-Shabaab, Boko Haram and ISIS).[30] As socio-economic situation worsened (Souleimanov 2011, 157–158), crime intensified and violence escalated (smuggling, slavery, kidnappings, assassinations, terrorism) (King 2008, 237–238), this undermined the ontological security of the state and pushed the Islamists towards a radical path. Led by Shamil Basayev and Dokka Umarov, the Islamists became progressively more radical.[31] State interaction had a crucial role in this. While Abkhazia—for instance—interacted with Turkey and in a limited way with the EU and Russia, the CRI was recognized by Taliban-led Afghanistan and forged close relations with the Gulf countries and the extremists in North Caucasus (Schaefer 2010, 127–128; Bullough 2010, 400–401). To attract support and 'earn' recognition Abkhazia tried to present itself as a democratic, law-abiding and responsible member of the international community, while CRI was obliged to present itself as a model Islamic state—an identity that was becoming increasingly difficult to sustain externally in the face of the overall collapse of the Chechen society.

In order to resolve this cognitive dissonance and restore the ontological security, the Islamists abandoned the goal of implementing *sharia* in the morally bankrupt nationalist CRI. If the society was to be purified, honour was to be washed with blood and changing one governmental elite with another would not have sufficed. A new identity—the Caucasus Emirate that included all of Muslim North Caucasus—was invented. To bring about the Emirate, the Chechen Islamist militants started behaving more and more irresponsibly, resorting to terrorism and destabilising the region, which Russia could not accept. The 1999 invasion of Dagestan by the Chechnya-based Islamic International Brigade was the most delusional attempt to put this idea of the Emirate in practice and should be read as a moral crusade to save Chechnya from the state into which it has fallen (Hughes 2013, 153–157). It was a plan that badly misfired, triggered the Second Chechen War and the eventual re-incorporation into Russian Federation.

---

[30]Following the death of Aslan Maskhadov, who was trying to keep control over CRI but was progressively losing control to Islamists, YuliaLatynina wrote in the Moscow Times: "The extremists enjoy a significant moral advantage as well. The authorities in the North Caucasus are fantastically corrupt and cowardly. Their betrayal of their own people knows no bounds. The post of future imam is not for sale. The election can't be rigged and unacceptable candidates can't be stricken from the ballot by obedient judges. The new imam's qualities will not be those the Kremlin uses to choose regional leaders—cowardice, corruptness and a lack of principles—but the qualities esteemed by the culture of the North Caucasus".

[31]Wilhelmsen (2005, 52) argued that behind this radicalisation "there were more pragmatic reasons, such as funding and fighters".

5 Conclusion

In this contribution we have claimed that the majority of scholarship on de Facto states has either (1) ignored the question of identity of de Facto states, (2) viewed identity as fixed (mostly in forms of negative stereotypes) or has (3) altogether denied the agency of de Facto states by presenting them as mere puppets of their patrons. Our main argument states that in some cases, de Facto states have pursued self-identity needs in order to preserve their ontological security, which—as the case of CRI demonstrates—compromised their physical existence to the point of physical destruction and formal reincorporation of the entity.

The case study supported our arguments laid out in the theoretical part in several ways. It showed that while other post-Soviet de Facto states embarked on state-building projects, Chechnya's divided political elites competed for control over the state, undermining its ontological security. The case illustrates that ontological security can become compromised even in de Facto states with strong national unity and ethnically homogenous population. Next, the weakening of ontological security took place in the context of increasing interaction with radical Islamic movements and regimes resulting in mutual radicalisation of domestic and foreign policy, which testifies to the fact that distinction between domestic and foreign policy has become blurred in de Facto states. It also highlights the fact that identity of de Facto states exists before interaction, but that interaction can (re-) shape their identity. Furthermore, the case underlined the importance of honour for the de Facto states in the Caucasus and showed how the entity resorted to violence to restore its honour and regain its ontological security by reinventing itself as the Caucasus Emirate. Finally, the case has buttressed our main argument that in some cases, the de Facto states have acted in a way as to fulfil their self-identity needs and preserve their ontological security, sometimes even to the point of compromising their physical existence.

In conclusion, we would like to propose a few ways in which scholars working on de Facto states could make use of the growing body of literature on ontological security in their future research. First, the ontological security could help us explain the continued existence of de Facto states. It can do so through exploring the relationship between foreign and domestic politics of de Facto states and the role of routines that have become entrenched and emotions (honour, glory, shame) that have become invested into the state-building. Second, it can help us gain better understanding of the 'new'[32] de Facto states: ISIS, People's Republic of Donetsk and People's Republic of Lugansk where radical changes in directions of state-building[33] suggest a degree of ontological insecurity. Third—and perhaps most important—is that ontological security perspective reveals that "behind the routines of daily life, chaos lurks (Mitzen 2006, 346)," which does not translate into

---

[32]Mylonas and Ahram (2015) call them 'unbound'.

[33]The two de facto states in East Ukraine at first expressed the wish to become part of Russia. When this was rejected they united to form Novorossiya—a project that was abandoned soon after.

"behind sovereignty lies anarchy" (as Realists would like us to believe), but it indicates that we risk real chaos if we get rid of routines—the procedures and practices that define interactions between actors and provide them with ontological security.

References

Balzani Lööv, J. (2014, June). *Sweden hosts world cup tournament for unrecognized nations*. Eurasianet. http://www.eurasianet.org/node/68556. Accessed November 2, 2015.

Bar-Tal, D. (1986). The Masada syndrome: A case of central belief. In N. A. Milgram (Ed.), *Stress and coping in the time of war* (pp. 32–51). New York: Brunnor/Mazel.

Blakkisrud, H., & Kolstø, P. (2012). Dynamics of de Facto statehood: The South Caucasian de Facto states between secession and sovereignty. *Southeast European and Black Sea Studies, 12*(2), 281–298.

Broers, L., Iskandaryan, A., & Minasyan, S. (2015). Introduction: The unrecognized politics of de Facto states in the post-Soviet space. *Caucasus Survey, 3*, 1–8.

Bullough, O. (2010). *Let our fame be great: Journeys among the defiant people of the Caucasus*. London: Penguin Books.

Campana, A. (2006). The effects of war on the Chechen national identity construction. *National Identities, 8*(2), 129–148.

Caspersen, N., & Stansfield, G. (Eds.). (2011). *Unrecognized states in the international system*. Routledge: London.

Caspersen, N., & Herrberg, A. (2010). *Engaging unrecognized states in conflict resolution: An opportunity or challenge for the EU?*. Brussels: Initiative for Peacebuilding.

Cooley, A., & Mitchell, L. A. (2010). Engagement without Recognition: A New Strategy toward Abkhazia and Eurasia's Unrecognized States. *The Washington Quarterly, 33*(4), 59–73.

Dembinska, M. (2009). Briser les logiques du «gel»: Approche différenciée et transformative en Abkhazie et en Transnistrie. *Étudesinternationales, 40*(4), 611.

De Waal, T. (2003). *Black Garden Armenia and Azerbaijan through Peace and War*. New York: NYU Press.

Frear, T. (2014). The foreign policy options of a small unrecognised state: The case of Abkhazia. *Caucasus Survey, 1*(2), 83–107.

Gammer, M. (2006). *The lone wolf and the bear, three centuries of chechen defiance of Russian rule*. Pittsburgh: University of Pittsburgh Press.

Geldenhuys, D. (2009). *Contested states in world politics*. Basingstoke: Palgrave Macmillan.

Giddens, A. (1984). *The constitution of society*. Berkeley: University of California Press.

Giddens, A. (1991). *Modernity and self-identity*. Palo Alto: Stanford University Press.

Graham, B. A. T., & Horne, B. (2012). *Unrecognized States: A Theory of Self-Determination and Foreign Influence*. Los Angeles: University of Southern California.

Grono, M. F. (2010). *Georgia's conflicts: What role for the EU as a mediator? Initiative for peacebuilding, mediation cluster*. http://www.initiativeforpeacebuilding.eu/pdf/Georgia_March2010.pdf. Accessed November 28, 2013.

Hansen, S. J., & Bradbury, M. (2007). Somaliland: A new democracy in the horn of Africa? *Review of African Political Economy, 34*(113), 466.

Hale, H. (2000). The parade of sovereignties: Testing theories of secession in the Soviet setting. *British Journal of Political Science, 30* (1), 31–56.

Hughes, J. (2013). *Chechnya: From nationalism to Jihad*. Chicago: University of Pennsylvania Press.

Inayatullah, N., & Blaney, D. L. (1996). Knowing encounters: Beyond parochialism in international relations theory. In Y. Lapid & F. Kratochwil (Eds.), *The return of culture and identity in IR theory*. Boulder, CO: Lynne Rienner Publishers.

Isachenko, D. (2012). *The making of informal states: Statebuilding in Northern Cyprus and Transdniestria*. Basingstoke: Palgrave Macmillan.

Jaimoukha, A. (2004). *The chechens: A handbook*. London: Routledge.

King, C. (2001). The benefits of ethnic war: Understanding Eurasia's unrecognized states. *World Politics, 53*, 524–552.

King, C. (2008). *The ghost of freedom: A history of the Caucasus*. Oxford: Oxford University Press.

Khintba, I. (2010). *The EU and the conflicts in the Eastern Neighbourhood: The case of Abkhazia*. Berlin: Heinrich Böll Foundation.

Laing, R. D. (1990). *The divided self*. New York: Penguin Books. (Original work published 1960).

Lebow, R. N. (2012). *The politics and ethics of identity: In search of ourselves*. Cambridge: Cambridge University Press.

Lynch, D. (2004). *Engaging Eurasia's separatist states: Unresolved conflicts and de Facto states*. Washington: United States Institute of Peace Press.

Mitzen, J. (2006). Ontological security in world politics: State identity and the security dilemma. *European Journal of International Relations, 12*(3), 341–370.

Mylonas, H., & Ahram, A. I. (2015). De Facto states unbound. *PONARS Eurasia Policy Memo 374*. 1–6.

O'Loughlin, J., Kolossov, V., & Toal, G. (2013). Inside Abkhazia: Survey of attitudes in a de Facto state. *Post-Soviet Affairs, 27*(1), 1–36.

O'Loughlin, J., Kolossov, V., & Toal, G. (2015). Inside the post-Soviet de Facto states: A comparison of attitudes in Abkhazia, Nagorny Karabakh, South Ossetia, and Transnistria. *Eurasian Geography and Economics, 55*, 1–34.

O'Neill, B. (1999). *Honor, symbols, and war*. Ann Arbor: University of Michigan Press.

Pegg, S. (1998). *De Facto states in the international system. Institute of International Relations*. Vancouver: University of British Columbia.

Popescu, N. (2006). *Democracy in secessionism: Transnistria and Abkhazia's domestic policies*. Bucharest: Open Society Institute.

Popescu, N. (2007). *Europe's unrecognised neighbours: The EU in Abkhazia and South Ossetia*. CEPS working document no. 260.

Rutland, P. (2007). Frozen conflicts, frozen analysis. Paper presented at the *ISA's 48th Annual Convention, Chicago*, 1st March 2007.

Rumelili, B. (2015). *Conflict resolution and ontological security: Peace anxieties*. London: Routledge.

Rywkin, M. (1995). The Western Borderlands of the Former Soviet Union: Issues and Problems. *American Foreign Policy Interests. 17*(1), 5–12. Chicago.

Schaefer, R. W. (2010). *The Insurgency in Chechnya and the North Caucasus from Gazavat to Jihad*. Santa Barbara, Calif.: Praeger Security International.

Souleimanov, E. (2011). The Caucasus Emirate: Genealogy of an Islamist Insurgency. *Middle East Policy, 18*(4), 155–168.

Stanislawski, B. H. (2008). Para-States, quasi-states, and black spots: Perhaps not states, but not "ungoverned territories", Either. *International Studies Review, 10*, 366–396.

Steele, B. J., & Amoureux, J. L. (2005). 'NGOs and monitoring genocide: The benefits and limits to human rights panopticism. *Millennium: Journal of International Studies, 32*(2), 401–432.

Steele, B. J. (2008). *Ontological security in international relations: Self-identity and the IR state*. New York, Routledge: The New International Relations.

Svensson, I. (2009). The Nagorno-Karabakh conflict: Lessons from the mediation efforts. *Initiative for peacebuilding*. http://www.initiativeforpeacebuilding.eu/pdf/Nagorno_Karabakh_conflict_mediation_efforts.pdf. Accessed November 22, 2013.

Swirszcz, J. (2009). The role of Islam in Chechen national identity. *Nationalities Papers, 37*(1), 59–88.

Tekushev, I., Markedonov, S., & Shevchenko, K. (Eds.). (2013). *Abkhazia: Between the past and the future*. Prague: Medium Orient.

Terlinden, U. (2008). Emerging governance in Somaliland: A perspective from below. In E. M. Bruchhaus & M. M. Sommer (Eds.), *Hot spot horn of africa revisited: Approaches to make sense of conflict* (pp. 51–67). Münster: Lit Verlag.

Trier, T., Lohm, H., & Szakony, D. (2010). *Under siege: Inter-ethnic relations in Abkhazia*. New York: Columbia University Press.

Wilhelmsen, J. (2005). Between a rock and a hard place: The Islamisation of the Chechen separatist movement. *Europe-Asia Studies, 57*(1), 35–59.

Yiftachel, O., & Ghanem, A. (2004). Understanding 'ethnocratic' regimes: The politics of seizing contested territories. *Political Geography, 23*, 647–676.

Author Biography

Urban Jakša is a Ph.D. candidate in Politics at the University of York and a Fulbright visiting research student at Columbia University. His interests include de facto states, geopolitical competition and conflicts in post-Soviet Europe. In his research, Urban focuses on how perceptions and interpretations of non-recognition influence interactions between Abkhazia and recognized actors in the international community.

Contemporary Referendum on Independence (RI) and Linguistic Aspects of an Intelligible Referendum Question (RQ)

Přemysl Rosůlek

The contribution is primarily focused on the evolution of the wording of the referendum question (RQ) on independence in a clearly delineated period (1980–2014) in which referendums on independence (RIs) became a frequent process accompanied secessionist process throughout the continents. For having sufficient amount of relevant samples, investigation and subsequent evaluation and comparison of the RQs are divided into four secessionist groups—emerging democracies; mutually negotiated and internationally supervised binding referendums proceeded mostly in post-colonial world; seceding micro-states in Pacific and Caribbean; and liberal democratic realm in the West.

The text will proceed as follows: first, normative criteria on a good RQ will be defined. Next, the wording of the RQ constructed for RI in four above-mentioned groups of entities will be introduced and closely analysed. Finally, the RQs will be confronted with the four-dimensional pattern which can be articulated by four research questions: first, *Purely evolutionary dimension*: Is there any impact of general norms linked to an intelligible RQ?; second, *time-spatial dimension*: Does the RQ differ in four different groups investigated in the text?; third, *liberal democratic dimension*: Is the RQ formulated for the RI in liberal democracy more intelligible than the one formulated in non-democratic units?; and fourth, *negoti-*

The original version of this chapter appeared in The Annual of Language & Language of Politics and Identity (2016), 10, 49–72. This article is updated and reprinted with permission from the copyright holders.

The publishing of this article was supported by the institutional support for the long-term conceptual development of the research organization—Department of Political Science and International Relations, University of West Bohemia in 2017.

P. Rosůlek (✉)
Department of Political Science and International Relations, Faculty of Arts and Humanities, University of West Bohemia, Pilsen, Czech Republic
e-mail: rosulek@kap.zcu.cz

ating dimension: Is the RQ formulated in cases of negotiated secession more intelligible than the one formulated by secessionists unilaterally?

1 Evolution of the Principles of Intelligibility of a Referendum Question (RQ)

Originally, the work on principles of a fair RQ submitted in the survey and for referendum dates back to first half of twentieth century (Gallup 1941). Since then, academicians from various scholarly fields contributed with an extensive literature on the wording of the RQ and its effect on peoples' decisions (Tversky and Kahneman 1981; McNeil et al. 1982, 1260–1261). They argued that the question formula can have a strong impact on citizens' preferences. Finally, in the early 1990s, scholars, international institutions, courts and expert bodies launched debate on a fair principle of a RQ in the sphere of politics related to secession.

Initially, scholars and institutions were strongly influenced by the two strongly biased RQs submitted to voters in Québec for RI in 1980 and 1995. Scholars sought criteria for a clear RQ in reaction to barely understandable (Flanagan 2011) and intentionally manipulated RQs by secessionists (LeDuc, no date, 19). Scholars criticized excessively long (Globus 1996, 149) RQ which contains vague and confusing terms as "*sovereignty*", "*sovereignty within offer of political and economic partnership*" or "*sovereignty-association*" (Dion 1998; Moore 2004[2001], 216; Globus 1996; Howe 1998, 34).

The clearness of the RQ started to define also federal institutions. The Supreme Court of Canada clarified that clear RQ on independence "*must be free of ambiguity*" (Supreme Court Judgments 1998, 88) and subsequent Clarity Act approved by the federal parliament stressed that RQ cannot have a long and confusing sentences as "*mandate to negotiate*" or would not contain "*other possibilities in addition to the secession (…) such as economic or political arrangements with Canada*" (Clarity Act 2000, 3).

Next, international organization Venice Commission, an advisory body of the Council of Europe, and non-governmental International Institute for Democracy and Electoral Assistance (IDEA) based in Stockholm contributed to the issue of RQ although their effort was aimed at wave of constitutional and European referendums across the Europe, and therefore, it lacked specificities related to RQ designed for voting on independence.

The Venice Commission worked on the issue of an intelligibility of a RQ between 2001 and 2007. Already in 2001, it published set of criteria emphasizing that fair RQ "*must be clear (not obscure or ambiguous); it must not be misleading; it must not suggest an answer; electors must be informed of the consequences of the referendum; voters must answer the questions asked by yes, no or a blank vote (…)*" (Venice Commission 2001, 4). Between 2005 and 2007, the Venice Commission added that the RQ must be non-leading (Venice Commission 2005a, b, 34–35), "*clearly phrased*" (ibid., 43), simple, not long and difficult to understand.

Table 1 Electoral Commission and principles of intelligible RQ

Clear and simple (easy to understand)	Concise and its language is easy to understand by voters
To the point	Focused on independence only; straightforward to answer
Unambiguous	Cannot create another RQ for voters; its wording must be properly understood by voters
Neutral	Not suggesting an answer; the formula cannot encourage people to prefer one response over the another
Not to mislead voters	Voters must understand both the meaning of particular words and the RQ as a whole

Source The Electoral Commission (2013a, b, c)

Moreover, the intelligible RQ should contain one subject only and offer voters clear "*Yes*" or "*No*" response options (Elo 2005; Venice Commission 2007).

In 2008, the IDEA clarified that RQ should be precise, clear and "*have one goal and interpretation only*". The IDEA condemned the RQ to be vague and applied for neutral formulation of the RQ which may be difficult to achieve in practise (IDEA 2008, 54–55).

Finally, the UK Parliament established institutional framework for contemporary rules on the designing intelligible RQ in 2000 by the Political Parties, Elections and Referendums Act (The PPERA 2000, 80–81). Subsequently, the Electoral Commission issued "*question assessment guidelines*" in 2002 and updated it by Referendum Question Assessment Guidelines in 2009. By then, the Electoral Commission formulated the criteria of the intelligible RQ as follows: "*should present the options clearly, simply and neutrally. So it should: be easy to understand; be to the point; be unambiguous; avoid encouraging voters to consider one response more favourably than another; avoid misleading voters*" (The Electoral Commission 2009). Before the Scottish RI, the Electoral Commission defined a criteria for intelligible RQ outlined above more properly (Table 1).

In the text, these criteria established by the Electoral Commission in the UK will be used for judging RQ investigated in the text. Reasoning for their pre-selection will be done in the next section.

2 Selection of Secessionist Groups for Investigation

At the end of the twentieth century, there were held over fifty RIs in the world (see Qvortrup 2014b, 58–59; Baldacchino 2010, 191). Around quarter of the RI took place on the territory of the communist and early post-communist federations and related republics which qualifies this group for proper investigation. In the case of the Soviet Union, early seceders—Lithuania, Latvia and Estonia—who left the Soviet Union prior to the attempted *coup d'état* August 1991 will be investigated together with the early secessions of republican units—Slovenia, Croatia, Macedonia, Bosnia and Herzegovina—from federative Yugoslavia.

Second, from the 1990s, there were held several RIs by which international community assisted which happened mostly—but not only—in a post-colonial world. Namely, the RQ formulated in Eritrea, East Timor, Montenegro and South Sudan will be surveyed.

Third, RQs formulated in post-colonial micro-states in Caribbean and Pacific deserve special attention for numerous occurrence of secessions there and for their often non-ambition goals of free association only. In the text, Nevis, Palau and Tokelau will be under survey.

Fourth, the secessions and attempted secessions in liberal democracies will be investigated as these entities have not been immune to secessionist course either. In the text, it applies for Québec, Scotland and Catalonia (Table 2).

Table 2 Referendums on independence (RIs) 1980–2014

Seceding unit	Parent country		Negotiated	Seceded
Post-communist federations				
Lithuania	Soviet Union	1991	No	Yes
Estonia	Soviet Union	1991	No	Yes
Latvia	Soviet Union	1991	No	Yes
Slovenia	Yugoslavia	1991	No	Yes
Croatia	Yugoslavia	1991	No	Yes
Macedonia	Yugoslavia	1991	No	Yes
Bosnia	Yugoslavia	1992	No	Yes
Internationally supervised				
Eritrea	Ethiopia	1993	Yes	Yes
East	Indonesia Timor	1999	Yes	Yes
Montenegro	Serbia-Montenegro	2006	Yes	Yes
South Sudan[a]	Sudan	2011	Yes	Yes
Micro-states				
Palau	USA	1983–1993[b]	Yes	Yes[c]
Nevis	St. Kitts & Nevis	1998	*no need*[d]	No
Tokelau	New Zealand	2006, 2007	Yes	No[e]
Northern America, Europe				
Québec	Canada	1980, 1995	No	No
Scotland	Great Britain	2014	Yes	No
Catalonia	Spain	2014	No	No

Source (Qvortrup 2014a, 58–59; Baldacchino 2010, 191), modified

[a]In South Sudan, only the Int. Org. for Migration (IOM) was participated but not on the issue of designing the RQ

[b]In Palau, altogether seven referendums were held to ratify negotiated Compact of Free Association

[c]In Palau, voters did not opt for independence but for the Compact of Free Associated State of the USA

[d]In Nevis, unlike other cases, the unilateral secession is guaranteed by constitution

[e]In Tokelau, voters did not opt for independence but for the Treaty of Free Association with New Zealand

Yet there have been RIs exceeding beyond the scope of investigated goals of this text. Following attempted secessions hardly match to any of the four categories introduced above as, e.g., series of attempted secessions of regional and subregional units ignored by both central political authorities of the post-communist federations or successive republics and international community. Furthermore, highly controversial RI in non-recognized entity Somaliland and non-binding and multiply choice ballot designed for RI in Puerto Rico were also ignored for the purpose of this text.

3 Emerging Democracies: The Soviet Union and Yugoslavia

At the turn of the 1980s and 1990s, Yugoslavia and the Soviet Union were plagued by serious, even critical internal crises or even by armed conflicts. During the process of the break-up of these post-communist federations, many RIs were held in their constitutive republics and subregional units. Generally speaking, referendums were organized unilaterally by secessionists regardless of the opposing opinion of the central authorities. Therefore, for the international community it became a matter of concern how to judge the legality of such referendums. At the outset, the international community emphasized the importance of territorial integrity of the Soviet Union and Yugoslavia. International organizations did not formulate any ethical standards regarding the prospects of establishment of the new states on the territory of the disintegrating Soviet Union.

3.1 Disintegration of the Soviet Union

The constitutions from the Soviet era have contained a provision on the justifiability of secession already from the time of the early Bolshevik rule until the demise of the Soviet Union (Tishkov 1997, 234; Duchacek 1977, 20). In fact, the right to secede was included in the legal framework of the federation only formally. The constitution lacked any detailed guidelines governing the process to be followed if any group would have decided to take the path towards independence. On the contrary, after they have consolidated power, the Bolsheviks started to associate separation with bourgeois nationalism (Tishkov 1997, 29–30). Despite the fact that the right to secede continued to be a part of propaganda and constitutions of the individual entities (ibid., 234), any such attempts were harshly persecuted until the demise of the federation (Duchacek 1977, 20).

The final years of the Soviet Union were characterized by turmoil, chaos and secessionist attempts. All 15 constitutive republics of the Soviet federation declared their sovereignty prior to the 1991 attempted anti-Gorbachev putsch (Kisangani and

Hesli 1995, 506). Nevertheless, unlike the Baltics together with Georgia, early seceders which intended to leave existing state, the other constitutive republics of the Soviet Union, claimed their independent statehood only after this unsuccessful *coup d'état* against Mikhail Gorbachev. Therefore, the latter cases do not match to the category of secessions from a larger state but rather to runaway, *sauve qui peut separatismus* (Buchanan 2010, 364, 367), from a state which entered in uncontrolled and irreversibly process directed towards dissolution.

In Lithuania, the RI was known as the Popular Survey about the independence of the Republic of Lithuania and the RQ submitted to voters read (Lietuvos Respublikos Seimas 1991):

> *Do you agree with preposition of new Constitution of Lithuania that is under preparation: The State of Lithuania shall be an independent, democratic republic.* Yes/No.

In comparison with Lithuania, there was almost no difference in the wording of the question in Latvia (Currie and Provost 2015, 276):

> *Do you support the democratic and independent statehood of the Republic of Latvia?* Yes/No.

Only the Estonian case differed from the previous two formulas. The RQ was constructed as a reminder of the past annexation and consequent occupation by Soviet Union under Stalinist rule. The related popular vote was considered here not primarily as a RI but as a ballot on the restoration of the previous state of affairs (ibid.; Eesti Vabariigi põhiseadus 2012):

> *Do you want restoration of the Independence of the Republic of Estonia?* Yes/No.

3.2 Dissolution of Yugoslavia

Similar to the Soviet case, Yugoslavian constitutions of 1963 and 1974 have contained provisions guaranteeing the individual republican units right to secession (Iglar 1992, 219). However, the preservation of territorial integrity of the federation was the supreme value in socialist Yugoslavia (Radan 2000, 73). Moreover, the constitution also contained provisions contradictory to other passages in the text which were favourable to secession. Namely, the articles 5(1) and 5(3) emphasized the indivisibility of territory and the impossibility of changing borders of the federation without the approval of all the republics and the autonomous provinces (Radan 2000, 66). However, regardless of the restrictive provisions in the constitution, things took a completely different turn after the 1990 elections when in other republics multi-party systems emerged which further strengthened tendencies towards a confederative model of Yugoslavia and/or independence. At that time, the Serbian political leader, Slobodan Milošević, abandoned the envisaged plan of a more decentralized Yugoslavia for the vision of a *"Greater Serbia"* (Oproiu 2011, 153). This factor further deepened the centrifugal tendencies in the federation.

Slovenia and Croatia were the first entities moving towards independence to be followed shortly after by Macedonia and Bosnia and Herzegovina. On the contrary, the political elites of the last remaining republic of Montenegro decided to stay with Milošević's Serbia.

In Slovenia, voters were presented with a short RQ (Slovenia Times 2015):

Should the Republic of Slovenia become an independent and sovereign state? Yes/No.

In Croatia, two RQs were submitted to voters and both were quite long (Vidmar 2013, 276; Izbori.hr 1991):

Do you agree that the Republic of Croatia, as a sovereign and independent state which guarantees a cultural autonomy and all civil liberties of Serbs and members of other nationalities in Croatia, shall enter into an association of sovereign states together with other republics (according to the suggestion of the Republic of Croatia and the Republic of Slovenia for solving of the state crisis in the SFRY?).

Do you agree that the Republic of Croatia shall remain in Yugoslavia as a unitary federal state (according to the suggestion of the Republic of Serbia and the Socialist Republic of Montenegro for solving of the state crisis in the SFRY?). For/Against.

In the Republic of Macedonia, the RQ reads (Koneska 2014, 65; Radio Slobodna Evropa 2011):

Are you in favour of sovereign and independent Macedonia, with the right to enter into future union of sovereign states of Yugoslavia?

With respect to Bosnia and Herzegovina, the Badinter Commission endorsed a RI in early 1992 arguing in its Opinion no. 4 the importance of *"the will of the peoples of Bosnia–Herzegovina (…) by means of a referendum of all the citizens of the SRBH without distinction, carried out under international supervision"* (Badinter Commission In: Türk 1993, 75–76).

Subsequently, the following RQ was submitted to voters (OSCE 1992, 9; N1 2015):

Are you for a sovereign and independent Bosnia and Herzegovina, a state of equal citizens, the peoples of Bosnia and Herzegovina-Muslims, Serbs, Croats, and members of other nations living in it?

3.3 Summary

There can be hardly any doubt that the voters did not know what it meant voting for independence after several generations were forced to live for decades under the Soviet and Yugoslav authoritarian regimes. The RQs on secession from Yugoslavia emphasized not only independence but also the sovereign character of the new entities. Due to the historical experience, the RQs on independence in Estonia stressed the term restoration of statehood. On the other hand, in Lithuania and Latvia, the RQs emphasized their democratic characters in the future. The RQs in

Croatia and Bosnia promised multi-ethnic character and peaceful coexistence in their newly independent entities. As for independence, the term in the RQs could be regarded as clear enough in most of the RQs examined above (Lithuania, Latvia, Estonia, Slovenia, Croatia, Macedonia and Bosnia and Herzegovina) in the form either independence or independent.

The Slovenian wording of the RQ formulated in 1991 meets the best standards for a short and clear question because its wording contained only one additional and redundant word—"*sovereignty*". Similarly, the RI in all of the three Baltic republics can be positively evaluated. All the three RQs focused primarily on "*independence*" (Vidmar 2013, 276, note 100). Apart from that crucial term, Lithuania and Latvia placed emphasis on democratic character of their states or statehood, respectively. In Lithuania, an unnecessary sentence mentioning constitution did not significantly dilute the term "*independent*" which was—alongside with the phrase "*democratic republic*"—the gist of the formula. Contrary to both cases mentioned above, in Estonia, the wording of the RQ did not present to the voters an emerging, newly independent and democratic country but rather a return to *status quo ante*. The Estonian political elites designed the question in a way so it was clear that there was independent state already in the past and that its termination caused by the Soviet annexation was illegal. Due to its historical consequences, the term "*restoration of the Independence*" can be classified as quite straightforward. In the Baltics, several extra words beyond necessity do not pose any threat that the RQ could become ambiguous.

In the case of Bosnia and Herzegovina, the RQ was straightforward, although its latter part contained a marketing design rather than rational formula as the formula of the RI was promising multi-ethnic paradise hardly achievable.

The RQ could not have been quite clear to voters in Macedonia and particularly in Croatia. In these cases, important factor which could jeopardize straightforwardness of the RQ could be related to their excessive length combined with controversial formulas.

In the cases of Macedonia and Croatia, lack of straight forwardness of the RQ can be partly observed. The RQs on the ballots there were not only focused at independence but simultaneously left the door open for a possible reunification (or staying in) with confederation-like Yugoslavia in the future. In any case, at the time of the RI in Macedonia and Croatia, there was no clear draft of reformed Yugoslavia on the table and, therefore, voters could not have any idea about the perspective of reformed confederative Yugoslavian model in the future.

However, unlike the Croatian case, voters in Macedonia genuinely opted for independence, as they had only one RQ on the ballot and it was much shorter than the one in Croatia. If a clear-cut RI ballot shall be designed by one question only, the case of Croatia cannot qualify to be good examples of such a ballot. In Croatia, there were two quite long and mutually interrelated RQs on ballot, which were misleading in several ways. The only important differentiations were placed in brackets at the end of both formulations. Neither of the two questions was topically linked directly to independence. The most important goal of the RQ was rather lost in the vague wording of both formulas. The ultimate goal of both RQs, or more precisely options, was not independence, but its achievement would be only the first step on the way towards re-entering Yugoslavia either in "*an association of sovereign states together with other republics*" or as "*a unitary federal state*". Although in the latter case the option of "*remain*" was emphasized, political elites counted with independence already before the RI. There were more contradictions in how the two options were formulated. The first one was confusing because it was de facto not asking for a vote on "*a sovereign and independent state*" as that was considered *fait accompli* in the RQ but, nominally, the paramount goal of the RI was about the option of joining the confederative model of Yugoslavia ("*Croatia shall enter into an association of sovereign states together with other republics*"), which, however, can barely ever turn into prospective statehood. In both theory and practice, the confederations are temporary units established during the stage of their unification or break-up. The second option on the ballot in Croatia was also not free from ambiguity. Voters could have opted for an option to "*remain in Yugoslavia*", which meant to remain in "*a unitary federal state*". However, a state can be virtually either unitary or federal by its character and cannot by characterized by both contradictory features simultaneously.

Except from Slovenia where the RQ started with the neutral phrase "*Should…*", all other RQs would have failed to meet contemporary criteria of neutrality for lacking impersonal formulas. Most of the RQs started with too personal wording which could not be considered as neutral: "*Do you agree…*" (Croatia), "*Do you support…*" (Latvia), "*Are you in favour…*" (Macedonia), "*Are you for…*" (Bosnia), "*…Do you give…*" and "*Do you want…*" (Estonia).

4 Internationally Supervised RI: From Eritrea to South Sudan

After the Second World War, international community associated self-determination with secession on a very limited scale linked to colonialism. In these cases, apart from a few exceptions from a general rule, declarations on independence of former colonies in Africa and Asia were internationally legalized only under the condition of compliance with the *uti possidetis* principle (Raić 2002, 219). Generally, the preservation of territorial integrity of existing states was protected by all possible means which included also use of military power by the central state which could rely on support of the UN (Weller 2008, 23) and the OAU (Munya 1999, 539, 542).

After the end of the Cold War, the international community did not depart significantly from its previous strongly reserved stance towards secessionist attempts. However, the international community was now more willing to accept newborn states if their secessions were negotiated with the central political authorities. All such events were special cases related either to previous annexations (East Timor), unimplemented autonomy (Eritrea) or to previous mistreatment

(South Sudan) by a larger state. Finally, outside the post-colonial context, negotiated independence as the ultimate solution imposed on last remaining republican unit of former Yugoslavia (Montenegro) represents a special case of supervision conducted by the EU.

4.1 Eritrea

After decades under Italian colonial rule (1890–1941), Eritrea became a part of the British protectorate during the Second World War. As a consequence of the failure of the Big Four to find a solution regarding the Italian ex-colonial territories after the Second World War, the Eritrean case was committed to the General Assembly of the UN (UNGA). Subsequently, the UNGA decided that Eritrea shall be autonomous part of Ethiopian federation (UNGA 1950). In 1952, the Federation of Ethiopia and Eritrea was established. Ten years later, however, federation was dissolved unilaterally by Ethiopia and Eritrea was annexed by Ethiopia. As a result, Eritrea launched a complicated and on some occasions armed and bloody struggle for its independence (Bereketeab 2007, 401–406).

After significant gains of the Eritrean People's Liberation Front in Eritrea and in conjunction with the fall of the Mengistu Haile Mariam regime in 1991, a provisional government in Eritrea was formed and, with the approval of the Ethiopian political elites, the USA and the UN supported an RI in Eritrea. The United Nations Observer Mission to Verify the Referendum in Eritrea (UNOVER) (UN 2005, 87) participated in organizing a legally binding referendum alongside with the Organization for African Unity (OAU), the Arab League and the Non-Alignment Movement (Villicana and Venkataraman 2006, 551). The wording of the RQ was also formulated by an international committee (Qvotrup 2014a, 62). In Eritrea, the RQ on the ballot was submitted to the voters in three official languages—Tigrinya, Arabic and English—complemented by symbols in colour due to the existing degree of illiteracy in the region. The RQ reads (New World Encyclopedia, no date):

> *Do you approve Eritrea to become an independent, sovereign state?* Yes/No.

4.2 East Timor

Timor was a part of the Portuguese colony from the sixteenth century until East Timor's Fretilin party declared independence in 1975. Shortly afterwards, Indonesia invaded Timor and incorporated its territory. When President Suharto resigned in 1998, his successor in the presidential office, Bacharuddin Jusuf Habibie, agreed to hold a referendum on East Timor's independence. Subsequently, three legal documents negotiated and signed by the United Nations Mission in East

Timor (UNAMET), Portuguese and East Timor governments, set political and security guidelines for the referendum procedure (Stephens 2015, 149). The agreement between the Republic of Indonesia and the Portuguese Republic on the question of East Timor, abbreviated as the East Timor Agreement (UN 1999), established political agenda, legally binding RI and the wording of the RQ. In this case, the mission UNAMET strongly influenced the RQ (UN 2005, 10) and the symbols on the ballot which were consulted with the local political parties (ibid.). Voters on the territory of East Timor were offered two options in four languages—English, Bahasa Indonesia, Tetun and Portuguese. Due to a certain degree of illiteracy, voters had also a choice between flags of Indonesia and of East Timor (Qvortrup 2014a, 132). The two parts of the RQ read (UN 2005, 10):

> Do you accept the proposed special autonomy for East Timor within the Unitary State of the Republic of Indonesia?

> Do you reject the proposed special autonomy for East Timor, leading to East Timor's separation from Indonesia? Accept/Reject.

4.3 Montenegro

The republic has been a part of Yugoslavia from its foundation in 1918 but only under J. B. Tito after the Second World War it has become a constitutive unit of the socialist federation. During the process of state dissolution in the 1990s, unlike Slovenia, Croatia, Macedonia and Bosnia and Herzegovina, the smallest federative republic of Montenegro became the last one which remained loyal to Milośević's Yugoslavia. Subsequently, political elites of Montenegro and Serbia established a new state—the Former Republic of Yugoslavia (Vuković 2012, 10). However, from the late 1990s, the new Montenegrin political elites took the opposite course as they started to head towards independence.

In 2003, State Union of Serbia and Montenegro was established as *"an EU-sponsored compromise"* (Vidmar 2007, 95). The constitution of the de facto confederative state contained a provision on a possible RI of a member-state *"after the end of the period of three years"* in article 60/1–3 (ibid.). Moreover, during the foundation of the Serbia-Montenegro, it was declared that any potential act of secession in the future must be preceded by adopting a law on referendum by a member-state *"bearing in mind internationally-recognized democratic standards"* (ibid., 97). Hereby, the act of potential secession was legally frozen at least until 2006. Just after the above-mentioned period has expired, the secession has taken place.

The EU actively participated in this RI, having helped to draft and pass the Law on Referendum on the State-Legal Status of the Republic of Montenegro prescribed in the constitution (ibid., 97–98). In this law, the entire procedure regarding the RI was delineated. The EU helped to draft wording of the RQ in Montenegro also (Qvortrup 2014b, 62).

The final wording of the RQ reads (RTCG, no date; OSCE 2006a, b, 7):

Do you want the Republic of Montenegro to be an independent state with full international and legal personality? Yes/No.

4.4 South Sudan

In 1956, Sudan gained independence. The country had previously been a part of an Anglo-Egyptian condominium and became the most extensive state territory in Africa which, moreover, incorporated diverse groups of people with diverse ethnicity, language and religion. In the south, which was rather distinct from rest of the country, although also not ethnically unified, the English language and Christianization were introduced, while the central political authorities in Khartoum attempted to construct a unified Sudanese nation through the policy of "Arabization" and "Islamification" (Christopher 2011, 127). As a result, two consecutive civil wars paralysed the country, while the imposition of the Shari'a law throughout the entire country led to further alienation of the southern part from the Islamic north and the central government which secured and protected the northern interests.

In the late 1990s, the right to self-determination of South Sudan was firstly recognized by the permanent representative of Sudan in the UN (1999). In 2002, the right to exercise self-determination through an *"internationally monitored referendum"* in order to *"to determine their future status"* (UNMIS 2005, 20, 22) was granted to the people of South Sudan in the Machakos Protocol (ibid., 17–26) mutually agreed by the central government and secessionists in the south. In 2005, both players agreed on an Interim National Constitution (2005) which outlined a detailed schedule before the RI would be held. In 2005, the Comprehensive Peace Agreement was signed. The agreement followed a long mediation effort of regional and international players between the northern National Congress Party (NCP) and the southern Sudan People's Liberation Movement and Army (Carney 2007).

As for the wording of the RQ, the Machakos Protocol contained the notion on the choice for the people of South Sudan between confirming *"the unity of the Sudan"* or *"to vote for secession"* (UNMIS 2005, 22). Three years later, the Interim National Constitution only slightly amended rough attribute of intended RQ. In the 222(2) art. of the constitution, the phrase *"voting to adopt"* was amended to *"voting to sustain"*. Therefore, the phrase linked to the option of preserving unity remained to be formulated in a rather complicated manner: *"confirm unity of the Sudan by voting to sustain the system of government established under the Comprehensive Peace Agreement and this Constitution"* (Republic of the Sudan Gazette 2005, 97). In 2009, the first clear recommendation on the design of the ballot came through the Southern Sudan Referendum Act. The definition of the ballot was given as a *"means the ballot paper issued by the Southern Sudan Referendum Commission to enable the voter to choose either to confirm the unity of Sudan or secession"*

(Southern Sudan Referendum Act 2009, 2). The act explicitly stated that the RI shall be organized "*to choose between two options*" (ibid., 5)—(a) "*confirmation of the unity of the Sudan by sustaining the form of government established by the Comprehensive Peace Agreement and the Constitution,* or(b) *secession*" (Southern Sudan Referendum Act 2009, 9).

Subsequently, the wording of the RQ accompanied by the symbols for illiterate voters was completely within the competences of the Southern Sudan Referendum Commission. Members of the commission were Sudanese by birth (Sudan Tribune 2011). The commission was obliged to "*prepare, design and print the ballots for the referendum so they are clear and easy to understand*" (Southern Sudan Referendum Act 2009, 9). The commission introduced ultimate version of the referendum ballot as follows (Vidmar 2012, 552):

"Unity" or "Secession".

4.5 Summary

In the case of 2006 Montenegrin referendum, the RQ submitted to voters would pass the criteria of intelligibility, although the RQ was rather long and could puzzle some voters by unnecessary formula in the second part of the RQ stressing "*full international and legal personality*". However, it was still clear enough and superfluous part of the formula did not increase its ambiguity.

In Eritrea, the RQ was quite clear, but despite the rather short and simple RQ, still some doubts prevailed if the RQ was fully clear to voters for two reasons. First, the RQ was formulated in the three official languages used in Eritrea. Arabic sources claimed that there is a question on independence only. Arabic-speaking expatriates in Qatar and Saudi Arabia perceived the RQ asking as "*Do you support a free Eritrea?*" or as "*Do you want Eritrea to be independent?*", respectively. Due to the high level of illiteracy in Eritrea, there were symbols on the ballot that had strong political connotations. Second, the ballot papers were coloured blue for "*Yes*" and red for "*No*" where red colour symbolized blood. For example, one local radio reported that the RI was a choice between freedom and slavery, essentially asking people if they want to be free (Immigration and Refugee Board of Canada 2001).

In East Timor, Accept/Reject response options on the ballot replaced less neutral and frequently used Yes/No options, but it cannot save the formula from criticism (Qvortrup 2014a, 143). Similar to Croatian case, the evidence of de facto two RQs on the ballot determined formula to be biased. However, there are other reasons decreasing the value of the RQ in Eritrea. Apart from the personal formula "*Do you accept...*", the main gist of the RQ was to stress a "*special autonomy*" within Indonesia in the phrase which could have encouraged voters to opt for this outcome —being expected to acquire at least some knowledge about what the special autonomy really mean—instead of voting for "*separation from Indonesia*".

The term "*separation*" not only substitutes a more direct and precise term "*independence*" but—more importantly—it evokes insecurity and instability. The pro-independence option was formulated in a negative sense—the voters had to reject special autonomy if they wished "*separation*", which had negative connotation.

In South Sudan, the RQ on the ballot was clear and simple. Most likely the shortest RQ ever submitted on RI, more precisely two one-word options, gave voters choice between "*unity*" and "*secession*". However, there could not have been a balanced relationship between both terms. Contrary to secession, which is by definition negative in Western political discourse from the time of Abraham Lincoln (Lindsay and Wellman 2003, 115–119; Buchanan 1997, 306; 1991, 338; Philpott 1995, 354) and does not necessary mean subsequent recognition by international community (Wood 1981, 111), the term unity is associated with positive images such as collective membership, family and strength. For that reason, the RQ did not meet standards of neutrality there as the term "*secession*" shall be replaced by "*independence*".

Additionally, these RQs would fail to meet strict criteria of pure neutrality based on impersonal wording of the RQ. It applies for Eritrea ("*Do you approve…*"), East Timor "*Do you accept…*" and Montenegro ("*Do you want…*"). Similarly, the criteria apply also for not neutral response option based on Yes/No alternatives in Eritrea and Montenegro.

5 Micro-states

As a consequence of ongoing decolonization in Caribbean and Pacific, in the period of the late 1960s, there were two major tendencies. First, that era was marked by the rise of mini-states (Duchacek 1970, 2, 69–71). There have been secessionist tendencies in various parts of Caribbean area disrespectable of the fact that newborn states were of insignificant size (Premdas 1996, 5). Second, parallel to that development, there was evidence of "*upside down decolonization*" when many inhabitants of small islands or archipelagos many considered post-Second World War "*membership*" in trusteeship mandate system more advantageous—or less risky—than independent status. In the Pacific, paradoxically, in number of cases, entities boycotted decolonization entirely (Qvortrup 2015, 70) and future perspective in a form of associated statehood rather than independence (Grant 2009, 34).

For example, in the Pacific, Tokelau struggled for extended post-colonial relationship with the New Zeeland and the quasi-RIs were de facto enforced on those micro-states from above. In the case of Palau, neither locals nor the USA had interest to support its full independence. On the contrary, in the Caribbean, decolonized Nevis found not to be fully satisfied in federation with St. Kitts and attempted to secede completely despite of its small size. In this part, RIs and RQs of the three tiny entities mentioned above will be analysed.

5.1 Nevis

In 1967, after demise of West Indies Federation (1958–1962), a former British colony Nevis became together with Saint Kitts and Anguilla a self-governing state associated with Great Britain. Anguilla seceded from the unit shortly thereafter, and from 1983, the two islands gained full independence under the official name Federation of Saint Kitts and Nevis (Columbia Electronic Encyclopedia 2016). By the constitution, it is not a federation between St. Kitts and Nevis but between Nevis and St. Kitts on the one hand and between St. Kitts and Nevis on the other (Phillips 2002, 136). That federal constitution is rare example in the world (Premdas 2013, 1) granting Nevis not only high degree of autonomy but also option to secede peacefully without the consent of the centre or neighbouring and larger St. Kitts island. There are only two constitutional conditions which must be met for successful "*exit*". First, independence cannot be achieved unless it is approved by two-thirds of five elected members of the Nevis Island Assembly and, second, decision must be taken not by less than the two-thirds of voters in a RI. The procedure related to wording of a RQ or designing a ballot is not mentioned in the constitution but implicitly the Supervisor of Elections and Electoral Commission are in charge of it (St. Kitts and Nevis Constitution 1983, art. 113). In 1996, Nevis Island Administration under the Premier Vance Amory and Concerned Citizens Movement (CCM) triggered the RI. Although overwhelming number of voters supported independence, two-thirds majority approval threshold was not met in 1998 RI. It is not clear whether secession bill would be approved by two-thirds majority of Assembly's elected members after the Nevis Reformation Party blocked it originally (St. Kitts and Nevis 2000). The RQ submitted to voters reads (Radan 2007, 228):

> *Do you approve of the Nevis secession bill and Nevis becoming an independent state separate from St Kitts?* Yes/No.

5.2 Palau

Prior to the end of the Second World War, Palau was occupied by several colonial powers. After Spain, Germany and Japan, the USA seized islands during the Second World War and, in 1947, Washington was given Palau under an UN Trust Territory in the Pacific. During the Cold War, Palau served as a strategic area security interests for the US administrative in Western Pacific. In the late 1970s, Palau rejected to enter Federated States of Micronesia. In 1986, Palau was last entity of the former UN Trust Territory in the Pacific with unresolved political status (Hinck 1990, 921–923). The process of decolonization was delayed by various specific reasons. First, Palau is not a good example of a "*unified political entity*" (Gerston 1989, 177) geographically nor politically. Palau is a group of 8 principal and around 250 either small or very small islands 600 miles east of the Philippines populated by some 20 thousand people (Hinck 1990, 918). As for "*political system*", except for rule of extended families, clans, high-clan families, local tribes, traditional internal cleavages and domination exercised by various colonial powers, Palau never experienced self-rule (Gerston 1989, 177). Second, there were no regular political parties nor plural media system (ibid., 178). Third, under the US trusteeship, Palau was formally transformed into political system similar to the US federation. Fourth, in economic terms, with a significant unemployment rate, Palau represented underdeveloped economy with majority of employees in national bureaucracy strongly relying on the US government which was, however, insufficiently aimed at development of self-sufficient economy (ibid., 178–179). Fifth and perhaps most importantly, the USA have had no intention to negotiate future status of Palau if the agreement would had been against its strategic interests in the Pacific (Hinck 1990, 955). For Palauans, strong economic dependence on the US state grants meant that the status of full independence was out of question (ibid., 956). Given the fact that Palauans' opinion on self-determination associated with right to control own land and with nuclear free constitution conflicted with the superpower's strategic interests in Palau, easy transition originally expected by the US advisors was far from reality. The USA required to keep one-fourth of land and to keep nuclear materials on their soil and harbours (ibid.). Yet another complication came with series of seven subsequent voting (!) on a free associated state with the USA. In any of these referendums after 1983, simple majority in favour of agreement was always reached; however, number of voters in favour of compact never crossed 75% approval quorum required by the constitution (Hinck 1990, 916). Finally, constitutional amendment decreased the legal hurdle to simply majority in 1992. In a following year, political status of Palau was finally resolved as voters approved the Compact of the Free Association with the USA (United Nations Chronicle 1990). In 1994, Palau finally gained political status of Free Association with the USA which, unilaterally and without prior consent of the UN and after use of economic coercion (and allegedly corrupted state officials in Palau also) (Hinck 1990, 943–960), "*retained responsibility for defence and the right to operate military bases*" in Palau which became a member of the UN (BBC 2015).

In 1983, the first referendum on Compact of the Free Association in Palau was held. The RQ reads as follows (Hinck 1990, 927):

Do you approve of Free Association as set forth in the Compact of Free Association? Yes/No.

5.3 Tokelau

Tokelau, atolls of a very small size in the Pacific, were annexed by British at the end of the nineteenth century. In 1926, Tokelau was transferred to New Zealand's administration which lasts until now (nzherald.co.nz 2006).

In 1960, the UN called for full accomplishment of decolonization policy. New Zealand willingly cooperated with the UN on dropping its unincorporated territories from the UN-led list of Non-Self-Governing Territories (Hooper 2008, 332). Unlike the Western Samoa, Cook Islands and Niue, Tokelau remained dependent territory (Parker 2006). From the 1970s, Wellington and the UN speeded up the process of political emancipation on Tokelau in order to finish colonial status of atolls. New Zealand promoted establishment of basic political institutions there and the UN Special Committee for decolonization made more official missions to Tokelau than to any other unincorporated territory on its list (ibid.). Nominally, there were three options for islanders on the table—full independence, quasi-independence in the form of a free association, or territorial integration with New Zealand. Disrespectable of their distinct language and identity, islanders were well aware that economy of Tokelau has been dependent by around 80% of budget on the New Zealand's assistance. Due to absence of capital and developed political institutions, Wellington did not support full independence either because Tokelau would have become the smallest state in the world comparable to Vatican only (Qvortrup 2015, 70) given the fact that a three tiny Tokelauan atolls in Polynesia are inhabited by less than one thousand people.

Political quasi-institutions in Tokelau had no intention to change current relationships with New Zealand until the early 1990s (Hooper 2008, 333) despite the fact that New Zealand and frequent UN missions on atolls supported internal political emancipation and awareness of external self-determination. The process of internal self-governance was completed between years 1994 and 2003 when public service, political—inclusive a law making—powers and administrator's competencies were fully delegated to Tokelau's political institutions. In 1994, the national head *ulu* introduced to the UN Visiting Mission document titled "Tokelau's Voice: 'New Wind, New Voters, New Sail—The Emerging Nation of Tokelau'" where he clearly suggested perspective of the free associated state with New Zealand (UN 2007).

In 2003, document "The Principles of Partnership" was signed with the government of New Zealand. A year later, document on economic support was signed. Both documents paved a way for approval of self-determination package in 2005 containing the Draft Constitution of Tokelau and the Treaty of Free Association between New Zealand and Tokelau (UN 2006). The document deals with the Relationship of Free Association between Tokelau and New Zealand in a detailed way and stipulates that apart from "*self-government in free association with New Zealand*", stating that other options "*including independence or integration with New Zealand*" cannot be excluded for the future (art. 11). Self-determination package introduced referendum rules including ballot design and the RQ submitted to voters. Ballot titled as "Voting Paper for Referendum on Self-Determination of Tokelau" reads (Government of Tokelau, no date):

> *The Proposal: That Tokelau become a self-governing state in free association with New Zealand on the basis of the Constitution and the Treaty.* I agree with the Proposal/I reject the Proposal.

5.4 Summary

In Nevis, the RQ is formulated clearly and unambiguously. In Nevis, both *"independent"* with positive connotations and *"separate"* with negative once were used in the RQ formula. Straightforwardness of *"independent state"* in the RQ is slightly shadowed not only by *"separate from"* but also by *"secession bill"*.

In Palau and Tokelau, logically, the RQ was determined to be unclear already because these entities were not headed towards fully independent political status. Citizens voted on far less clear *"free association"*. The fact is much more precarious for voters than voting on black and white alternatives. As a consequence, the RQs were constructed in a more explanatory way and their length was more demanding for voters. Logically, the RQ and related campaign in Palau and Tokelau had to be designed more carefully so voters know that the RQ is pointed at drifting from colonial status to somewhere between full independence and intrastate autonomy. As a consequence, voters could be suspicious when notion on *"the free association"* was followed by the reference to *"the Constitution and the Treaty"* in the case of Tokelau and to the *"Compact"* in the case of Palau. Interestingly, in Tokelau, the phrase "free association" was clarified as attached to *"with New Zealand"* but in Palau, the associate country [the USA] was not even mentioned in the RQ.

Yet, there are differences favouring intelligibility of the RQ in Tokelau over the Palauan RQ.

In Tokelau, unlike majority of other cases investigated, the wording of the RQ started neutrally *"The Proposal: That Tokelau become…"*. Secondly, the extensively formulated response options in Tokelau (*"I agree with the Proposal"*/*"I reject the Proposal"*) represents unique case of all investigated in the text which makes the RQ comparable only to recent recommendations done by the Electoral Commission towards the RQ linked to the "Brexit".

In Palau, due to the fact that another RQ was put on the ballot to voters at the same time (*"Do you approve of the Agreement concerning radioactive, chemical, and biological materials concluded pursuant to section 314 of the Compact of Free Association?"*) (Hinck 1990, 927), the principle of intelligibility of the sovereignty RQ was rather decreased.

Additionally, contemporary criteria of neutrality and impersonality in RQs would not be met in Palau and Nevis (*"Do you approve…"*). The contemporary criteria of neutral response option avoiding Yes/No response would not be met in Nevis nor in Palau.

6 Liberal Democracies

Liberal democratic countries are far less prone to experiencing dangerous conflicts and secessionist attempts compared to the post-colonial world. In the West, secessions seemed to be quite unlikely until recently (Dion 1996). Nevertheless, it has become quite clear that even Western Europe and North America are not immune to serious secessionist demands originating and being formulated on their peripheries. Linguistic and ethnic agenda have been usually the major driving force of secessionist movements. Established liberal democratic states have been usually willing to accommodate ethno-linguistic diversity by the means of federalism (Belgium), devolution (the UK) or regionalization (Spain). On the other hand, they strongly defend their territorial integrity and the principle of indivisibility and usually strongly disagreed with secessionist demands within their state borders and condemned them as illegal (Spain) or prescribe difficult constitutional conditions for secessionists (Canada). From the beginning of the twentieth century, there have been only a few cases in which states were established on the grounds of peaceful and mutually negotiated secession (Norway, Iceland).

In a following part, the RQ constructed for RI in Québec, Scotland and Catalonia will be investigated.

6.1 Québec

Sovereignty started to be an issue in Québec from the second half of the 1960s. At that time, the term independence was frequented among secessionists. Later, after the Parti Québécois (PQ) came to power in November 1976, it *"added an associative dimension with the rest of Canada that led to the 'sovereignty-association' project"* and promised a referendum on sovereignty-association (Yale and Durand 2011, 243). At the time of referendum, the PQ, aware of public opinion preferences, modified its *"sovereignty-association"* project and shifted it towards a *"mandate to negotiate"* (ibid.) which was more acceptable for the public. Given these circumstances, the RQ submitted to voters in 1980 reads (Canada History 2013; Radio Canada 2008):

> The Government of Québec has made public its proposal to negotiate a new agreement with the rest of Canada, based on the equality of nations; this agreement would enable Québec to acquire the exclusive power to make its laws, levy its taxes and establish relations abroad—in other words, sovereignty—and at the same time to maintain with Canada an economic association including a common currency; no change in political status resulting from these negotiations will be effected without approval by the people through another referendum; on these terms, do you give the Government of Québec the mandate to negotiate the proposed agreement between Québec and Canada. Yes/No.

After the failure of the *"Yes"* platform in 1980, the Canadian government of Pierre Elliot Trudeau promoted all-Canadian nationalism with the tangible outcome being the Charter of Rights and Freedoms and the Constitution Act of 1982. Trudeau's policy was not perceived favourably even among the Québec federalists, not to mention the separatists. Subsequently, the failure of the Meech Lake Accord process in 1987–1990 represented another landmark which stirred the nationalists in Québec into action. More specifically, several provinces refused to ratify the initiative of federal government which would bring the Québec province back *"into the constitutional family*" (Choudhry and Biens 2007, 179) guaranteeing the province the status of a distinct society. Finally, the failure of the Charlottetown Accord proposing a *"minimal"* federalism (Lluch 2010, 348) in a 1992 nation-wide referendum was considered by the majority of Francophones in Québec as a hostile move against their province. Afterwards, the Parti Québécois together with Action Démocratique du Québec and a new separatist party in the federal parliament—Bloc Québécois—decided to hold another referendum on sovereignty-partnership in 1995.

The Québec RQ in 1995 read (Pue 2012; The Canadian Encyclopedia 1995; Radio Canada, no date):

> *Do you agree that Québec should become sovereign, after having made a formal offer to Canada for a new economic and political partnership, within the scope of the Bill respecting the future of Québec and of the agreement signed on 12 June 1995?* Yes/No.

6.2 Scotland

Scotland became a part of England in 1707 on the basis of the Acts of Union passed separately by the English and Scottish legislatures. The first article of the document stated that union will be *"forever"* (Pittock 2012, 13). Since then, the most important event in the Scottish constitutional history has been the process of devolution in the late twentieth century.

In 1997, successful referendum on devolution enabled Scotland to reinstall Parliament after two centuries and to receive tax-levying powers (Tierney 2013, 360). In 2007 and 2011, the success of the Scottish National Party (SNP) in two consecutive elections to the Scottish Parliament enabled the SNP to launch and heat a national debate on the idea of independence and, at the same time, it recognized referendum device as an essential method of how to proceed towards the desired independence (The Scottish Government 2007, 130, 136, 139). Analogously, the Scottish Government suggested a multiple choice referendum in which voters would opt *"between independence, the status quo, and significant additional devolution"* (Scottish Executive 2007, 33). Apart from the perspective of status quo versus independence options on the referendum ballot, the SNP debated seriously the opinion of a multiple choice referendum for a long period (The Scottish Government 2007, 137–138; The Scottish Government 2010, 6; The Scottish Government 2012, 8). The head of the SNP, Alex Salmond, suggested that the multi-option sovereignty referendum to be *"decided by proportional representation"* in which a third of voters backing the winning option would be sufficient number (Gordon 2011). Furthermore, the Scots also did not rule out two consecutive sovereignty referendums of which the first shall be initiatory and the latter one ratificatory (Scottish Executive 2007, 34). Initially, in the framework of national-wide debate on sovereignty referendum, Scottish Government offered several preliminary wording of the RQ aimed either at independence only (Scottish Executive 2007, 46) or on multiple choice option (The Scottish Government 2010,

20–22). However, although the Scottish Government did not exclude multiple choice referendum at the beginning of 2012, it has proposed the RQ which would *"comply with the Electoral Commission's guidelines which state that referendum question should present the options clearly, simply and neutrally"* (The Scottish Government 2012, 10). Therefore, it has suggested RQ aimed at independence only as follows (The Scottish Government 2012, 11): *"Do you agree that Scotland should be an independent country?"* Yes/No.

In 2012, the UK government strongly condemned the sovereignty referendum proposal based on the two RQs *"for a number of reasons"* (The Secretary of State for Scotland 2012, 19), reasoning that such a RQ would *"deal with two entirely separate constitutional issues"* (ibid.). Consequently, two different RQs would generate four possible outcomes. *"Having four different campaigns would not help to generate clarity"* and voters in Scotland could have barely made an informed decision on the issue (ibid.). The UK Government condemned the preliminary RQs for being too *"long and complex"* (ibid.) and recommended the Scottish Government to formulate *"simple question in consultation with the Electoral Commission"* (The Secretary of State for Scotland 2012, 19). In October 2012, the crucial Edinburgh Agreement was signed by the Prime Minister of Britain, David Cameron, and the First Prime Minister of Scotland, Alex Salmond. The document outlined a firm basis for the entire RI procedure and also the instructions for the *"Scottish Parliament to legislate for a referendum with one question on independence"* held before the end of 2014. Additionally, it was also concluded that the wording of the RQ would be reviewed by the Electoral Commission (HM Government, The Scottish Government 2012).

Subsequently, the Electoral Commission analysed the RQ proposed by the Scottish side and concluded that its wording lacks neutrality and is more favourable to supporters of independence as the formula could lead voters to prefer the *"Yes"* option. In particular, the phrase *"Do you agree…?"* (The Electoral Commission 2013a, b, c, 1) shall be amended into a more neutral RQ also in order not to *"ask for a judgment of someone else's view or decision"* (ibid., 33). The commission suggested a more neutral wording of the RQ (ibid., 1) which simultaneously keeps the condition of being simple, short and direct (ibid., 33). The Scottish Government accepted the recommendation and the RQ appeared on the ballot. The final formula reads (ibid., 33; Tierney 2013, 365):

Should Scotland be an independent country? Yes/No.

6.3 Catalonia

The post-Franco Spanish model of the State of Autonomies based on the 1978 Constitution was designed as almost a federal or quasi-federal state (Rius-Ulldemolins and Zamorano 2015, 168) but complete federalism was not implemented in order to preserve the Spanish unity and protect the state from potential separatist tendencies of the individual historical regions (ibid., 173). The Constitution of Spain does not allow secession, and legal authority for holding sovereignty referendums is conferred only on the central government. That competence was not only confirmed but also strengthened by the decision of the Spanish Constitutional Court in 2008 declaring it illegal to hold a sovereignty referendum in the Basque autonomous community (Muñoz and Guinjoan 2013, 44). Furthermore, the constitutional principle of indivisibility of Spain which explicitly rules out secession could also be seen as the factor. Furthermore, the Constitutional Court decision in 2010 found several provisions of the Catalonian autonomy approved by the Catalonian Parliament some years earlier illegal (ibid., 49) and its ruling de facto reshaped the competencies of the central power (Rius-Ulldemolins and Zamorano 2015, 181).

Strong opposition of the central political authorities in Madrid towards the scope of autonomy required by Barcelona is sometimes called "*recentralization policy*" (ibid., 178), and the long waiting period for the Spanish Constitutional Court's ruling on that issue kept the agenda well alive in Catalonia (Muñoz and Guinjoan 2013, 49). In the following years, it became a top political issue (Bourne 2014, 95). Consequently, starting in the small town of Arenys de Munt, local municipalities across Catalonia organized unofficial RI. At that time, the mainstream Catalonian nationalism shifted from its over century-long moderate and autonomist tendency in favour of secession (Lluch 2010, 344; Muñoz and Guinjoan 2013, 48).

Despite the systematic pressure exerted by the Spanish executive, legislative and supreme judicial body on the regional government not to organize any RI, Catalonia insisted on voting on the issue of independence. Nevertheless, after enduring criticism, it decided to hold only a non-binding "*popular consultation*" (DW 2014). The wording of the RQ for the Catalonian RI was prepared jointly by the leaders of five pro-Catalonian parties. Irrespective of demands put forth by the Catalonian civic organizations to formulate clear and unequivocal RQ linked straightforward to independence, diverse political elites in Catalonia prioritized to demonstrate their united position on the issue at the expense of a clear RQ. The compromise reached by the five nationalist political parties resulted in two RQs submitted to the voters in consultative RI (Jot Down Magazine 2014):

Do you want Catalonia to be a State? Yes/No.

In case of the voters' positive response written on the ballot as "*if so*", they continued to answer the other RQ:

Do you want this State to be Independent? Yes/No.

6.4 Summary

Logically, as the criteria set by the Electoral Commission shall be considered as the norm in the text, the RQ formulated for RI in Scotland have to meet criteria of intelligibility without any doubt. The RQ was precisely constructed in a deliberative way on which the Scottish Government cooperated together with the UK Government and the Electoral Commission. Rather surprisingly, apart from the Scottish RQ, there is no one case of surveyed in the text aimed solely at *"independence"*. The other investigated cases either substituted independence by another word or the proper term was accompanied in the RQ by other words usually beyond necessity. Second, except for Scottish RQ with *"Should"* at the beginning of the RQ, only two other RQs avoided being too personal—in Slovenia and Tokelau. In Scotland, any of the words of the RQ were analysed by experts and confronted to focus groups. Therefore, after a careful analysis, *"be"* prevailed over *"become"* and *"country"* over a *"state"*. Several versions of RQs were tested but ultimately, *"Should Scotland be an independent country?"* was identified as the best option. The Scottish case alongside with the Baltics, Slovenia and Nevis proved that a short formula rapidly increases the unambiguity of the RQ. Despite of praise, the RQ designed for the Scottish referendum had two shortcomings. Less seriously, in the Scottish case, the Electoral Commission did not condemn Yes/No response options for lack of neutrality and favoured advocates of independence (allegedly everyone wants to vote for *"Yes"* because it is nicer than to vote in negative way for *"No"*). The Electoral Commission rejected suggestions of scholars Matt Qvortrup and Ron Gould who argued that *"Yes"* and *"No"* response options formulated for Scottish RI should be replaced by less neutrally formulated alternatives *"I agree"* or *"I do not agree"* (The Electoral Commission 2013a, b, c, 21). Paradoxically, for the "Brexit" RQ, the Electoral Commission changed its opinion and retrospectively, the "Scottish" RQ can be also considered as slightly biased. More seriously, it should be taken into account that even properly defined RQ could be misleading for voters. More seriously, timing of the vote is important. Scottish voters can feel being deceived as many of them might have voted in RI de facto for Scotland to remain in the EU not for Scotland being independent and out of the EU.

In Catalonia, apart from unclear formulations, the two mutually conditioned questions reduced voters' ability to understand the language of the question. Initially, voters had to figure out what does it mean to vote for *"to be a State"* if that is not an independent state. Only after challenging that puzzle, voters would have to catch the sense of the second and more lucid RQ: *"Do you want this State to be Independent?"* Perhaps, although not explicitly mentioned, the first RQ was aimed at federalization of the entire country but, legally, it does not make much sense to ask for that issue prior to an all-Union debate. After East Timor and Croatia, neither Catalonia can qualify to be intelligible RQ for lacking one single question only.

In the 1980 and 1995 Québecs' sovereignty referendums, the RQs were most ambiguous of all compared. The goal of the referendum question was not clear. In general, there are many options on the scale of the term *"sovereignty"*, which was preferred on the ballot over the word *"independence"* which can represent only one and quite clear-cut type of sovereignty. In 1980, a common currency issue unbounded with the issue of independence could have been a very puzzling proposition for the voters. Of course, the length of the RQ makes its reading difficult. In the 1995 Québec referendum, the RQ was shorter, however not sufficiently to become unequivocal. Most strikingly, the term sovereignty again substitutes the term independence on the ballot. Moreover, voters were not giving a mandate to the government as in 1980 but this time, they had to have proper knowledge of the content of the Bill offered to Canada which proposed "*a new economic and political partnership*". And similarly, no clear dividing line between independence and a vaguely introduced sovereignty was drawn in the RQ. The RQs which do not contain the word independence may—although it does not necessarily have to—increase the likelihood that the RQ would not be properly apprehended by voters. The word independence was substituted several times by other terms and there is a question if that is necessary and adequate. For example, instead of independence, "*sovereignty*" [mandate to negotiate] or "*sovereign*" [a new partnership] was used in Québec 1980 and 1995 referendums, respectively. In the cases of South Sudan and East Timor, instead of independence, "*secession*" or "*separation*" appeared on the RI ballot. Another factor which could have effect on straightforwardness of the RQ is linked to its excessive length combined with more controversies. This applies to the sovereignty referendum in Catalonia and both 1980 and 1995 Québec RQs.

Additionally, impersonal formulas appeared in 1980 and 1995 Québecs' RI ("*...Do you give...*"/"*Do you agree...*") and in Catalonian RI ("*Do you want...*").

7 Concluding Remarks

The primary objective of this contribution was to find answers on the research questions formulated alongside four dimensions.

7.1 Purely Evolutionary Dimension

There have been either none or at most a limited and indirect impact of evaluation of norms on the RQs formula in the examined period 1980–2014. In emerging democracies, counting Slovenia and the Baltic republics (1990–1991), the RQs were much more intelligible than in both 1980 and 1995 Québec referendums. However, all of these RQs were formulated prior to the process of careful evaluation of the norms of a clear RQ—this era started after the second sovereignty referendum in Québec. In general, there was an improvement of the wording of the RQ in the internationally supervised RI (1993–2011), although the RQs used during these secessions were still partly biased. Both the "*Canadian*" and the CoE principles emphasizing the clear RQ and criticizing vaguely defined RQs may had —though indirectly—influenced RQ in South Sudan, the most recent of all internationally supervised RI examined in the text where the shortest formula of the RQ ever submitted to voters. However, the formula of the RQ on the ballot in the liberal democratic Catalonia submitted to voters in 2014 represented a radical setback.

7.2 Time-Spatial Dimension

Hereby, final design of the RQs revealed certain similarities although they hardly prevail over differences. In the Baltics, *"independence"* was important for all of the investigated RQs while the notion *"democratic"* for two of them (Lithuania, Latvia). All the three RQs were only slightly biased. In the case of seceding republics from Yugoslavia, all four surveyed RQs (Slovenia, Croatia, Macedonia and Bosnia) emphasized *"independence"* and *"sovereignty"*. However, quite intelligible RQ formulated in Slovenian RI is contrasting to partly biased RQs in Macedonia and Bosnia and strongly biased RQ in Croatia. Nevertheless, all these RIs took place at the same time between years 1991 and 1992 when—moreover— the RQ designed for RI was not evaluated yet in international area nor in liberal democracies. For that reason, RQs in a post-communist area can be mutually confronted in a timely evaluation only to other groups.

As for micro-states, unlike quite intelligible RQ formulated in attempted RI held in Nevis prior to clear rules on the clear RQ in both international area and liberal democratic world, RQs in Palau and Tokelau could not be intelligible enough given the fact that voting was aimed at, first, forced decolonization and, second, at quasi-independence status only. Therefore, despite the constructing RQ in 1983 or 2006, it can barely avoid even double confusing formulations in its RQs. In Palau, voters have to challenge *"Free Association"* and *"Compact of Free Association"* in the wording of the RQ, while in Tokelau voters face terms as *"free Association"* and *"Constitution and the Treaty"* in the RQ.

Internationally supervised and assisted referendums have been much more scattered both geographically and mentally. Tracking the outcomes in relatively wider period investigated here (1993–2011), the most intelligible RQ was constructed in earliest case of East Timor in 1993 far before any principles of a clear RQ started to be elaborated while the most biased RQ was designed for RI in East Timor. Certain shortcomings also applied for most recent RQ submitted in 2011 South Sudan RI. In liberal democratic countries, most biased RQ in 1980 Québec's RI was followed by slightly more intelligible RQ in 1995. The Scottish RI in 2014 represents almost ideal reference point, however, contrasts to strongly biased RQ formulated for Catalonian RI at the same time "advanced" enough for mature RQs.

7.3 Liberal Democratic Dimension

The question whether the RQs formulated for the RI were more intelligible in liberal democratic secessionist units rather than in non-democratic once cannot be clearly confirmed. The RQs were quite clearly formulated for RI held in emerging democracies in the early 1990s already—in the three Baltic republics and Slovenia. On the contrary, some strongly biased RQs were formulated in liberal democratic secessionist units regardless of the timeline as were the early case of Québec in 1980 and later case of Catalonia in 2014.

7.4 Negotiating Dimension

Only the fourth of the searched dimensions bring clear results for the RQs investigated in the text. The RQs formulated in cases of negotiated secessions are far more intelligible than the RQs constructed unilaterally by secessionists. There have not been seriously biased or unclear RQs in any of the four internationally supervised RI held in Eritrea, East Timor, Montenegro and South Sudan or in micro-states (Palau, Tokelau) which strongly contrasted to biased RQs formulated for RI unilaterally by secessionists in liberal democracies as Québec, Catalonia. On the contrary, carefully negotiated RQ in Scotland represents only entity from liberal democratic units investigated in the text with intelligible RQ. Surprisingly, the most notable exemption from the rule here clearly formulated RQs designed unilaterally by secessionists in majority of emerging democracies (the three Baltic republics, Slovenia).

In the near future, other RQs submitted to voters for RI can more clearly prove whether there is raising awareness among secessionists throughout the world willing to adopt norms and principles of intelligibility of RQ. And the prospect does not have to be pessimistic only. On the eve of the 20th anniversary of the 1995 Québec-biased sovereignty referendum, at the end of October 2015, the leader of the Parti Québécois Pierre Karl Peladeau said—apparently influenced by the Scottish model—that the next RQ in Québec could read: *"Should Québec be an independent country?"* (Jocelyne 2015).

References

Baldacchino, G. (2010). Upside down decolonization. *Subnational Island Jurisdiction*: Questioning the "post" in postcolonialism. *Space and Culture, 13*(2), 188–202.
Bereketeab, R. (2007). When success becomes a liability: Challenges of state building in Eritrea (1991–2005). *African and Asian Studies, 6,* 395–430.
Bourne, A. K. (2014). Europeanization and secession: The cases of Catalonia and Scotland. *JEMIE, 13*(3), 94–120.
Buchanan, A. (1991). Toward a theory of secession. *Ethics, 101*(2), 322–342.
Buchanan, A. (1997). Self-determination, secession, and the rule of law. In R. McKim & J. McMahan (Eds.), *The morality of nationalism* (pp. 301–323). New York and Oxford: Oxford University Press.
Buchanan, A. (2010). *Justice, legitimacy, and self-determination. Moral foundations for international law*. Oxford and New York: Oxford University Press.
Canada History. (2013). *Referendum 1980*. http://www.canadahistory.com/sections/eras/trudeau/1980_referendum.htm. Accessed November 1, 2015.
Carney, T. (2007). *Some assembly required. Sudan's comprehensive peace agreement*. Special report 194. USIP, Washington. http://www.usip.org/sites/default/files/sr194.pdf. Accessed November 1, 2015.
Choudhry, S., & Gaudreault-Des Biens, J.-F. (2007). Frank Iacobucci as constitutional maker: From the Quebec Veto reference to the Meech Lake Accord and the Quebec secession reference. *University of Toronto Law Journal, 57*(2), 165–193.

Christopher, A. J. (2011). Secession and South Sudan: An African precedent for the future? *South African Geographical Journal, 93*(2), 125–132.
Clarity Act. (2000). *S.C. 2000, c. 26*. http://laws.justice.gc.ca/PDF/C-31.8.pdf. Accessed November 25, 2015.
Columbia Electronic Encyclopedia. (2016). *Saint Kitts and Nevis*, 6th Edn. Q2.
Currie, J. H., & Provost, R. (2015). *The Canadian yearbook of international law* (Vol. 51). Vancouver: UBC Press.
CVK (Centrālā vēlēšanu komisija). Iedzīvotājuaptauja par LatvijasRepublikasneatkarību. Drukas versija. http://www3.lrs.lt/pls/inter2/dokpaieska.showdoc_l?p_id=1062&p_query. Accessed January 10, 2016.
Dion, S. (1996). Why is secession difficult in well-established democracies? Lessons from Quebec. *British Journal of Political Science, 26*(2), 269–283.
Dion, S. (1998). *Letter to Premier Lucien Bouchard on the need to respect the supreme court's decision in its entirety* (translation). http://www.solon.org/Constitutions/Canada/English/Arguments/dion-3.html. Accessed December 18, 2015.
Duchacek, I. D. (1970). *Comparative federalism. The territorial dimension of politics*. New York: Holt, Rienehart and Winston.
Duchacek, I. D. (1977). Antagonistic cooperation: Territorial and ethnic communities. *Publius, 7*(4), 3–29.
DW (Deutsche Welle). (2014). *Rebuking Madrid, Catalans vote to secede from Spain*. http://www.dw.com/en/rebuking-madrid-catalans-vote-to-secede-from-spain/a-18050684. Accessed November 12, 2015.
Eesti Vabariigi põhiseadus. (2012). Kommenteeritud väljaanne. Sissejuhatus. Lühiülevaade põhiseadusea jaloost. http://www.pohiseadus.ee/sissejuhatus/. Accessed November 16, 2015.
Elo, M. (2005). *Referendums: Towards good practices in Europe*. Doc. 10498. Report Political Affairs Committee Rapporteur: Mr, Finland, Socialist Group, 8 April 2005. Author(s): Parliamentary Assembly. http://www.assembly.coe.int/nw/xml/XRef/X2H-Xref-ViewHTML.asp?FileID=10820&lang=en. Accessed December 11, 2015.
Flanagan, T. (2011). *Clarifying the clarity act. The globe and mail*. http://www.theglobeandmail.com/opinion/clarifying-the-clarity-act/article586395/. Accessed June 10, 2016.
Gallup, G. (1941). Question wording in public opinion polls. *Sociometry, 4*(3), 259–268.
Gerston, L. N. (1989). Policymaking by referendum in Palau: Grassroots democracy or political paralysis? *Asian Affairs, 16*(4), 175–185.
Globus, P. (1996). Questioning the question: The Quebec referendum. *A Review of General Semantics, 53*(2), 148–151.
Gordon, T. (2011). *Westminster vows not to block SNP independence vote*. Herald Scotland. http://www.heraldscotland.com/news/13029672.Westminster_vows_not_to_block_SNP_independence_vote/. Accessed November 4, 2015.
Government of Tokelau. (no date). http://www.tokelau.org.nz/About+Us/Government/Self+Determination+Package.html. Accessed July 13, 2016.
Grant, T. D. (2009). Regulating the creation of states. From decolonization to secession. *Journal of International Law and International Relations, 5*(11), 11–57.
Hinck, J. (1990). The Republic of Palau and the United States: Self-determination becomes the price of free association. *California Law Review, 78*(4), 915–971.
HM Government, The Scottish Government. (2012). *Edinburgh agreement*. Edinburgh: HM Government—The Scottish Government. http://www.gov.scot/Resource/0040/00404789.pdf. Accessed November 9, 2015.
Hooper, A. (2008). Tokelau: A sort of 'self-governing' sort of 'colony'. *Pacific Currents. The Journal of Pacific History, 43*(3), 331–339.
Howe, P. (1998). Rationality and sovereignty support in Québec. *Canadian Journal of Political Science, 31*(1), 31–59.
IDEA (International Institute for Democracy and Electoral Assistance, Stockholm). (2008). *The international IDEA handbook. Direct democracy*. Stockholm. http://www.eods.eu/library/IDEA.Direct-DemocracyEN.pdf. Accessed November 9, 2015.

Iglar, R. F. (1992). The constitutional crisis in Yugoslavia and the international law of self-determination: Slovenia's and Croatia's right to secede. *Boston College International and Comparative Law Review, 15*(1), 213–239.

Immigration and Refugee Board of Canada. (2001). Ethiopia: Exact wording of question for referendum of April 1993 regarding Eritrean independence; Whether or not the question made reference to a choice between slavery and freedom. *Refworld*. http://www.refworld.org/docid/ 3df4be300.html. Accessed November 19, 2015.

Izbori.hr. (1991). *Izbori. Arhiva*. http://www.izbori.hr/arhiva/pdf/1991/1991_Rezultati_Referendum. pdf. Accessed December 21, 2015.

Jocelyne, R. (2015). Peladeau already planning 'clear' question for next sovereignty referendum. In *The Star.com*. http://www.thestar.com/news/canada/2015/10/30/peladeau-already-planning-clear-question-for-next-sovereignty-referendum.html. Accessed November 12, 2015.

Jot Down Magazine. (2014). ¿Quiere que Cataluña sea un Estado? ¿Y que este sea un Estado independiente? http://www.jotdown.es/2014/11/quiere-que-cataluna-sea-un-estado-y-que-este-sea-un-estado-independiente/. Accessed November 12, 2015.

Kisangani, F. E., & Hesli, L. V. (1995). The disposition to secede. An analysis of the Soviet case. *Comparative Political Studies, 27*(4), 493–536.

Koneska, C. (2014). *After ethnic conflict: Policy-making in post-conflict Bosnia and Herzegovina and Macedonia*. Routledge: Ashgate.

LeDuc, L. (no date). *Referendums and elections: How do campaign differ?* https://ecpr.eu/ Filestore/PaperProposal/e3c91233-daf8-40a7-896b-969a94eb0826.pdf. Accessed February 16, 2016.

Lietuvos Respublikos Seimas. (1991). Dėl Lietuvos Respublikos gyvento jųapklausos. Numeris: I-956. http://www3.lrs.lt/pls/inter2/dokpaieska.showdoc_l?p_id=1062&p_query. Accessed January 10, 2016.

Lindsay, P., & Wellman, C. H. (2003). Lincoln on secession. *Social Theory and Practice, 29*(1), 113–135.

Lluch, J. (2010). How nationalism evolves: Explaining the establishment of new varieties of nationalism within the national movements of Quebec and Catalonia (1976–2005). *Nationalities Papers, 38*(3), 337–359.

McNeil, B. J., Pauker, S. G., Sox, H. C., Jr., & Tversky, A. (1982). On the elicitation of preferences for alternative therapies. *The New England Journal of Medicine, 36*(21), 1259–1262.

Moore, M. (2004). *The ethics of nationalism*. Oxford and New York: Oxford University Press.

Muñoz, J., & Guinjoan, M. (2013). Accounting for internal variation in nationalist mobilization: Unofficial referendums for independence in Catalonia (2009–11). *Nations and Nationalism, 19* (1), 44–67.

Munya, P. M. (1999). The organization of African unity and its role in regional conflict resolution and dispute settlement: A critical evaluation. *Boston College Third World Law Journal, 19*(2), 537–592.

N1. (2015). BiH obeležava Dan nezavisnosti. http://rs.n1info.com/a39217/Svet/Region/BiH-obelezava-Dan-nezavisnosti.html. Accessed November 30, 2015.

New World Encyclopedia. Eritrean war of independence. http://www.newworldencyclopedia.org/ entry/Eritrean_War_of_Independence. Accessed November 19, 2015.

Oproiu, M. (2011). Slobodan Milosevic and the violent transformation of borders in former Yugoslavia. *Eurolimes, 11,* 142–156.

OSCE. (1992). The referendum on independence in Bosnia-Herzegovina February 29–March 1, 1992. 102st Congress, 1st session. http://www.csce.gov/index.cfm?FuseAction=Files.Download &FileStore_id=331. Accessed November 7, 2015.

OSCE. (2006a). Interim report 1. 28 Mar 2006–20 Apr 2006. OSCE, Podgorica. http://www.osce. org/odihr/elections/montenegro/18845?download=true. Accessed November 7, 2015.

OSCE. (2006b). Kancelarija za demokratske institucije I ljudska prava. Republika Crna Gora. Referendum o Državnom statusu.Posmatračka misija za referendum OSCE/ODIHR-a.

Konačniizvješta. Warszsawa. http://www.osce.org/sr/odihr/elections/montenegro/20099?download= true. Accessed November 7, 2015.
OSN [UN]. (2005). *Fakta a čísla OSN. Základní údaje o Organizaci Spojených národů*. UN, Praha.
Palau Profile—Timeline. (2015). *BBC*. http://www.bbc.com/news/world-middle-east-15446663. Accessed August 17, 2016.
Parker, I. (2006). Birth of a nation? *New Yorker, 82*(11).
Phllips, F. (2002). *Commonwealth Caribbean constitutional law*. London: Cavendish Publishing.
Philpott, D. (1995). In defense of self-determination. *Ethics, 105*(2), 352–385.
Pittock, M. (2012). National identities, Scottish sovereignty and the union of 1707: Then and now. *National Identities, 14*(1), 11–21.
Premdas, R. (1996). *Ethnicity and identity in the Caribbean: Decentering a Myth*. Working Paper#234. Kellog Institute. The Hellen Kellogg Institute for International Studies. https://kellogg.nd.edu/publications/workingpapers/WPS/234.pdf. Accessed July 28, 2016.
Premdas, R. (2013). Secession in the contemporary world. In *ISA eSymposium for sociology* (pp. 1–11). http://www.isa-sociology.org/uploads/files/EBul-Premdas-Jul2012.pdf. Accessed August 17, 2016.
Pue, K. (2012). *Democratic governance. reference re: Secession of Quebec, in Context*. Centre for Constitutional Studies. University of Alberta. http://ualawccsprod.srv.ualberta.ca/ccs/index.php/constitutional-issues/democratic-governance/652-reference-re-secession-of-quebec-in-context. Accessed December 28, 2015.
Qvortrup, M. (2014a). *National and ethnic conflict in the twenty century: Referendums and ethnic conflict*. Philadelphia: University of Pennsylvania Press.
Qvortrup, M. (2014b). Referendums on independence, 1860–2011. *Political Quarterly, 85*(1), 57–64.
Qvortrup, M. (2015). *Referendum and ethnic conflict*. Pittsburgh: University of Pennsylvania Press.
Radan, P. (2000). Post-secession international borders: A critical analysis of the opinions of the Badinter Arbitration Commission. *Melbourne University Law Review, 24*(1), 50–76.
Radan, P. (2007). *Creating New States. Theory and practice of secession*. Hampshire: Ashgate.
Radio Canada. (2008). Référendum 1980: l'avenir du Québec en question. In *Archives de Radio-Canada*. http://archives.radio-canada.ca/politique/provincial_territorial/dossiers/1294/. Accessed November 2, 2015.
Radio Canada. (no date). Point de rupture. La question référendaire. http://ici.radio-canada.ca/nouvelles/dossiers/pointderupture/Chapitre_4_1.shtml. Accessed November 2, 2015.
Radio Slobodna Evropa. (2011). 20 godini nezavisnost. http://www.makdenes.org/content/article/24321916.html. Accessed December 20, 2015.
Raić, D. (2002). *Statehood and the law of self-determination*. The Hague, London and New York: Kluwer Law International.
Republic of the Sudan Gazette. (2005). Special Supplement. No. 1722. Interim National Constitution of the Republic of the Sudan. In *Ministry of Justice*. https://unmis.unmissions.org/Portals/UNMIS/CPA%20Monitor/Annexes/Annex%201-%20Interim%20National%20Constitution%20of%20Sudan%20-%20FIXED.pdf. Accessed December 1, 2015.
Rius-Ulldemolins, J., & Zamorano, M. M. (2015). Federalism, cultural policies, and identity pluralism: Cooperation and conflict in the Spanish Quasi-Federal system. *Publius: The Journal of Federalism, 45*(2), 167–188.
RTCG. Law on the referendum on state-legal status of the Republic of Montenegro. http://www.rtcg.org/referendum/regulativa/zakon_o_referendumu.pdf#search=%22zakon%20o%20referendumu%20o%20dr%C5%BEavno-pravnom%20statusu%22. Accessed December 7, 2015.
Slovenia Times. (2015). *Slovenia's road to independence*. http://www.sloveniatimes.com/slovenia-s-road-to-independence. Accessed November 14, 2015.
Southern Sudan Referendum Act. (2009). https://unmis.unmissions.org/Portals/UNMIS/Referendum/SS%20Referendum%20MOJ-Englis.pdf. Accessed December 1, 2015.
St. Kitts and Nevis Constitution. (1983). http://pdba.georgetown.edu/Constitutions/Kitts/kitts83.html. Accessed December 4, 2015.

St. Kitts and Nevis. (2000). Background notes on countries of the world 2003, 10495517. *St. Kitts and Nevis. Academic Search Complete.*

Stephens, C. (2015). Operationalising reciprocity in secessionist referenda. *University of Quennsland Law Journal, 34*(1), 139–165.

Sudan Tribune. (2011). *South Sudan referendum voting process.* http://www.sudantribune.com/spip.php?article37536. Accessed December 1, 2015.

Supreme Court Judgments. (1998). *Reference re secession of Quebec.* [1998] 2 SCR 217.SCC Case Information 25506. http://scc-csc.lexum.com/scc-csc/scc-csc/en/1643/1/document.do. Accessed November 8, 2015.

The Canadian Encyclopedia. (1995). *Quebéc referendum 1995.* http://www.thecanadianencyclopedia.ca/en/article/quebec-referendum-1995/. Accessed November 7, 2015.

The Electoral Commission. (2009). *Referendum question and assessment guidelines.* http://www.electoralcommission.org.uk/__data/assets/pdf_file/0006/82626/Referendum-Question-guidelines-final.pdf. Accessed October 16, 2015.

The Electoral Commission. (2013a). *Referendum on independence for Scotland advice of the Electoral Commission on the proposed referendum question.* Edinburgh, London: Electoral Commission. http://www.electoralcommission.org.uk/__data/assets/pdf_file/0007/153691/Referendum-on-independence-for-Scotland-our-advice-on-referendum-question.pdf. Accessed November 9, 2015.

The Electoral Commission. (2013b). *Referendum on independence for Scotland.* Advice of the Electoral Commission on the proposed referendum question January 2013. http://www.electoralcommission.org.uk/__data/assets/pdf_file/0007/153691/Referendum-on-independence-for-Scotland-our-advice-on-referendum-question.pdf. Accessed October 16, 2015.

The Electoral Commission. (2013c). *Referendum on the United Kingdom's membership of the European Union.* Advice of the Electoral Commission on the referendum question included in the European Union (Referendum) Bill. http://www.electoralcommission.org.uk/__data/assets/pdf_file/0004/163282/EU-referendum-question-assessment-report.pdf. Accessed October 16, 2015.

The PPERA (Political Parties, Elections and Referendums Act). (2000). http://www.legislation.gov.uk/ukpga/2000/41/pdfs/ukpga_20000041_en.pdf. Accessed October 12, 2015.

The Scottish Executive. (2007). Choosing Scotland's future. A National conversation. In *Independence and responsibility in the modern world.* Edinburgh. http://www.gov.scot/Resource/Doc/194791/0052321.pdf. Accessed November 2, 2015.

The Scottish Government. (2007). *Your Scotland, your voice: A national conversation.* Edinburgh. http://www.gov.scot/Resource/Doc/293639/0090721.pdf. Accessed November 2, 2015.

The Scottish Government. (2010). *Scotland's future: Draft referendum (Scotland) bill consultation paper choosing Scotland's future.* Edinburgh. http://www.gov.scot/resource/doc/303348/0095138.pdf. Accessed November 2, 2015.

The Scottish Government. (2012). *Your Scotland, your referendum.* Edinburgh. http://www.gov.scot/Resource/0038/00386122.pdf. Accessed November 9, 2015.

The Secretary of State for Scotland. (2012). *Scotland's constitutional future. A consultation on facilitating a legal, fair and decisive referendum on whether Scotland should leave the United Kingdom.* https://www.gov.uk/government/uploads/system/uploads/attachment_data/file/39248/Scotlands_Constitutional_Future.pdf. Accessed November 9, 2015.

Tierney, S. (2013). Legal issues surrounding the referendum on independence for Scotland. *European Constitutional Law Review, 9*(3), 359–390.

Tishkov, V. (1997). *Ethnicity, nationalism and conflict in and after the Soviet Union: The mind aflame.* London, Thousand Oak and New Delphi: Sage Publications.

Türk, D. (1993). Recognition of states: A comment. *European Journal of International Law, 4*, 66–91. http://www.ejil.org/pdfs/4/1/1227.pdf. Accessed December 9, 2015.

Tversky, A., & Kahneman, D. (1981). The framing of decisions and the psychology of choice. *Science. New Series, 211*(4481), 453–458.

UN. (1960). *Declaration on the granting of independence to colonial countries and peoples.* 1514 (XV). http://daccess-dds-ny.un.org/doc/RESOLUTION/GEN/NR0/152/88/IMG/NR015288.pdf?OpenElement. Accessed November 21, 2015.

UN. (1999). *Agreement between the Republic of Indonesia and the Portuguese Republic on the question of East Timor.* http://peacemaker.un.org/sites/peacemaker.un.org/files/ID%20TL_990505_AgreementOnEastTimor.pdf. Accessed December 4, 2015.

UN. (2006). *Professor Tony Angelo (New Zealand).* Discussion paper. Yanuca, Fiji, 28–30 November 2006. http://www.un.org/en/decolonization/pdf/dp_2006_angelo.pdf. Accessed September 8, 2016.

UN. (2007). GA/COL/3164 16.10.2007. *United nations to observe referendum on self-determination in non-self-governing territory of Tokelau*, from 20 to 24 October. http://www.un.org/press/en/2007/gacol3164.doc.htm. Accessed November 10, 2015.

UNGA. (1950). *Report of the United Nations Commission for Eritrea; Report of the Interim Committee of the General Assembly on the Report of the United Nations Commission for Eritrea.* http://daccess-dds-ny.un.org/doc/RESOLUTION/GEN/NR0/059/88/IMG/NR005988.pdf?OpenElement. Accessed December 1, 2015.

United Nations Chronicle. (1990). Trusteeship mission reports on Palau voting, 02517329, 27 (2). *Academic Search Complete.*

UNMIS. (2005). *Sudan comprehensive peace agreement.* https://unmis.unmissions.org/Portals/UNMIS/Documents/General/cpa-en.pdf. Accessed December 2, 2015.

Venice Commission. (2001). *Guidelines for constitutional referendums at national level.* http://www.venice.coe.int/webforms/documents/default.aspx?pdffile=CDL-INF%282001%29010-e. Accessed December 11, 2015.

Venice Commission. (2005a). *Referendums in Europe—An analysis of the legal rules in European States.* http://www.venice.coe.int/webforms/documents/default.aspx?pdffile=CDL-AD%282005%29034-e. Accessed September 11, 2015.

Venice Commission. (2005b). *Opinion on the compatibility of the existing legislation in Montenegro concerning the organisation of Referendums with applicable international standards.* http://www.venice.coe.int/webforms/documents/default.aspx?pdffile=CDL-AD%282005%29041-e. Accessed December 11, 2015.

Venice Commission. (2007). *Comparative analysis of the legal rules on referendums in Europe. Code of Good Practice on Referendums.* http://www.venice.coe.int/webforms/documents/default.aspx?pdffile=CDL-AD(2007)008-e). Accessed December 11, 2015.

Vidmar, J. (2007). Montenegro's path to independence: A study of self-determination, statehood and recognition. *Hanse Law Review, 3*(1), 73–101.

Vidmar, J. (2012). South Sudan and the international legal framework governing the emergence and delimitation of New States. *Texas International Law Journal, 47*(3), 541–559.

Vidmar, J. (2013). Notes and Comments/Notes et commentaries—The Scottish independence referendum in an international context. In J. H. Currie & R. Provost (Eds.), *The Canadian yearbook of international law* (Vol. 51, pp. 259–288). Vancouver: UBC Press.

Villicana, R. L., & Venkataraman, M. (2006). Public policy failure or historical debacle? A study of eritrea's relations with Ethiopia since 1991. *Review of Policy Research, 23*(2), 549–571.

Vuković, I. (2012). Political dynamics of the post-communist Montenegro: One party show. In *4th ECPR graduate conference, Bremen, Jacobs University, July 4–6, 2012.* https://ecpr.eu/Filestore/PaperProposal/c9d05d30-f11a-4225-965b-c6724a4f71d5.pdf. Accessed November 1, 2015.

Weller, M. (2008). Why the legal rules on self-determination. Do not resolve self-determination disputes. In M. Weller, B. Metzger (Eds.), *Settling self-determination disputes. Complex power-sharing in theory and practice* (pp. 17–45). Leiden and Boston: Martinus Nijhoff Publishers.

Wood, J. R. (1981). Secession: A comparative analytical framework. *Canadian Journal of Political Science/Revue Canadienne de Science Politique, 14*(1), 107–134.

Yale, F., & Durand, C. (2011). What did quebeckers want? Impact of question wording, constitutional proposal and context on support for sovereignty, 1976–2008. *American Review of Canadian Studies, 41*(3), 242–258.

Author Biography

Přemysl Rosůlek is a Political Scientist and Associate Professor at University of West Bohemia, Faculty of Philosophy and Arts, Department of Political Science and International Relations. Author is focused primarily on nationalism, ethnic conflicts, secession in theory and practice, contemporary problems of political philosophy and South-eastern Europe.

(Super)Power Rule: Comparative Analysis of Parent States

Martin Riegl and Bohumil Doboš

The post-World War II era faced an unprecedented turn towards the support of the territorial integrity of sovereign states that was only overcome by the principle of self-determination during the decolonization process. The principle of territorial integrity and unchangeable nature of borders remain at the centre of international politics with the opposing principle of self-determination as a tool for ending the era of colonialism still being valid and sound. The secessionist movements outside the context of decolonization (e.g. Katanga, Biafra, West Papua, Cabinda, Southern Rhodesia, East Timor in 1975, Bougainville, Republika Srpska Krajina, Tamil Eelam, Chechnya) usually faced hostile reactions from the international community that is strongly biased towards the support of sovereignty and indivisibility of territory. The obligation to provide the justification of its case is usually on the side of secessionist movements and only rarely examples of internationally supported divisions of territory or support for such future divisions can be found.

A sharp change in the nature of the international recognition from negative to positive in accordance with the colonial right for self-determination[1] (Fabry 2010) was accompanied not only by an increase in the number of members of the international community with full recognition, but also by an increase in the number of entities with de facto statehood yet without full international recognition. These entities remained trapped in the anomaly position of the binary logic of contemporary geopolitics (recognition versus non-recognition).

This chapter is dedicated to the Charles University Research Development Schemes, programme PROGRES Q18—Social sciences: from multidisciplinary to interdisciplinary.

---

[1]Decolonization was allowed and even mandated by international law (Peters 2014, 107).

M. Riegl · B. Doboš (✉)
Faculty of Social Sciences, Institute of Political Studies,
Charles University, Prague, Czech Republic
e-mail: bohumil.dobos@gmail.com

© Springer International Publishing AG 2017
M. Riegl and B. Doboš (eds.), *Unrecognized States and Secession in the 21st Century*, DOI 10.1007/978-3-319-56913-0_6

A dynamic development of political map corresponds to the dichotomist tension between the principles of (external) self-determination and territorial integrity with none of these applied systematically or dogmatically by the international community. M. Fabry pointed out this dichotomy in the context of the attitude of the international community towards recognition of the new political entities. Fabry argues that between 1815 and 1950 this recognition held negative character when state recognition was an acknowledgement of an achievement of de facto statehood by a people desiring independence, while since the 1950s the key to foreign recognition has not been the attainment of de facto statehood but rather a prior international acceptance of their asserted right to independence (Fabry 2010). Nevertheless, even *"the current self-determination/recognition regime"* (Fabry 2010, 225) based on the UN Resolution 1514 (A/RES 1960) is not applied consistently as can be demonstrated by the SADR case in the 1970s in which the geopolitical interests of external actors dominated over the principles, or by the ambiguous Somaliland case when the decision was "delegated" to the regional body.

Friction between the sovereignty first approach (Williams et al. 2015) and the ad hoc attitude towards secessionism by the international community leads to the existence of unrecognized entities that are labelled by F. McConnell as being *"in consistently negative terms (as illegal, pathological and clandestine) and with regard to what they fail to achieve (sovereign territorial statehood)* (McConnell 2009, 344–345)".[2] These entities have been a part of the political environment for decades despite the fact that *"(c)urrent legal and normative doctrine forbids de jure recognition to those territorial units whose political leadership has been resisted by metropolitan central authorities* (Berg 2009, 219)".

Despite a clear lack of consensus, a clear demarcation of borders or spheres of influence among influential world powers leads to destabilization of some regions due to ad hoc enforcement of their political goals. M. Fabry refers to the situation as follows—"self-determination cannot be made into a universal positive right—aptly captured by former UN Secretary-General Boutros Boutros-Ghali's statement that if every ethnic, religious or linguistic group claimed statehood, there would be no limit to fragmentation (Fabry 2010, 219)".

While taking into account the importance of the analysis of the justification of the secessionist cases by different movements,[3] this paper aims to present a different attitude towards the study of territorial disintegration. Our paper aims to present selected cases of internationally supported territorial disintegration that was either de facto successful and de iure accepted (Bangladesh, South Sudan, Eritrea, etc.) or has yet to materialize (either de facto or de iure) (the Western Sahara, Palestine, Kosovo, etc.) and to search for the factors that are common for their parent states. By comparison of the parent states, we seek to examine the factors that are common

---

[2]See also Peg and Kolsto (2014).

[3]And different level of actual following of that justification—see Kopeček et al. (2016).

for these countries and to lay basis for the theoretical understanding of the factors influencing the acceptance of territorial disintegration *vis-à-vis* the parent states.

The aim of the paper is thus to analyse the reasons for and the context of full or partial acceptance of the secessionist claims out of the decolonization process. This riddle should be solved by answering the question why the international community applies in some cases a policy of *collective recognition,* while in other cases the principle of *collective non-recognition* (Oeter 2014) with the focus on the position of the parent state. The basic assumption is that the international regime after 1945 generally accepts the use of force measures by the parent state[4] (as recently in the case of Mali[5]) in the cases of secession (e.g. Cabinda, Katanga, South Kasai, Bougainville, South Rhodesia, Chechnya, Herzeg-Bosna, Western Bosnia, Republika Srpska Krajina, Tamil Eelam), but in ad hoc cases, the use of force is pronounced illegitimate. This illegitimacy is then the first step towards the loss of territorial integrity (Kosovo, South Sudan, and Western Sahara).

The paper is structured as follows. First, we present some basic theoretical models that lie at the core of our research. Following this part, we present the cases that have been chosen for our empirical research and their brief historical development. Third, the comparison of the major factors connected to separatism with a focus on similar and different conditions of parent states is made. Finally, we deduce some broader implications based on the comparison.

1 Theoretical Background

The contemporary research on unrecognized states usually focuses on the geopolitical discussions related to geopolitical agents, such as the parent, patron states and external players, justification, legality, and legitimacy of the attempts to fragment the political map by the bids for independence. D. Geldenhuys summed up the major claims justifying secession as they appear in scholarly literature,[6] but pointed out the fact that *"(a)lthough a secessionist entity might improve its chances of*

---

[4]"Often the government involved in a secessionist conflict asks for and receives military assistance from abroad (Nigeria from UK/USSR, Papua New Guinea, Ethiopia from Iran/Israel) (Tancredi 2014, 81)".

[5]"The UN Security Council in Res. 2071 (2012) stressed the primary responsibility of the Malian authority for ensuring…the unity in its territory (Tancredi 2014, 75)".

[6]"Secession should have a just cause,… among such are genocide, cultural extinction (also called ethnocide), oppression,… secession is a final resort solution,… secession is the only way in which the minority concerned can exercise its right of self-determination in a democratic fashion,… the internal and external legitimacy of the central government has been widely questioned due to its authoritarian and repressive nature,… the group should have historic claims to the territory,… the new state has to be constituted on a democratic basis, guarantee individual and minority rights on its soil,… the putative state should have a relatively effective central government that has provided order,… the emerging state has reasonable prospects of survival and economic prosperity,… the remainder state's economy will not be substantially weakened (Geldenhuys 2009, 40–42)".

international recognition by meeting the criteria just listed there is no guarantee that the world community will oblige (Geldenhuys 2009, 40–42)". He reflects not only the 1980s debate between H. Beran and A. Birch, who summed up the most common arguments used by elites, but also the so-called new set of normative criteria that are based on a principle of conditional recognition and were first applied by the European Community during the dissolution of Yugoslavia. These rules are also reflected in the policy of collective recognition which according to S. Oeter *"relies on a set of normative criteria as a guideline for such common action"* and collective non-recognition in relation to an unrecognized state[7] (Geldenhuys 2009; Oeter 2014), the latter being applied *vis-à-vis* Katanga, Biafra, Rhodesia, South African homeland states and the Turkish Republic of Northern Cyprus (Geldenhuys 2009, 22) or the Eurasian unrecognized states.[8] The principle of territorial integrity is also a part of the criminal code of many states—e.g. in 2005 the Third Session of the Tenth National People's Congress of the People's Republic of China adopted the Anti-Secession Law (Tancredi 2014, 74) or in 2013 Russia amended its criminal code to establish penalties up to six years in prison for calls for separatism and other acts that might lead to a disruption of the territorial integrity of the Russian Federation (Maleshin 2014).

The scholarly literature also tends to accept that the international community, fearing unlimited fragmentation of the political map as was voiced during the establishment of microstates[9] or by the UN Secretary-General B.B. Ghali, has preferred the principle of territorial integrity over the right of external self-determination. This has been evident in the cases of Congo and Mali, where the UN and an international coalition led by France in the latter case, militarily intervened in order to prevent secession of Katanga (1960–1961) and Azawad.[10] This approach is, however, not applied consistently which has led to the successful cases of secession outside the context of decolonization. Some authors (Walter et al. 2014) point out that the international community failed to establish codified procedural rules for secession in the cases of Bangladesh or the Kosovo secession; therefore, the establishment of a universal set of requirements for accepted secession is still lacking and unlikely to be developed (Copp 1998). As noted by Pavkovič and Radan, *"(h)owever, the initial seceders from Yugoslavia and from the USSR differed in the readiness of the international organizations and their member*

---

[7]"… they all experience collective non-recognition in the sense of being deliberately excluded from UN membership … non-recognition was deliberately extended from a unilateral basis to a broader representation of the international community (Geldenhuys 2009, 7, 23)".

[8]"Russia's recognition of Abkhazia and South Ossetia in the aftermath of Western recognition of Kosovo demonstrated that even precedent-sensitive foreign policy justifications may not achieve their desired effect if they are not accepted by major powers (Fabry 2010, 224)".

[9]While the Maldives were accepted into the UN (in the same year, when the declaration of independence was declared) Nauru, which in the year of declaration of independence had a population of only 3100 inhabitants (Rosůlek 2014), was not accepted into the UN until 1999.

[10]"Secessions of Katanga and Azawad were rejected by the UN Security Council and Security Council of the AU in the latter case (Tancredi 2014, 82–83)".

states to intervene on their behalf. The Republic of Western Bosnia was overrun in August 1995 by the Bosnian Muslim army and Croatian army in a joint operation with NATO. In the same operation the Croatian army and the Bosnian Muslim forces, together with NATO ground troops (under the UN flag) and NATO air force, attacked the Serb Republic (...) (b)ut in contrast to Bosnia Herzegovina, in this case NATO military intervention secured a de facto secession: that of Kosovo from Serbia (Pavkovič and Radan 2007, 153)".

Some authors have attempted to theoretically approach the acceptance of secessionist entity by the international community and in this regard it is important to point out two works in this field—a new political theory of secession based on (super)power rule of M. Sterio and the concept of earned sovereignty of P. Williams. Our paper is based on M. Fabry's thesis on the evolution of the nature of international recognition since the 1950s and a modified Sterio's (super)power rule, who defined the factors leading to the successful secession as:

1. That it has suffered heinous human rights abuses;
2. Its mother's state central government is relatively weak;
3. The international community has already gotten involved through a form of international administration of the secessionist territory; and
4. It enjoys the support of most of the great powers (Sterio 2013).

Sterio concludes in her analysis that the key to success may lie in the geopolitical goals of external actors, which is contrary to the usually stressed importance of legitimacy of the secessionist bid or its ability to establish a de facto statehood and to follow the rules based on the new set of normative criteria developed after the end of the bipolar world order. "*In other words, why were the great powers supportive of East Timor, Kosovo, and South Sudan, and not of Chechnya, the Georgian provinces, or Tibet? One plausible explanation, albeit cynical one, is that the great powers seem intent on helping groups, movements, and states when it is in their own geopolitical interest to do so* (Sterio 2013, 66)".

Our modification of the (super)power rule works with the assumption that secession will not be successful if the parent state enjoys a strong and effective support from the guarantor who is able to project his power in a manner effective enough to deny the secessionist entity a de facto independence or an acceptance by the majority of the international community. Unlike Sterio, we believe that the remaining criteria are of secondary importance. Our hypothesis is based on the understanding that the fate of the secessionist entities is decided by the role of the (super)power(s) in the region and its/their international acceptance and recognition is based both on the role of the patron state and the normative criteria. The (super)power decision to support one or the other side of the conflict is thus a sufficient condition for de facto success/failure of the secession while the support of (super)power is a necessary condition for the full de iure recognition given the role of the United Nations Security Council. Limited de iure recognition will be enabled by the collective recognition process that is usually also started by the (super)power and is influenced by the normative strength of the secessionist claim and the soft power of the supportive (super)power.

In the following comparison, we will present five factors—analysis of the internal situation in the parent state; geopolitical position of the parent state; origins and legitimacy of the secessionist claims; analysis of the parent state's reaction to the claims; and the international approach towards the secession. Analysing these five points, we aim at reaching an understanding of the nature of international recognition in relation to the nature of the parent state.

2 Case Selection and Description

Selection of the cases for our research has been an intriguing task as the case selection is crucial for the validity of our generalizations. The cases researched in the following text are those that were widely internationally accepted (however, not always fully recognized) at the time of writing this paper, as these cases would be all internationally recognized according to the competing logic of the crucial role of normative rules. We look deeper into the above-described factors to analyse whether the moral question is the crucial one or whether the approach and attitude of the (super)powers play a significant role. Case selection was thus based on two principles. First, the secessionist entity was not absorbed into its parent state and maintains its secessionist claims until the present times (unlike, e.g., Katanga, Tamil Eelam, or Biafra) and has obtained significant or full international recognition (unlike, e.g., South Ossetia or Abkhazia). The case of Taiwan has been omitted as the de facto entity is not an outcome of secession but a split following a civil war in mainland China that ended in 1950. On the other hand, case of the Western Sahara is not a case of secession but has been affected by the same principles as traditional secessionist movements with the parent state occupying its territory.

There are four post-World War II examples that can be understood as successful (both de facto and de iure) cases of secession—Bangladesh, Eritrea, South Sudan, and East Timor. These cases succeeded in winning de facto independence from their parent states and in receiving full international recognition outside the colonial context. Out of the cases that have not yet achieved full recognition by the international community or de iure independence, we have selected the cases of Kosovo (de facto independence, wide international recognition), Palestine (wide international recognition and semi-autonomous status), Sahrawi Arab Democratic Republic (SADR) (wide international recognition), and Bougainville (planned independence referendum). All of these cases are, additionally, interconnected by the past or present violent reaction of their respective parent states (Pakistan, Ethiopia, Sudan, Indonesia, Serbia, Israel, Morocco, Papua New Guinea) countering their movements towards independence.

2.1 Bangladesh

After the independence and partition of the British India in 1947, Bangladesh became part of Pakistan as the East Pakistan. Despite the importance of the province for the country as a whole, West Pakistani elites, according to Bennett Jones, refused to give the Bengali population of Bangladesh a proper representation and kept it impoverished. The authoritarian government, however, enabled somewhat fair and free elections to take place in 1970 that were overwhelmingly won by the Awami League—a party representing the Bengalis. This was unacceptable for the military leadership of Pakistan that in 1971 launched an incursion into East Pakistan, starting a bloody civil war. With the Indian support and direct military intervention in favour of what was to become Bangladesh and the complicated logistical support for Pakistani troops from the West Pakistan given the unsuitable terrain in the country, Bangladesh was able to defeat the Pakistani troops out and win its de facto independence (Bennett 2009, 140–180). "*… although the intervention was legally justified on grounds of self-defence and humanitarian intervention, it was mostly condemned, both in Security Council and in the UN General Assembly, where many states re-affirmed their adherence to the principle that nothing can justify armed action against the territorial integrity of a member state* (Tancredi 2014, 91)". Throughout 1972, many countries recognized the independence of Bangladesh (even the Pakistani ally, the USA) and in 1974 Bangladesh was accepted into the United Nations.

2.2 Eritrea

Eritrea was united with Ethiopia after World War II during the process of decolonization. Various forces rebelled against this union from the beginning, and the region was caught up in a protracted civil war. After decades of fighting, the Eritrean and Ethiopian rebel forces succeeded in 1991 in making significant military victories that forced the Ethiopian government to organize an independence referendum. After the overwhelming support for the independence by the Eritrean population had been confirmed by the referendum results (with only 0.17% voting against) (African Elections Database 2011), the newborn country declared independence in 1993. Eritrea has since then been an accepted member of the international community.

2.3 East Timor

East Timor as part of the Portuguese colonial empire was decolonized at a later stage compared to the British or French territories. It gained independence from

Portugal in the mid-1970s but was soon invaded and occupied by the Indonesian forces. It is important to point out that its first bid for international recognition in 1975 was not accepted by the international community due to the geopolitical importance of the parent state for the USA (Simms 2013). Ever since the occupation East Timor fought the war of separation against the government in Jakarta that was often very violent. International pressure led, however, to the separation at the turn of the twentieth and the twenty-first century and East Timor was accepted as a fully independent and sovereign state in 2002.

2.4 South Sudan

Sudan as a multi-ethnic country had suffered from a problematic relationship between its Arab and sub-Saharan population since the creation of the colonial entity under the British rule. After achieving independence in 1956, the country was dominated by the Arab population which led to the first war against the southern separatists and the supporters of a larger role of non-Arabs in the country. This first civil war ended in 1972 but was rekindled in 1983 mainly over the issues concerning the relocation of funds obtained through the drilling of oil in the southern territories. After a protracted civil war, the Arab elites in 2005 accepted a peace plan that included an independence referendum to be held in 2011. Despite the original acceptance by the Southern elites of autonomy inside the unified Sudan, a later shift towards the push for full independence led the voters to overwhelmingly demonstrate their preference for the creation of a new state, and the fully recognized entity was established the same year (Idris 2013).

2.5 Kosovo

Kosovo became a focal point of the international attention due to the ethnic war in former Yugoslavia and the subsequent ethnic conflict in the late 1990s with the Serbian forces that led to the bombing of targets inside Serbia by the NATO forces in 1999. Unlike the previous three cases, the process of recognition of Kosovo is not globally accepted. Despite the pleas from the Kosovar elites and some members of the international community (headed by the USA), Kosovo did not receive full recognition as an independent state in 2008 and its status has been mainly challenged by Russia. Even though the case is sometimes compared to that of East Timor,[11] the case of Kosovo remains a controversial one, and despite obtaining a certain level of international acceptance and independence (mediated by the EU), it is not a member of the UN and does not hold full international recognition.

---

[11]See Scheffer (2009).

2.6 Palestine

The issue of Palestine is connected to the post-World War II decolonization process and the hostility of the Arab states towards the state of Israel. Despite the original plan to create both Israel and Palestine, the invasion of the Arab forces onto the territory of the Jewish state in 1948 led to the occupation of Palestine by the Israeli forces that continues until today. Throughout the time, Palestine has been able to secure an increasing amount of international support and is recognized by majority of countries as an independent state despite the fact that it does hold only a limited authority over its territory. Palestine is also a member of many international organizations. Its main international opponent is the USA which uses a similar veto right in this case as Russia does in the case of Kosovo.

2.7 SADR

The Western Sahara is a former Spanish colony. In the mid-1970s, the Spanish retreated from the territory under international pressure, which was followed by the annexation of the unit by Morocco and Mauritania (which soon retreated from the occupied territories). This annexation was directly succeeded by an insurgency led by Polisario movement which presents itself as a SADR's government in exile. The civil war officially ended in 1991 by a ceasefire agreement between Polisario and the Moroccan government. This accord promised referendum over the future status of the Western Sahara. However, the referendum has never been held which causes further distress in the region with occasional outbursts of violence. Another effect of the dispute in the Western Sahara is the Moroccan absence from the African Union (as the only African state) due to the support of many African states for the Polisario cause (coming most strongly from Algeria). SADR thus remains a partially recognized state with a limited control over its own territory.

2.8 Bougainville

Bougainville became part of Papua New Guinea during the process of decolonization in Southeast Asia and Pacific in the 1970s. The island, as the site of major gold and copper mining operations, became dissatisfied with the lack of autonomy and the low share from the income produced by the islands outputs, which triggered insurgencies that were suppressed by the central government's armed forces and hired mercenary forces. During the peace process that began in the late 1990s, the island received a political autonomy and local administration was established. The island is to hold an independence referendum in 2019 that is agreed on with the central government and is expected to become an independent state after the referendum has taken place.

3 Comparison

3.1 Pakistan

The first researched factor is the internal situation in the parent state by the time the international community began inclining towards the possibility of the acceptance of secession. We will focus on the level of democracy in the parent state, the provision of basic freedoms, and the level of state effectiveness. The first studied case is Pakistan in the late 1960s and early 1970s. As noted in the previous chapter, Pakistan was by that time ruled by the military regime (situation more or less observable until recent times) and the basic freedoms were withheld from the population—especially in the former East Pakistan. A low level of adherence to democratic principles was also demonstrated by the refusal to accept the outcome of the elections that were won by the Awami League and the violent reaction to the protests in Bangladesh (Bennett Jones 2009, 140–180). Pakistan, for the entire period of its existence, might also be called a failing or weak state. Its economy is weak, the level of education low, and the state institutions backward.[12] State institutions and functions were and are to a large extent dependent on foreign aid (mainly from the USA or China).

As for the geopolitical situation, Pakistan as a country created by the partition of the British India in 1947 was in a complicated geopolitical position. Not only has it had to deal with an unfavourable geographical and demographic structure (Kaplan 1994), but it has also faced constant challenges from the hostile Soviet-backed India and unstable Afghanistan. Pakistan was on the other hand supported by the USA which in the wake of the Bengali crisis tried to bolster the Pakistani army and even sent its aircraft carrier into the Bay of Bengal (Bennett Jones 2009, 140–180). However, following the atrocities conducted by the Pakistani forces in Bangladesh and in the attempt to improve relations with India, the USA did not prevent the establishment of independent Bangladesh. Besides, the Bangladeshi independence was directly supported by the Indian forces which intervened in the crisis.

As for the causes of secession, the case of Bangladesh, as noted above, was based on the issue of exclusion of the Bengalis from the Pakistani political system. Pakistan as a geographically divided country faced challenges related not only to the cooperation between the West and East Pakistan, but also a challenging ethnic composition of the West Pakistan. The latter issue dominated the political life and thus the Bengalis felt excluded—an issue worsened by the nullification of the electoral victory of the Awami League and the consequent forceful reaction to the

---

[12]For data see http://data.worldbank.org/country/pakistan.

public protests. Bangladesh thus based its independence bid on the issue of the lack of representation and oppression.

Pakistan reacted harshly to the Bangladeshi calls for independence and its military action in the East Pakistan caused widespread bloodshed. A huge wave of refugees entered India which forced the Indian government to militarily intervene in the conflict. Despite the forceful military reaction, the Pakistanis were unable to pacify the region and defeat the intervening Indian forces (Bennett Jones 2009, 140–180).

As previously noted, the Pakistani military action in Bangladesh was not received well in the region or on the international stage. India launched a direct military intervention and even the USA as the supporter and ally of Pakistan did not act strongly on its behalf. The United Nations Security Council (UNSC) was divided concerning the solution to the conflict and thus decided not to further deal with the question and to refer it to the General Assembly.[13] Bangladesh was accepted as a member of the UN in 1974.

3.2 Ethiopia

Since 1974, Ethiopia was under the rule of Haile Mengistu who in the first four years of his rule started the so-called Red Terror in which he massacred scores of his opponents (Tegegn 2012). Mengistu, however, successfully maintained his power until 1991 when rebel forces captured the capital Addis Ababa, forcing him into exile. We, therefore, might point out the fact that at the time of the Eritrean secession Ethiopia was an autocratic state, repressing basic freedoms. The Horn of Africa in the 1980s was also plagued by some of the worst famines in modern history. All these factors show the inefficiency of the state in providing the basic functions and goods.

At an early stage of the Ethio-Eritrean conflict, the decolonization of Eritrea was opposed by the Western powers. Despite the previous opposition of the Soviet bloc, Ethiopia was supported by the former eastern bloc countries of the Soviet Union and Cuba during the reign of Haile Mengistu. These countries supported not only the government but also its struggle against both the Eritreans and from some point also Somalia (Tegegn 2012; Lewis 2008, 27–70; Giorgis 2014, 99–103). Following the fall of the USSR, the Eritrean separatists were able to defeat the government forces, force Mengistu out of the country, and establish independent Eritrea.

As for the justification of secession, Eritrea was an entity forcefully incorporated into Ethiopia during the process of decolonization. Its call for independence thus follows the reasoning of unjust occupation of its territories by Ethiopian forces and the right of self-determination (Giorgis 2014, 117–120). This reasoning was

---

[13]See UNSC Resolution 303 (1971) at http://daccess-dds-ny.un.org/doc/RESOLUTION/GEN/NR0/261/63/IMG/NR026163.pdf?OpenElement.

accepted by the international community based on the military victory of the rebels, as evident by the general acceptance of the 1993 independence referendum.

Similarly to the previous case, Eritrean independence calls were met with a forceful reaction and a consequent rebellion that led to a prolonged internal conflict. This conflict was ended only when the rebel forces were able to achieve a major military advance and aid the Ethiopian opposition to conquer the capital of Addis Ababa (Giorgis 2014, 117–154).

The Eritrean case was mediated by the UN as the neighbouring states did not directly intervene in the situation in Ethiopia. The international community accepted the 1993 referendum and the UNSC recommended the General Assembly to accept Eritrea[14] in its aftermath, which resulted in the Eritrean UN admission the same year.

3.3 Indonesia

East Timor became part of Indonesia as an occupied territory, which is according to many authors perceived as a case for legitimate secession (e.g. Geldenhuys 2009), under the dictatorship of General Suharto. While the Suharto regime fell a year before East Timor independence referendum, it must be noted that during its existence the basic freedoms and democracy were both very limited or absent. Furthermore, the region of East Timor was plagued by constant violence perpetrated by the Indonesian armed forces (Robinson 2011). On the other hand, Indonesia as a federation was quite stable and unlike the previous cases may not be considered a failed state despite the fact that provision of state functions has been and still is uneven and some of the state functions are still limited.

Indonesia was supported by the USA during Suharto's rule as a bulwark against communism in Southeast Asia and as a part of its containment strategy (Robinson 2011). Following the collapse of the Communist bloc, however, Suharto lost most of its Western backing and was forced by the United Nations and the world powers to resign and Indonesia to cede East Timor.

East Timor was in a way similar to Eritrea occupied by Indonesia and struggled for decades to regain its independence. Its claims are thus similar as well—illegal annexation, oppression, and exclusion. Despite the fact that the independence bid in 1975 was ignored (28 November 1975, however, is called the Independence Declaration Day up to today and it has been celebrated[15]) and that the Indonesian stand was supported throughout Suharto's rule by the USA, the East Timor argumentation for secession was in the end globally accepted.

---

[14]See UNSC Resolution 828 (1993) at http://daccess-dds-ny.un.org/doc/UNDOC/GEN/N93/309/72/IMG/N9330972.pdf?OpenElement.

[15]See http://www.easttimorgovernment.com/history.htm.

East Timor was also a victim of central government's military campaign. Consequently, the island faced internal conflicts between supporters of independence and pro-Indonesian groups. East Timor civil war is another case of the heavy-handed approach to the secessionist issues by the central government.

The international reaction to the independence referendum in the East Timor was —as in the Eritrean case—quite welcoming. In 1999, the UN established a transitional UN mission designed to help the newly emerging country with the establishment of working institutions based on the referendum outcome.[16] The mission was active until 2002 when the East Timor proclaimed its independence that was accepted by the UN[17] and the East Timor was admitted as a member.

3.4 Sudan

Since its independence, Sudan has been a country dominated by the Arab population and the military that has been repressing the basic rights of the non-Arabs in the country. The non-Arabic population predominantly lives in what is now South Sudan and in the Darfur province. Not only have the non-Arabs been largely unrepresented in the central institutions, but they have also been marginalized in their own provinces, and their rights repressed even by military means (Idris 2013). Sudan is also a long-term member of the group of the least stable countries according to the Fund for Peace's analysis.[18]

Sudan has been under pressure from the West since the end of the Cold War. This is due to the support provided by the Khartoum regime to terrorism—e.g. preserving safe haven for Osama bin Laden—and also due to the policies towards South Sudan. The USA became a major supporter of the South's independence and a major backer of the independence referendum. Sudan at the same time lacked important international support. International opinion was thus largely anti-Sudanese and pro-independence (Riegl and Doboš 2014).

The South Sudan secession bid was backed by the issue of under-representation and oppression stemming from religious and ethnic differences. The South Sudanese argued by pointing out the long-shared history of oppression that escalated in two post-colonial civil wars and the overall virtual absence of non-Arabs in the government structure, army, etc. The more protracted and bloody the second civil war became, the more attention this argumentation received (Idris 2013).

The reaction to the South Sudanese secession also follows the same pattern. The central government conducted two bloody civil wars against the South and was

---

[16]See UNSC Resolution 1272 (1999) at www.un.org/en/ga/search/view_doc.asp?symbol=S/RES/1272(1999).

[17]See UNSC Resolution 1392 (2002) at http://www.un.org/en/ga/search/view_doc.asp?symbol=S/RES/1392%282002%29.

[18]See http://fsi.fundforpeace.org/.

unprepared for any major concessions until the pressure of the international community and its military inability to suppress the rebellion led to the acceptance of the independence referendum (Idris 2013).

The South Sudanese peace project was supported by the UN and the organization accepted the outcome of Comprehensive Peace Agreement in 2005.[19] In 2011, the UNSC voted for the prolongation of the peacekeeping mission in the region[20] and consequently supported the establishment of the independent South Sudan with a strong UN presence in the newborn country.[21] In the same year, South Sudan was accepted as a UN member.

3.5 Serbia

Unlike the previous cases, Serbia was regarded as a free country with a reasonable level of democracy and respect for basic freedoms in the years before the 2008 Kosovo declaration of independence.[22] Serbia was also a reasonably stable country that was deemed moderate/warning by the Fund for Peace in the years of the Kosovo secession.[23] The position on the chart can be explained by the power struggle between the factions loyal to the former Milosevic regime and new pro-Western forces, as well as by the Kosovo issue. The Kosovo independence came at the time when the country was stabilizing itself and introducing larger freedoms for its citizens.

As for the geopolitical position, during the Kosovo crisis Serbia was in the transitional phase. On the one hand, it received a strong backing from Russia and the Russian government was the most outspoken opponent of the Kosovo independence; on the other hand, it slowly began a transition towards establishment of closer relations to the EU with the prospect of future membership. Despite this fact and the disagreements concerning the recognition of Kosovo even among the Western countries, Russia remained the most forceful defender of the Serbian territorial integrity.

The main argumentation in the case of Kosovo touches on the issue of the right of self-determination and oppression from the side of Serbia. The first issue was connected to the ethnic composition of Kosovo that is mainly inhabited by ethnic Albanians. The second issue was connected to the violent campaigns that were in the past launched against the Kosovar population by Serbia and the history of ethnic

---

[19]See UNSC Resolution 1627 (2005) at http://www.un.org/en/ga/search/view_doc.asp?symbol=S/RES/1627%282005%29.

[20]See UNSC Resolution 1978 (2011) at http://www.un.org/en/ga/search/view_doc.asp?symbol=S/RES/1978%282011%29.

[21]See UNSC Resolution 1996 (2011) at http://www.un.org/en/ga/search/view_doc.asp?symbol=S/RES/1996%282011%29.

[22]See https://freedomhouse.org/report/freedom-world/2008/serbia.

[23]Link in note no. 2.

violence in the post-Yugoslavian region. In its Declaration of Independence, the Assembly of Kosovo based its argumentation on the history of violence, the principle of self-determination, and democracy and effectiveness (Krasniqi 2008).

The Serbian reaction to the Kosovo case is twofold. First, in the 1990s the Serbian forces conducted a major military campaign against the Kosovo rebellion that led to the 1999 NATO campaign targeting Serbian infrastructure and military in order to protect the Kosovar civilian population that arguably faced ethnic cleansing. On the other hand, the 2008 bid for independence was not faced by any major military campaign and the protests against this act were and are mainly diplomatic.

As noted above, the international opinion on Kosovo independence was divided. On the one hand, the USA together with some Western European countries stood as a firm supporter of the Kosovar bid, on the other, some EU members refused to recognize Kosovo mainly from the fear of their own secessionist regions. Russia and other countries took a firm stand against the Kosovo bid for independence. Kosovo has never been admitted as a member state of the UN.

3.6 Israel

Palestine is an issue relevant for the entire post-World War II period, but the international opinion has in recent years been increasingly supportive of its attempts to establish an independent state. Israel can be regarded as a democratic state with competitive elections and basic freedoms provided for most of its inhabitants. However, the Palestinian territories are exempted from the general elections as they fall under the limited jurisdiction of the Palestinian Authority that is de facto divided between the government located on the West Bank and Hamas which rules in the Gaza Strip. It thus might be said that Israel without Palestinian territories can be labelled a democratic and free state.[24] It is also a rather well-functioning country that has been able to remain stable since the last intifada.

For the most of its existence, Israel has been protected by the strong US support. Even though most of the Western countries still back Israel in the Palestine question, this support has been slowly waning as Palestine enters an increasing number of international organizations and has even been fully recognized by Sweden—an EU member. Given the geographical and geopolitical position of Israel, which is surrounded by hostile nations, it remains probable that the US support will not be significantly reduced as this could mean annihilation of the country itself.

The Palestinian case is rooted in calls for independence based on the original treaty that in 1948 divided the former British Palestine between Palestine and Israel with Jordan on their eastern borders. Palestinian bid for independence is based in the right of self-determination, illegal occupation, and oppression. This view is

---

[24]See https://freedomhouse.org/country/israel.

present, for example, in the 1988 Declaration of Independence as prepared by Yasser Arafat and the Palestine Liberation Organization that argues using the basis of illegal occupation and principle of self-determination.[25]

The Israeli reaction to the Palestinian independence calls is a combination of diplomatic effort based on the issue of security and limited military actions against the Palestinian territories. Israel uses its international backing and geopolitical situation as a diplomatic leverage pointing out the security threat caused by the independent Palestine. On the other hand, in case of a (perceived) crisis the Israeli Army is able to penetrate the areas and use force to achieve some of its goals against undesirable Palestinian groups.

The Palestinian attempts to enter the UN have been blocked in a similar fashion by the opposition of the USA. Despite these setbacks, Palestine was able to negotiate a position of non-member observer state in the UN General Assembly in 2012.[26] Palestine is also a member of many international organizations, such as UNESCO. Even the EU member states have recently become more welcoming towards the idea of the independent Palestinian state.

3.7 Morocco

Morocco witnessed steady democratization under the rule of monarchy that lasts until today. Despite the gradual attempts to reform the country throughout the twentieth century, the changes to the political system occurred mainly at the end of the 1990s and especially after Mohammed IV ascendency to the throne in 1999. Freedom House qualifies Morocco as partly free with many issues related to the traditional law and the influence of monarch.[27] Morocco also remains in the warning part of the Fund for Peace's table making it an average country signalling its relative stability.[28]

Because of the Western Sahara issue, Morocco is in isolation on the African continent as it is the only African country not admitted to the African Union; it thus faces analogical situation to that of collective non-recognition on the regional basis. It also faces major tensions with neighbouring Algeria. On the other hand, Morocco is perceived as one of the modernizing Arab countries and, therefore, does not face any sustained international pressure to resolve the issue, as the international attention is more focused on the stability of the country and the process of reformation of its political system. The Moroccan stability was and still is mainly supported by the USA and France, as they perceived Morocco as an important ally

---

[25]Full text available at: http://www.jewishvirtuallibrary.org/jsource/Peace/pncdec.html.
[26]See General Assembly Resolution 67/19 at http://unispal.un.org/UNISPAL.NSF/0/19862D03 C564FA2C85257ACB004EE69B.
[27]See https://freedomhouse.org/report/freedom-world/2015/morocco.
[28]Link in note no. 2.

against the communist influence in North Africa (Polisario is a radical leftist movement) during the Cold War and as an important ally in the war against terror nowadays (Mundy 2009; Novais 2009).

The Western Sahara is yet another region using the argument of illegal occupation. Since the Spanish withdrawal from the region, the Western Sahara has been under the occupation of Morocco and originally even by Mauritania. Polisario presents itself as a representative of the region that is illegally occupied and calls for a self-determination process. The claim is based on the idea of Sahrawi nation that was conceptualized throughout the second half of the twentieth century (Zunes and Mundy 2010, 92–3).

Morocco uses two strategies against the Western Sahara secessionist attempts. The first, as in previous cases, is a military campaign. The second is the re-population of the region by Moroccans so it ensures non-independence vote in any possible referendum that would be taken by the inhabitants of the Western Sahara, as the region is scarcely populated and the new population of Moroccans form quite a significant share of the total. Since the early 1990s, Morocco has agreed on the independence referendum but has not yet been able to agree on the rules of this referendum, and so the issue still remains unresolved (Zunes and Mundy 2010, 169–253).

As noted above, the issue of the Western Sahara is a hotly contested issue on the African continent. Morocco and Algeria have waged a war and Morocco is the only African country not to be admitted to the AU. In 1975, the UNSC issued a resolution urging Morocco not to conduct operations in the Western Sahara.[29] At the end of the 1980s and beginning of the 1990s, the UNSC supported the self-determination process in the region and in 1991 established the UN Mission for the Referendum in the Western Sahara.[30] The mission has been active until present.

3.8 Papua New Guinea

Since its independence in 1975, Papua New Guinea was attempting to establish democratic institutions, but this effort was complicated by the weakness of its central institutions, widespread corruption, etc. Furthermore, the state's capacities were limited and the state itself was not very effective in fulfilling any basic functions and in providing basic goods (Sepoe 2006). Papua New Guinea has received large amounts of international aid since becoming independent, especially from Australia (Department of Foreign Affairs and Trade 2015). Major breaches of the basic freedoms can be traced especially to the handling of the Bougainville

---

[29]See UNSC Resolution 379 (1975) at http://www.securitycouncilreport.org/atf/cf/%7B65BFCF9B-6D27-4E9C-8CD3-CF6E4FF96FF9%7D/MINURSO%20SRES380.pdf.

[30]See UNSC Resolution 690 (1991) at http://www.securitycouncilreport.org/atf/cf/%7B65BFCF9B-6D27-4E9C-8CD3-CF6E4FF96FF9%7D/MINURSO%20SRES690.pdf.

secessionism. By the end of the twentieth century, however, the country was ranked as free.[31]

Ever since it became independent, Papua New Guinea has retained strong ties to Australia and New Zealand and these countries have a significant influence in Papua. These links have further been strengthened by the importance and the amount of humanitarian aid entering Papua and fear of limitless fragmentation at the regional level shared, for example, by the government of Fiji, that was observable during the eight years of blockade imposed on the island of Bougainville by the central government of the parent state. However, as the result of the establishment of de facto statehood in Bougainville and the virtual inability of the parent state to restore its territorial integrity, these two regional powers also pushed the Papuan government to allow Bougainville to gain autonomy and conduct an independence referendum after they had ceased supporting the governmental actions against the territory.

Bougainville attempted to reach independence shortly after the decolonization of Papua New Guinea based on the right of self-determination. Another reason for the independence calls was the acutely perceived exploitation of its mineral wealth when only a small share of the profits was invested into the development of the island itself. The 1990 Declaration of Independence states that Bougainville is culturally distinct from Papua New Guinea, a victim of the economic blockade of the island by the parent state, in effective control of the island, and adhering to the democratic principle of self-determination.[32]

Papua New Guinea followed the suit of the previous cases and used military action against its separatist province. Due to the weakness of the Papuan military forces, it was even forced to hire a private military company to do some of the fighting for the government during the 1990s (Braithwaite 2010, 40–43). Papuan government was, however, forced by the international community (with a strong role of Australia) to abandon its military campaign after years of civil war and allow Bougainville autonomy with a prospect of the independence referendum.

Despite its original support for the mining operations on Bougainville, Australia took a stance as a major supporter of the political solution to the Bougainville conflict in the late 1990s. Since the mid-1990s, there have been several international peacekeeping missions deployed in the region.[33] In 1998, the UN established the UN Political Office in Bougainville. The UN, after the end of conflict, aims at the proper organization of the independence referendum.[34]

---

[31]See https://freedomhouse.org/report/freedom-world/1999/papua-new-guinea.

[32]Full text available at http://asopa.typepad.com/asopa_people/2014/07/the-1991-bougainville-unilateral-declaration-of-independence.html.

[33]See http://unpan1.un.org/intradoc/groups/public/documents/un/unpan022605.pdf.

[34]See http://www.pg.undp.org/content/papua_new_guinea/en/home/operations/projects/crisis_prevention_and_recovery/peace-building-in-bougainville.html.

4 Analysis

Table 1 sums up the findings of the comparison with a focus on the parent states.

As evident from the analysis, the cases differ in many important characteristics. We can see that the cases comprise democratic, democratizing, and non-democratic regimes. Also the internal effectiveness differs on a scale from ineffective entities (e.g. Ethiopia, Sudan) to a modern developed state (Israel). Even though the reaction to the secession was usually a military campaign, it is not true in all the cases as some of the researched states attempted to accommodate the independence movements by other means (Israel and Morocco). Also, the full international recognition is in some cases missing (Kosovo, Palestine, Western Sahara, and Bougainville between 1990 and 1997).

On the other hand, there are apparently some striking similarities. In case the secessionist movement was supported by some (super)power, the parent state was unable to suppress it without the support of another (super)power (e.g. Morocco does not need support as SADR lacks one as well). In the case of clash of interests of the two (super)powers, the one with stronger influence in the region succeeded in getting the upper hand (e.g. the USA in Kosovo). In case a UNSC permanent member disagrees with secession, the secessionist entity is unable to obtain full recognition (e.g. Palestine, Kosovo). (Super)powers possess the ability of bandwagoning—if they support secession, most of their allies will as well (e.g. Kosovo case).

We can see that it might be possible to draw a connection between violent suppression of secessions and the international support for independence bids, but this would not take into account the cases mentioned at the beginning of the paper where the violent suppression was supported or overlooked by the international community (e.g. Biafra, Tamil Eelam, Cabinda, or Katanga) and many accounts where even later successful secession movements remained unprotected from indiscriminate violence as they were out of (super)power attention or their parent states received (super)power support (e.g. East Timor, Bougainville). Furthermore, looking at the unrecognized states in the post-Soviet space (e.g. Abkhazia and South Ossetia) we might clearly observe that the bandwagoning ability of the USA might be stronger than that of Russia (the case of Kosovo); however, this is not a general rule as its position in case of Palestine receives only a limited support from the international community.

As the differences among these cases prove, there is no clear rule for international acceptance of secession and the diversity among successful entities is wide. Successful, complete, fully recognized secessions have obtained international recognition through the support of some important (super)power that was able to effectively project its power in the region (e.g. India in Bangladesh, the USA in South Sudan) and the parent state was not protected by another (super)power (e.g. the USA in Israel, Russia in Serbia) with normative justification of the case strong enough to bring support from the prevalent part of the international society. It is thus important to acknowledge that (super)powers may act as both enablers and

Table 1 Comparison of secessions

Parent state	Democracy freedom	Effectiveness	Parent state support	Secessionist support	Justification of secession	Parent state reaction	International recognition
Pakistan	Military dictatorship/lack of freedoms	Not effective	Limited, USA	Significant, India	Democracy, self-determination, exclusion	Military campaign	Yes
Ethiopia	Dictatorship/lack of freedoms	Not effective	During Mengistu rule Soviet bloc, the 1990s lack of support	None, the 1990s UN support	Illegal occupation, self-determination	Military campaign	Yes
Indonesia	Dictatorship/limited freedom	Limited effectiveness	USA, the 1990s lack of support	None, the 1990s UN support	Illegal occupation, self-determination, exclusion	Military campaign	Yes
Sudan	Exclusive illiberal democracy/ethnically exclusive	Not effective	Lack of support	None, the 1990s/2000s USA and UN support	Democracy, self-determination, exclusion	Military campaign	Yes
Serbia	Democracy/free	Limited effectiveness	Russia	USA, part of the EU	History of violence, self-determination, effectiveness, democracy	International pressure	Limited
Israel	Democracy/free	Effective	USA	Soviet bloc, significant	Self-determination, illegal occupation	Military campaign/accommodation	Limited
Morocco	Constitutional monarchy/partially free	Limited effectiveness	USA, France (limited)	AU	Self-determination, illegal occupation	Internal colonization	Limited
Papua New Guinea	Democracy/partially free	Limited effectiveness	Australia, the late 1990s lack of support	The late 1990s Australia and UN	Economic blockade, effectiveness, democracy, self-determination	Military campaign	Planned referendum

spoilers of secession and their actions are based on an ad hoc basis with a focus on their actual motivation that might transform throughout the time (e.g. USA in Indonesia). It cannot be said that parent states that contain a secessionist entity with wide or full recognition necessarily possess any major similarities or are in some important factors different from the cases of unaccepted secessions. Last but not least, it is important to point out that despite the fact that (super)powers with a greater amount of soft power are able to gain larger international support for their steps (a comparison of the USA in Kosovo and Russia in Abkhazia/South Ossetia), this is not an absolute rule as might be documented by the international approach towards the Palestinian issue. Effective (super)power support is thus a sufficient condition of the de facto secession while its positive influence on the international collective recognition process remains only one of the factors. In the process of de iure recognition, lack of (super)power opposition remains a necessary condition for the successful outcome.

5 Conclusion

As noted by D. Geldenhuys, recognition "*is a matter of political discretion, not a legal or moral duty* (Geldenhuys 2009, 42)". Despite the fact that since 1945 the nature of international recognition has evolved from negative to positive in accordance with the Resolution 1514 of the UN General Assembly from 1960, the implementation of new regulative norms is applied only on ad hoc basis. Looking at the cases of successful secessions that have been fully accepted (Bangladesh, Eritrea, East Timor, and South Sudan) by a significant part of the international community (Kosovo, Palestine, and Western Sahara), or where independence referendum has been agreed on (Boungainville), we can observe that issues of democracy, violent suppression, or right for self-determination are of secondary importance, as the cases similar in nature might lead to different approaches from the international community and the acceptance of secession might evolve throughout the time. Success of secession is thus based on the enabling and spoiling potential of the relevant (super)powers. We might observe that some (super)powers are able to facilitate collective recognition (the USA vs. Russia), but the collective (non-)recognition and support for (super)power's position is also based on moral justifications of secession (e.g. Palestine).

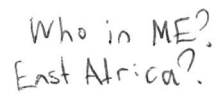

Secession will thus not succeed in case it directly contradicts the interests of the most influential (super)power in the region. Secession will usually not succeed without an external support from a (super)power. Secession will not gain collective recognition without a backing from a (super)power with strong soft power and/or without a strong normative imperative (Kosovo, Palestine vs. Abkhazia, South Ossetia). A UNSC permanent member's opposition will lead to blocking the full recognition. (Super)powers are acting as both spoilers (Palestine) and enablers (South Sudan, Kosovo) of secessions. If the secession appears in the region attracting no outside interest, the solution to the issue will be de facto delegated to the regional body (Espirito Santo, Union Island, Western Sahara, Somaliland, or Bougainville).[35] When there exists no external interest, secession might succeed in case of military victory over the central government (Eritrea). Internal effectiveness of the entity is not connected to the level of the international recognition (Somaliland vs. East Timor).

As evident from these findings, international recognition of secession is a highly ad hoc process. Proclaimed normative and legal standards are only of secondary importance, as the most decisive factor is the enabling/spoiler role of (super) powers. Success of secession is thus to a large extent determined by the geopolitical interests of relevant (super)powers in the region and their relative strengths and influence. Wide recognition, however, also depends on the fulfilment of some normative and moral grounds and in case of (super)power support for the secession on the perception of the legitimacy of such an approach. The importance of morality of secession is evident in the *"conflict between great powers over the normative criteria that are most appropriate for the recognition of secessionist regions as independent states* (O'Loughlin et al. 2014, 432)".

Wide international recognition of secession and/or de facto independence is thus only possible if: a) the parent state has lost its support from (super)power in its attempt to prevent secession with secessionist entities strong enough to prevail or with their own (super)power backing (Pakistan, Ethiopia, Indonesia, Papua New Guinea); b) the parent state lacks effective support of (super)power and the secessionist entity is backed by (super)power (Sudan, Serbia); c) the dominant (super)power desires a peaceful solution to the secession without abandoning the parent state (Israel); and d) no (super)power is interested in the region and the regional body supports the secessionist entity (Somalia and Morocco).[36] In addition to these first three criteria, the secession must be perceived as legitimate in the normative sense by the majority of the international community in order to obtain wide international justification.

References

African Elections Database. (2011). *Elections in Eritrea.* http://africanelections.tripod.com/er.html. Accessed January 25, 2016.

Berg, E. (2009). Re-examining sovereignty claims in changing territorialities: Reflections from 'Kosovo Syndrome'. *Geopolitics, 14*(2), 219–234.

Braithwaite, J. (2010). *Reconciliation and architectures of commitment: Sequencing peace in Bougainville.* Canberrra: ANU Press.

---

[35]"In 1979 the government of St. Vincent and the Grenadines invited troops from Barbados to counter the attempted breakaway of Union Island. Similarly, Vanuatu (New Hebrides) when facing the independents' struggle of the island of Santo, called in first British and French troops, and then troops from Papua New Guinea (Tancredi, 2014, 88)".

[36]Lack of regional support, for example, has prevented international recognition of otherwise effective and de facto independent Somaliland.

Copp, D. (1998). International law and morality in the theory of secession. *The Journal of Ethics,* 2(3), 219–245.

Department of Foreign Affairs and Trade. (2015). *Development assistance in Papua New Guinea.* http://dfat.gov.au/geo/papua-new-guinea/development-assistance/Pages/papua-new-guinea.aspx. Accessed October 8, 2015.

Fabry, M. (2010). *Recognizing states: International Society and the establishment of new states since 1776.* Oxford: Oxford University Press.

Geldenhyus, D. (2009). *Contested states in world politics.* London: Palgrave Macmillan.

Giorgis, A. W. (2014). *Eritrea at a crossroads: A narrative of triumph, betrayal and hope.* Houston: Strategic Book Publishing.

Idris, A. (2013). *Identity, citizenship, and violence in two Sudans.* New York: Palgrave.

Jones, O. B. (2009). *Pakistan: Eye of the storm.* Bodmin: Yale University Press.

Kaplan, R. D. (1994). The coming anarchy. *The Atlantic Monthly, 273*(2), 44–76.

Kopeček, V., Hoch, T., & Baar, V. (2016). De facto states and democracy: The case of Abkhazia. *Bulletin of Geography. Socio-Economic Series, 32*(32), 85–104.

Krasniqi, J. (2008). *Kosovo declaration of independence.* http://www.assembly-kosova.org/?cid=2,128,1635. Accessed November 7, 2015.

Lewis, I. M. (2008). *Understanding Somalia and Somaliland.* New York: Columbia University Press.

Maleshin, D. (2014). Chief editor's note on 2013 Russian legal events. *Russian Law Journal, 2*(1), 4–6.

McConnell, F. (2009). De facto, displaced, tacit: The sovereign articulations of the Tibetan Government-in-Exile. *Political Geography, 28*(6), 343–352.

Mundy, J. (2009). Out with the Old, in with the New: Western Sahara back to Square One? *Mediterranean Politics, 14*(1), 115–122.

Novais, R. A. (2009). An unfinished process: The Western Sahara as a post-scriptum of the colonial period. *Africana Studia, 12,* 59–66.

Oeter, S. (2014). The role of recognition and non-recognition with regards to secession. In C. Walter, A. von Ungern-Sternberg, & K. Abushov (Eds.), *Self-determination and secession in international law* (pp. 45–68). Oxford: Oxford University Press.

O'Loughlin, J., Kolossov, V., & Toal, G. (2014). Inside the post-Soviet de facto states: A comparison of attitudes in Abkhazia, Nagorny Karabakh, South Ossetia, and Transnistria. *Eurasian Geography and Economics, 55*(5), 423–456.

Pavković, A., & Radan, P. (2007). *Creating new states: Theory and practice of secession.* Aldershort: Ashgate.

Pegg, S., & Kolstø, P. (2014). Somaliland: Dynamics of internal legitimacy and (lack of) external sovereignty. *Geoforum, 66,* 193–202.

Peters, A. (2014). The principle of Uti Possidetis Juris: How relevant is it for issues of secession? In C. Walter, A. von Ungern-Sternberg, & K. Abushov (Eds.), *Self-determination and secession in international law* (pp. 95–138). Oxford: Oxford University Press.

Riegl, M., & Doboš, B. (2014). Secession in post-modern world: Cases of South Sudan and Somaliland. *Acta Geographica Universitatis Comenianae, 58*(2), 173–192.

Robinson, G. (2011). East Timor 10 years on: Legacies of violence. *The Journal of Asian Studies, 70*(4), 1007–1021.

Rosůlek, P. (2014). *Politický secesionismus a etické teorie. Allen Buchanan a jeho kritici.* Brno: Barrister & Principal.

Scheffer, D. (2009). Actrocity crimes framing the responsibility to protect. In R. H. Cooper & J. V. Kohler (Eds.), *Responsibility to protect: The global moral compass for the 21st century* (pp. 77–98). New York: Palgrave MacMillan.

Sepoe, O. (2006). Democracy in Papua New Guinea: Challenges from a rights-based approach. http://press.anu.edu.au/ssgm/global_gov/mobile_devices/ch22.html. Accessed October 8, 2015.

Simms, B. (2013). *Europe: The struggle for supremacy, 1453 to the present.* New York: Basic Books.

o, M. (2013). On the right to external self-determination: "Selfistans", secession, and the great powers' rule. *Minnesota Journal of International Law, 19*(1), 137–176.

Tancredi, A. (2014). Secession and use of force. In C. Walter, A. von Ungern-Sternberg, & K. Abushov (Eds.), *Self-determination and secession in international law* (pp. 68–95). Oxford: Oxford University Press.

Tegegn, M. (2012). Mengistu's "Red Terror". *African Identities, 10*(3), 249–263.

Walter, C., von Ungern-Sternberg, A., & Abushov, K. (2014). *Self-determination and secession in international law*. Oxford: Oxford University Press.

Williams, P. R., Avoryie, A. J., & Armstrong, C. J. (2015). Earned sovereignty revisited: Creating a strategic framework for managing self-determination based conflicts. *ILSA Journal of International & Comparative Law, 21*(2), 425–451.

Zunes, S., & Mundy, J. (2010). *Western Sahara: War nationalism and conflict irresolution*. New York: Syracuse University Press.

Author Biographies

Martin Riegl was born in 1980. He currently lectures at the Institute of Political Studies of Faculty of Social Sciences, Charles University. He graduated in 2010 at Faculty of Social Sciences, Charles University (programme political science), where successfully finished doctoral studies in the field of political geography. Since 2008 he has been lecturing at the Department of Political Science (FSS, UK), his academic research is focused on the institution of the sovereign state, geopolitics of political disintegration, secession, unrecognized states, and state failure. He actively participated at scientific conferences and workshops in the Czech Republic, Slovakia, Germany, Belgium, Poland, United Kingdom, Taiwan, etc.

Bohumil Doboš is a Ph.D. student at the Institute of Political Studies, Faculty of Social Sciences, Charles University. His research interest lies in areas of post-Westphalian geopolitics, New Middle Age theory, geopolitical anomalies, geopolitics of violent non-state actors, and astropolitics. He is also a Coordinator of the Geopolitical Studies Research Centre at the same institute and Employee at the Ministry of Defence of the Czech Republic—Defence Policy and Strategy Division.

Part II
Case Studies

Political Institutions in the Post-Soviet De Facto States in Comparison: Abkhazia and Nagorno-Karabakh

Vincenc Kopeček

De facto state, as the term has been recently coined and used in academic literature (Pegg 1998; Lynch 2004; Popescu 2006; Caspersen 2008; Berg and Mölder 2012; Kolstø and Blakkisrud 2012; von Steinsdorff and Fruhstorfer 2012; Toal and O'Loughlin 2013; Berg and Pegg 2016; Gerrits and Bader 2016), is a territorial entity which exists for a longer period of time (at least several years), controls most of the territory it lays claims to, and lacks but actively seeks wider international recognition (c.f. Kolstø 2006).[1] Most of the de facto states were formed as a consequence of unresolved armed ethnic or ethno-political conflicts between a central government and a separatist movement. Instead of a peace treaty, which would provide a basis for a post-conflict reconstruction, reconciliation and internationally accepted territorial solution, including incorporation of the separatist entity into the parental state or potential international recognition of the separated polity, these conflicts have, since the signing of a ceasefire, frozen in a no-war-no-peace situation, which has been lasting for decades.

The original version of this chapter appeared in The Annual of Language and Language of Politics and Identity (2016), 10, 73–99. This article is updated and reprinted with permission from the copyright holders. This article has been prepared as a part of the grant project de facto States in Northern Eurasia in the Context of Russian Foreign Policy (GACR 15-09249S) financed by the Czech Science Foundation.

[1]For a terminological discussion about de facto states, quasi states, etc., see, e.g. Riegl (2010).

V. Kopeček (✉)
University of Ostrava, Ostrava, Czech Republic
e-mail: vincenc.kopecek@osu.cz

At present, the post-Soviet area is the macroregion with the highest concentration of de facto states in the world.[2] In the first decade of the twenty-first century, a shift towards establishing a more democratic society has taken place in some of the de facto states, including Abkhazia and Nagorno-Karabakh (Caspersen 2009; Berg and Mölder 2012; Kolstø and Blakkisrud 2012; Kopeček et al. 2016). This shift was driven by an assumption of de facto states' political elite that democratic states *"have more chance of being recognized by the international community than others"* (Ghukassyan cited in Caspersen 2009, 55–56). As a result of this, Abkhazia and Nagorno-Karabakh have adopted many democratic institutions. They have approved fairly democratic constitutions, developed multiparty systems, regularly hold competitive elections and have established a local self-government. However, both entities are still far from Western liberal democracies in terms of quality of political rights and civil liberties (Freedom House 2015). They have remained somewhere in the grey or foggy zone (c.f. Carothers 2002) between authoritarianism and democracy and belong to the long list of hybrid regimes *"combining democratic and authoritarian elements"* (Diamond 2002, 167).

This study focuses on both democratic and non-democratic institutions the two concerned de facto states have developed. Though there are already studies analysing the formation of political institutions in both Abkhazia and Nagorno-Karabakh (Berg and Mölder 2012; Kolstø and Blakkisrud 2012; Bakke et al. 2014; Ó Beacháin 2012; Matsuzato 2008; Skakov 2005; Krylov 2002; von Steinsdorff 2012; Smolnik 2012), there are still at least two research gaps. First, in this chapter, both Abkhazia and Nagorno-Karabakh are treated as competitive authoritarianisms, a type of hybrid regime, *"in which formal democratic institutions exist and are widely viewed as the primary means of gaining power, but in which incumbents' abuse of the state places them at a significant advantage vis-à-vis their opponents"* (Levitsky and Way 2010, 5). Consequently, formal political institutions are highly unstable and a significant role is played by informal political institutions (Levitsky and Way 2010, 27–28; c.f. Morlino 2009, 276–277). Thus, after focusing on division of power, political parties, elections, and self-governing bodies, it is also the informal practices which are put under scrutiny.

Second, and more importantly, despite the fact that most of the studies analysing political institutions in de facto states are based on interviews, it is quite rare to hear authentic and critical voices of the political stakeholders—politicians, former politicians, civil society leaders, political analysts, journalists, etc. Thus, the main research question of this chapter is how political stakeholders in Abkhazia and Nagorno-Karabakh perceive selected political institutions. Do they reflect the hybrid character of political regimes in their home countries and the central role

---

[2]In present, there are at least six de facto states, four of them in the post-Soviet area (Abkhazia, Nagorno-Karabakh, South Ossetia, and Transnistria). The only two cases out of the post-Soviet space are Northern Cyprus and Somaliland. Some authors also mention Kosovo, Palestine, Western Sahara, or Iraqi Kurdistan; however, these cases do not meet definition criteria used in this article.

played by the informal political institutions? And if so, what measures should be, in their opinion, taken in order to overcome the institutional hurdles which impede further democratization of the concerned de facto states?

These questions are answered by a comparative analysis based on a field research in Abkhazia, Nagorno-Karabakh, and Armenia, which was carried out in August and October 2015. One of the interviews used in this chapter dates back to 2009 and was conducted during previous research in Abkhazia. In total, eighteen interviews were done, ten in Nagorno-Karabakh and Armenia, and eight in Abkhazia, and thirteen respondents were male and five were female. All the interviews were made in person and without an interpreter; eleven interviews were in Russian and six in English. Due to the sensitivity of the topic of the research and specific conditions in the two de facto states, the form of each interview differed, though, in general, they can be characterized as expert and semi-structured, framed to a four-stage elicitation process (Flick 2009, 165–169). At the beginning of the interview, each respondent was given an opportunity to speak freely about the political system of the respective de facto state in general and to identify the most pressing political problems. After that, the interview continued in order to cover selected parts of the political system—i.e. constitutions, political parties, elections, self-government and the informal practices. Ten respondents, namely those who were interviewed by the author during his previous researches, were contacted in advance and served as the gatekeepers who helped the author to select and contact other possible respondents by the snowball-sampling method (Biernacki and Waldorf 1981; Noy 2008). The aim of the author was to interview at least one person from the four selected categories, defined on the basis of author's previous experience from the field research in the South Caucasus, the de facto states in particular: politicians or former politicians, state servants, civil society leaders and journalists. As seen from the list of interviews, some respondents belong to two or even more categories. Their identities, however, are not revealed in order to protect their personal safety.

1 Abkhazia and Nagorno-Karabakh in a Nutshell

Abkhazia has de facto separated from Georgia in the early 1990s, and after merely two decades of its de facto existence, it has been recognized by Russia, Venezuela, Nicaragua and Nauru. Before the civil war, Abkhazia used to be a multiethnic region, where the ethnic Abkhaz comprised only a minority of the population. During the war (1992–1993), almost all the ethnic Georgians living in the capital of Sukhum(i) and other regions in central and northern Abkhazia were driven out. Those who remained were the Armenians, Russians, and Megrels, who use the Georgian as a literary language and are concentrated in the southern regions, where they constitute the majority. Russia, who supported Abkhazian separatists, is Abkhazia's patron state, protecting it militarily and providing Abkhazia with economic assistance.[3]

Nagorno-Karabakh, an autonomous region with ethnic Armenian majority, has separated from Azerbaijan after a long period of ethnic clashes leading to a bloody war in 1992–1994. All the ethnic Azeris and Kurds had to flee their homes, and unlike Abkhazia, Nagorno-Karabakh has become a mono-ethnic community. As of now, Nagorno-Karabakh has not been recognized by any UN member state. Its existence is facilitated by Armenia, which is Nagorno-Karabakh's patron state.[4]

Both countries are very small regarding their size and population. Abkhazia is slightly larger in population, with about 250,000 people living on 8660 km^2, whereas Nagorno-Karabakh controls larger territory (about 12,000 km^2) with smaller population of about 140,000 (Matsuzato 2008, 99).

2 Division of Powers

As shown by Hale (2015), all post-Soviet states with the sole exception of Moldova have adopted presidential or semi-presidential constitutions.[5] Some scholars even employ the term super-presidentialism, in which the executive represented by the president dominates over the legislature and the jurisdiction (Fish 1997). As shown by Ishiyama and Kennedy, super-presidentialism has to do more with the extended competences of the president and his/her control over the resources than with the formal division of power between the executive and the legislature. Thus, even countries with nominally semi-presidential constitutions such as Armenia (until the application of constitutional changes approved by the October 2015 referendum) or Ukraine can be treated as super-presidential (Ishiyama and Kennedy 2001, 1178).

In both Abkhazia and Nagorno-Karabakh, the position of the President of the Republic is eminent. In Abkhazia, this is due to the presidential character of the republic as defined by the Constitution (Конституция Республики Абхазия 2014), which, at least in theory, completely separates the legislative and executive power. The President and the Vice-President are elected simultaneously and directly by the people for a 5-year term. The President is not only the Head of State, but also the chief of executive, who appoints the Cabinet of Ministers and other state officials, including heads of executive bodies in individual districts and cities, which brings Abkhazia closer to the super-presidential model. The Parliament is a legislative

---

[3]For more on Abkhazia and the conflict with Georgia, see, e.g. Souleimanov (2013), Hoch and Souleimanov (2013), Trier et al. (2010), Francis (2011).

[4]For more on Nagorno-Karabakh and the Armenian-Azerbaijani conflict see, e.g. Souleimanov (2013), Croissant (1998), de Waal (2003).

[5]Henry Hale does not consider the Baltic states as "post-Soviet", though they used to be the part of the Soviet Union.

body, which approves, for example, the state budget or the presidential nominees for the Prosecutor General, the Chairman of the National Bank, etc.

Nagorno-Karabakh's political system is, on paper, closer to a semi-presidential model.[6] However, the reality seems to be different. According to the Constitution of the Nagorno-Karabakh Republic (2006), the President of the Republic is the Head of State directly elected by the citizens for a 5-year term. The President nominates candidate(s) for the Prime Minister for the National Assembly's approval. In comparison with the French Fifth Republic, however, which is considered the model of semi-presidentialism (Elgie 2007, 5), it is not the legislature, which has the final word in the process of formation of the government, but it is the president, who can form the government without the consent of the parliament. On paper, Karabakh's National Assembly has the right to pass a no confidence vote to the Government, but in such a case, the President shall dissolve the National Assembly and set the date for extraordinary parliamentary elections. The President also appoints and dismisses judges, nominates candidates for the Prosecutor General, Presidents of the Supreme Court and the Oversight Chamber, forms and presides over the National Security Council and appoints other state officials. Such model is, indeed, closer to post-Soviet super-presidentialism than to the French Fifth Republic. As one opposition MP said: *"The President decides on everything. He simply says who will be the Prime Minister, who will sit in the Government, who will become the Speaker of the National Assembly, etc. There is no discussion on it"*.[7]

Respondents in Abkhazia and Nagorno-Karabakh identified factors contributing, in their opinion, to the eminent powers of both Presidents. In Nagorno-Karabakh, respondents emphasized the negative experience their country had with the parliamentary system. *"The parliamentary system, which was the relic of the Soviet Union, proved to be weak in times of the 'Liberation War'. This was the reason for the establishing of the State Defence Committee. This executive body proved to be effective and its chairman, Robert Kocharyan, was elected President under the Law on the President of the Nagorno-Karabakh Republic. This is how* [Nagorno-Karabakh] *has switched to presidentialism"*.[8] Some respondents even mentioned a more distant past: *"The experience with the parliamentary system of the First Armenian Republic* [of 1918–1920] *was not good. The totalitarian Armenian SSR was also a parliamentary system. In 1991–1992 Nagorno-Karabakh was a parliamentary republic and during this time it lost vast territories"*.[9]

Other factor contributing to the formation of the presidential system mentioned by the respondents in Nagorno-Karabakh is the fear of war. Presidentialism is

---

[6]In February 2017, the change of the Nagorno-Karabakh's constitution towards a purely presidential model was approved by the referendum. The changes are to be applied in the forthcoming years.
[7]Interview No 1.
[8]Interview No 4.
[9]Interview No 7.

perceived as the system which can react faster than parliamentarism. For some, parliamentarism is a kind of luxury which Nagorno-Karabakh cannot afford due to its geopolitical situation, as explained, for example, by an opposition MP: "*We need a strong state, because we constantly live under the risk of war. And presidential system produces a strong state*".[10] An Armenian journalist put it in a very similar way: "*As long as the Karabakh conflict is not solved, Nagorno-Karabakh simply must have presidential or semi-presidential system. There is no other option.*"[11] In Abkhazia, the fear of war was not given as a reason why the presidential system should endure. Respondents were confident that after the Russo-Georgian war in 2008, the Georgian military incursion is simply ruled out.

For some respondents in both Abkhazia and Nagorno-Karabakh, the emergence of presidentialism was closely connected with the strong personalities which guided both of the concerned de facto states through the perils of war: Vladislav Ardzinba and Robert Kocharyan. According to an Abkhazian former politician, "[t]*he presidential system was suited for Ardzinba. He was the only leader and most of the competences were given to him as the President. Later, we realized that Ardzinba would not live forever and we started to think about reforms in the direction of parliamentarism.*"[12] An ethnic Armenian journalist expressed an opinion that "[a]*fter the war, in Karabakh, they vested all the powers in the hands of Kocharyan. This was because* [Karabakh Armenians] *were used to the system of GenSec* [Secretary General]—*one person who decides on everything*".[13]

3 Political Parties and Elections

Competitive authoritarianisms always have multiparty systems. Political parties can organize and operate freely; however, the playing field in which the opposition parties challenge the ruling parties is uneven (Levitsky and Way 2010, 9–10). Thus, political parties have to play a dual game. On the one hand, they have to focus on elections, by which they can acquire seats in legislatures. But elections are not the only game in town; incumbents use their resources to do their best in order to make the playing field uneven and prevent an opposition from winning elections.[14] So, on the other hand, opposition parties also have to undertake activities which undermine the ruling regime; that is, they criticize the uneven rules and organize public protests or boycotts, and simultaneously, they take part in the contest based on the rules they criticize (Levitsky and Way 2010, 29–32).

---

[10]Interview No 3.

[11]Interview No 7.

[12]Interview No 14.

[13]Interview No 7.

[14]For more on post-Soviet political parties and party systems, see Wilson (2005), Miller et al. (2000), Kitschelt et al. (1999).

In de facto states, this schizophrenic situation goes even further. Being internationally unrecognized or only partially recognized, lacking internationally guaranteed security provisions and living under a constant threat of parent state's military incursion, almost any division of opinions is perceived as a threat for the national independence (Hoch et al. 2010, 293–294). Thus, the opposition political parties have certain constraints in undermining the ruling regimes, and their chances to replace the ruling elite are considerably lower. In Abkhazia, for example, almost nobody dared to criticize President Vladislav Ardzinba, who was perceived as an unchallenged national leader and a war hero (Krylov 2002). The situation has changed only when his second term was coming to an end and the opposition forces were preparing to challenge Ardzinba's handpicked successor, the incumbent Prime Minister Raul Khajimba (Skakov 2005, 161–169). After the 2003 presidential elections, which were surprisingly won by Sergei Bagapsh, an opposition candidate, the situation turned around and it was the former pro-government forces, which called mass demonstration in their support and tried to change the election results. However, under the auspices of Russia, a compromise solution was negotiated. In repeated elections, Bagapsh ran for President, whereas Khajimba ran for Vice-President (Matsuzato 2008, 108). The need for preserving national unity was given a priority over deep political division between Bagapsh and Khajimba.

Although the oldest Abkhazian political party, *Apsny Azhlart Apartia* (Abkhazian People's Party), registered already in 1992 (Кучуберия 2008; Krylov 2002), political parties played only a minor role in Abkhazian politics for almost a decade. Even in the first years of the new millennia, handful of political parties co-existed with powerful sociopolitical movements such as the *Aitaira* (Revival), the *Amtsakhara* (Eternal Flame), the *Akhatsa* (Hornbeam) or the *Apsny* (Abkhazia) (Skakov 2005, 160–174). However, most of these movements have already transformed into political parties—the *Apsny* and the *Aitaira* did so in 2001. The *Amtsakhara* is probably the best example of how political parties are being formed in Abkhazia. It was founded as a union of war veterans; then in 2001, it was registered as a sociopolitical movement; and finally, in 2013, the *Amtsakhara* became a political party (Krylov 2002; Апсныпресс 2013). The problem is that parties of this kind largely represent only specific groups of population which they used to represent when they were registered as sociopolitical movements or non-governmental organizations. In the case of the *Amtsakhara*, it is war veterans. Though the *Amtsakhara* is registered as a political party, its central office in Sukhum(i) is still preoccupied with providing services for war veterans such as arranging proper health care, pensions, social benefits.[15]

In 1990s, it was common that one person was a member of more parties or sociopolitical movements. Maia Agrba was a good example; she served as one of the co-chairs of the Republican Party *Apsny* and was a member of the Communist Party at the same time (Krylov 2002). Also, the tradition of having two, three or even more co-chairs testifies to the lower relevance of political parties. Having

---

[15]Interview No. 18.

system of co-chairs, from the managerial perspective, causes contradictions in the party leadership and is far less effective than the system with one chairman and a few vice-chairmen. For example, the *Aitaira* had three co-chairs, the *Apsny Akzaara* (United Abkhazia), a coalition of forces opposing President Bagapsh, had also three co-chairs (Skakov 2005, 164, 170), and the People's Front of Abkhazia for Development and Justice, founded only in 2015, elected even four co-chairs (Абхазия-Информ 2015).

The relatively low importance of political parties in Abkhazia is mainly caused by two factors. First, the electoral system in Abkhazia has always been a majoritarian one and the right to nominate a candidate has always been given also to public organizations or groups of voters. This provision has always been frequently used and surely did not help to develop functional party systems (Ó Beacháin 2012, 168; Krylov 2002). Second, due to the single-issue character of Abkhazia's political regime, i.e. protecting the national independence, there are virtually no ideological differences among the parties. Instead on programmes, they seem to be based on personalities—a fact which will be discussed in the contribution dedicated to the informal political institutions.

Much of what has been stated about Abkhazian political parties is valid for the parties in Nagorno-Karabakh too. Parties are grouped around strong leaders, and ideology, with the exception of the *Hay Heghapokhakhan Dashnaktsutyun* (Armenian Revolutionary Federation) or, in short, the Dashnak Party, plays a secondary role, if any. The Dashnaks, a left-wing political party, however, are an exception among political parties in both Abkhazia and Nagorno-Karabakh. It is the local branch of an all-Armenian political party, which was founded in 1892 in Tbilisi and was the leading political force of the First Armenian Republic in 1918–1920, and after the sovietization of Armenia has moved to the Diaspora (Matsuzato 2008, 104–105).

The first decade of Nagorno-Karabakh's existence as the de facto state has seen only one relevant political party—the Dashnaks. In 2005, there was a boom of political parties in Nagorno-Karabakh. It was caused by two factors: the parliament passed a law on political parties, and the electoral system has been changed from a majoritarian to a mixed one, giving better chances to party candidates (Smolnik 2012, 158). There are now more parties in Nagorno-Karabakh; however, four of them seem to be more stable and popular than the others. The *Artsakhi Demokratakan Kusaktsutyun* (Democratic Party of Artsakh) and the *Azat Hayrenik* (Free Motherland) have always been the government parties. The Democratic Party used to be a power base of former President Arkadi Ghukassyan and is chaired by the long-lived Speaker of the Parliament Ashot Ghulyan. In 2015, it became an associated member of the European Free Alliance, a European political party representing regional parties and holding 12 seats in the European Parliament (Goetz 2015). The *Azat Hayrenik* was founded by businessman Araik Harutyunyan, who has been serving as Karabakh's Prime Minister since 2007. Nagorno-Karabakh's opposition parties often perceive the *Azat Hayrenink* as an artificial party which serves the purpose of grabbing votes from the "real" opposition (Matsuzato 2008, 105). It bears certain similarities to the Abkhazian Party for the Economic

Development, which was also founded by a businessman, Beslan Butba, in 2007 (Ó Beacháin 2012, 169; Кучуберия 2007). Interestingly, also Butba served as Prime Minister, although only for half a year.

The *Sharszhum-88* (Movement-88) and the Dashnak Party somehow stand between the government and the opposition. In 2002–2003, the Dashnaks cooperated with the Democratic Party, in 2004 and 2005 with the *Sharzhum-88* (Matsuzato 2008, 105–106); however, since 2007 they have been again part of the ruling coalition or at least they have supported the ruling parties.[16] The *Sharzum-88* is led by Edvard Aghabeghyan, who served as the Mayor of Stepanakert in 2004–2008. In 2007, the *Sharzhum-88* unexpectedly supported Bako Sahakyan, Ghukassyan's handpicked successor, a move that has de facto brought them to the pro-government platform (Matsuzato 2008, 106). However, in 2012 presidential elections, the *Sharzhum-88* supported Sahakyan's rival, a retired major-general Vitaly Balasanyan (RFE/RL 2012).

In 2015, one more political party, the *Azgayin Veratsnund* (National Revival), obtained seats in Karabakh's Parliament. It is chaired by Hayk Khanumyan, a political scientist, and together with the *Sharzhum-88*, it claims to be an opposition force.[17]

Local journalists and civil society leaders interviewed perceive political parties in both concerned de facto states in a very critical way. Above all, they point out the insignificant ideological and programme differences. An Armenian journalist claimed that "[b]*etween political parties in Nagorno-Karabakh, there are almost no differences. The National Revival seems to be a liberal party, the Dashnaks are a nationalist leftist party, and all remaining parties, except the Communists, are a moderate mixture of conservatism, liberalism and nationalism*".[18] Another journalist stressed the low level of inter-party competition: "*In fact, there is no competition between parties and ideologies. In Nagorno-Karabakh, a political party with an ideology is missing. All of them* [the political parties] *want basically the same things: national independence, development, etc. For me, as a journalist, the Parliament is an uninteresting institution. Several years ago, there used to be a political struggle—for example privatisation was an important topic. The Dashnaks wanted to preserve the state ownership of the strategic industries at least. However, in present, even the Dashnaks do not differ from the other parties.*"[19]

Similar perception of political parties prevailed in Abkhazia. A civil society leader shared his/her opinion that "[p]*olitical parties* [in Abkhazia] *are weak, they are not organized on an ideological or program basis. In fact, they are rather interest groups, and their members often change one party for another according to their interests.*"[20]

---

[16]Interview No 2.
[17]Interview No 1.
[18]Interview No 7.
[19]Interview No 9.
[20]Interview No 12.

Unsurprisingly, party members and MPs were less critical, however, even they agreed on some similarities between the parties, as one opposition MP did: "*All the parties agree on the basic principles of Karabakh's foreign policy. There are, of course, some differences in the domestic politics. Nevertheless, when we meet over a glass of brandy or 'chacha', we can overcome our disputes. After all, we all have fought together.*"[21]

Also, the role of strong personalities and personal interests was mentioned as an important factor in formation of political parties. According to a Karabakhi opposition MP "[i]*t were personal interests, not ideas, on which the political parties* [in Nagorno-Karabakh] *have been formed. The Azat Hayrenik is a good example. The party protects interests of several businessmen, and this is the reason why we have a corrupted Prime Minister.*"[22] The same was claimed by a Karabakhi activist: "*As almost everywhere in the post-Soviet area, political parties in Nagorno-Karabakh have been rather formed around leaders, not programs.*"[23] An Abkhazian activist and former politician sees the situation in his/her country in a very similar way: "*In fact, there are no political parties in Abkhazia. There are only groups around several strong personalities. They do not have any programs, on which a coalition agreement could have been signed.*"[24]

Interviewed opposition politicians, journalists and civil society leaders in Nagorno-Karabakh perceive the political playing field as uneven due to a disproportionately large allocation of resources to the ruling parties. This was, however, not mentioned by the respondents in Abkhazia. According to a Karabakhi opposition MP, "[t]*he Democratic Party and the Azat Hayrenik control almost all the resources. In fact, nothing can be done without a consent of these two parties. From local organs to the central government, everything goes in the line of the Democratic Party, or the Azat Hayrenik.* (…) *If you want to make a career in the state sector, you have to be a member of one of these two parties.*"[25] Another Karabakhi respondent added: "*You can be elected to the Parliament, you can become an MP, but the problem is that if you are not a member of a ruling party, people will not take you seriously. People respect only those* [MPs] *who support the government and have access to resources*".[26]

---

[21]Interview No 3.
[22]Interview No 1.
[23]Interview No 8.
[24]Interview No 14.
[25]Interview No 3.
[26]Interview No 8.

4 Self-Government

Both Abkhazia's and Nagorno-Karabakh's Constitution guarantee the right of self-government. In Nagorno-Karabakh, the Law on Local Self-Government was adopted in 1998 (NKR USA 2005, 14), and the basic principles of self-government are also specified in the Constitution. Self-governing communities consist of one or more settlements; members of the community elect a representative body—the Council of Elders—and the Head of the Community, who is vested with the executive power. There is no regional self-government in Nagorno-Karabakh; the heads of the regions are selected by the President.

In Abkhazia, the Law on Administrative Units (No. 375-c-XIII, 1997) and The Law on Elections to the Self-Governing Bodies (No. 1549-c-XIV 2006) set up the self-government on both the regional and local level. However, the head of the self-governing unit, be it a region or town, is selected (in theory) by the President from the ranks of the elected representatives of the self-governing unit. The law, however, is confusing, and the selected head of a town or regional administration often comes from a different town or region.[27] The head of regional administration is also the head of the administration of the regional capital and selects the heads of rural settlements from the ranks of their elected representatives.

Local stakeholders identified several problematic aspects of the local self-government in the both concerned de facto states. In Nagorno-Karabakh, the lack of financial resources was identified as the most serious obstacle limiting day-to-day operation of the self-governing units. The self-government *"receives almost all financial resources from the state"* and *"even small investments, e.g. repair of the holes in a school roof, have to be approved by the government instead of local bodies."*[28] Thus, local self-governing bodies *"do not have enough resources to deal with local problems"*, and, as described by an Armenian journalist, the local officials are *"people who just stamp documents"*.[29]

An opposition MP expressed an opinion that *"[t]he legal foundation of the self-government in Nagorno-Karabakh is good, but in reality, there are serious problems."* He or she illustrated them with the story of the former Mayor of Stepanakert. *"Abel Aghabeghyan, the leader of the Sharzhum-88, defeated the pro-government candidate and became the Mayor of the capital in 2004. However, soon, the problems had started. The government cut off his financial resources, limiting his capacity to govern the city, so that everyone could see what happens when the Mayor is from the opposition camp. And people do care about it, they would not vote for somebody who has bad relations with the government"*.[30]

---

[27]Interview No 13.
[28]Interview No 1.
[29]Interview No 7.
[30]Interview No 3.

In Abkhazia, the lack of financial resources was also mentioned, but one even more serious problem was perceived—the direct dependence of the local and regional executive bodies on the central government. In words of an Abkhazian local politician, "[t]*he main problem of our* [Abkhazian] *self-government is its factual non-existence. How can one speak about self-government, if there is no special law on it? At present, 'self-governing' bodies are defined by the law on administrative units, i.e. together with the local and regional administration. The crucial problem is that self-government is not separated from the administration. Consequently, we* [the self-governing units] *have a very limited budget, and we deal almost only with ethno-cultural or social work matters*".[31]

In both Abkhazia and Nagorno-Karabakh, the self-government, however, is often seen as a soil where seeds of more democratic politics can germinate. An Abkhazian activist expressed the opinion that the central government hinders the needed reform of the self-government; however, he or she thinks that "*there is an initiative from below—the elected representatives from towns and regions established a kind of 'soviet of local representatives' and formulated the proposals for reform by themselves.*"[32] In Nagorno-Karabakh, local journalist assessed the local elections as "*more democratic than the parliamentary elections. The ruling parties mostly win anyway, but from time to time there are surprises. I see them* [the local elections] *as a hope for the Karabakhi democracy from below. The question is how to transfer these surprises to the higher level.*"[33]

On the contrary, there were also quite pessimistic views on the local self-government and possible grass-roots reforms. In words of Yerevan-based Karabakhi journalist, "[p]*eople* [in Nagorno-Karabakh] *do not have a clue about how the self-government should work, and expect that the state will do everything. It is because they perceive the self-government as a part of the state. No wonder— the self-government units have almost no power. And the state shows no will to change it and prefers people to be passive. There is a true story about* [Nagorno-Karabakh's] *Prime Minister arriving at a village. On both sides of a road, there were gutters full of sewage, so it was not possible to cross it. The Prime Minister asked the dwellers, why they had not put at least some planks over the gutters, and he was answered that this was task of the government to erect some gangways.*"[34] An Abkhazian local politician provided a similar opinion: "*The older generation* [in Abkhazia], *but not only them, do not understand how self-government should work; or, rather they understand it in the Soviet style. Members of the lower Soviet had to fulfil orders from his/her superior. People do not understand that self-government is not subordinate to anybody, and has authorities of its own*".[35]

---

[31] Interview No 13.
[32] Interview No 12.
[33] Interview No 6.
[34] Interview No 9.
[35] Interview No 13.

5 Informal Political Institutions and Practices

Lauth (2000, 22 and 26) sees the presence of informal institutions in situations where there is a discrepancy *"between the behavioural norms of formal institutions and the actual behaviour of individuals"*. Informal political institutions are those which (1) shape *"modes of behaviour and attitudes at a stage prior to political participation"*, (2) *"have a direct impact upon political participation"*, or (3) *"make available additional channels of influence for political participation beyond formal institutions"*. Formal political institutions can thus be understood as the official, written rules, while informal political institutions as the unofficial, unwritten rules.

In Abkhazia and Nagorno-Karabakh, the interviewees identified several informal institutions, which are clearly visible through concrete practices of political actors and segments of the population. First, it is clientelism, which is based on a *"specific, personally stratified relationship"* (Lauth 2000, 20) leading to an unequal yet mutually beneficial relationship between the patron and the client. In fact, Abkhazia's and Nagorno-Karabakh's political parties, although they have legal foundations, are the outstanding examples of clientelism. As Lauth (2000, 33) puts it, in clientelist parties, "[t]*he loyalties involved remain linked to persons and are not transferred to formal institutions.*" Respondents commonly call these parties *grupirovki*, as did, for example, an Abkhazian civil society leader and a former politician: *"We* [in Abkhazia] *do not have political parties, but 'grupirovki' based on common financial interests."*[36] The parties, however, seem to be just part of a more complex pyramidal structure.

Some strong personalities prefer not to join any party and operate as independents. This is the case of most of the presidents. For example, Bako Sahakyan, the President of Nagorno-Karabakh, *"started his career as a dealer, then his friend, who was the Minister of Defence, made him responsible for supplying the army. For a while, he also used to informally represent the army in Moscow, but it seems he embezzled some money there, so he was called back to Karabakh and even taken into custody."*[37] *"In 1995 he left to Yerevan and then to Moscow, where he used to work in the intelligence service."*[38] *"[The then President] Ghukassyan who, after the unsuccessful assassination attempt on him, looked for loyal persons, made Sahakyan the Interior Minister and later the head of* [Nagorno-Karabakh's] *security service."*[39] Sahakyan has never been a member of any party, but, step by step, seems to have built his own power base. Finally, he was handpicked as Ghukassyan's successor. At present, in the words of one respondent, Sahakyan is *"the key person in the country. He decides on almost everything and everybody. (…) Almost every problem has to be discussed with the President, and his informal consent is always necessary, be it selecting candidates for ministers, influencing*

---

[36]Interview No 16.
[37]Interview No 8.
[38]Interview No 9.
[39]Interview No 8.

judges,[40] *or selling a state owned land."*[41] An interviewed journalist added another reason why Sahakyan became president: *"He is a very consensual person, he can get on with almost everyone, even with the radical opposition. Under his presidency, the ruling regime is very soft and open to incorporate anybody."*[42]

The same journalist described Nagorno-Karabakh's political elite: *"There are three main groups. First, the old guard, former Communist apparatchiki and members of the Komsomol. Second, the business people. I would not use the word oligarchy, they are not so rich to be called oligarchs like in Russia. For example, Prime Minister Harutyunyan owns some companies and estates and even he does not hide it. Third, people connected with the army. We have a large army, and men who are in the army, simply cannot be real citizens, because they are dependent on their superiors".*[43]

The Abkhazian political reality is often being explained by the clan logic. Allegedly, there are two main clans—north-western Gudauta (or Bzyp) and south-eastern Ochamchira (or Abzhua) clans. *"The unwritten law"*, Skakov (2005, 171) writes, *"demands that a native of Gudauta running for president must take an Ochamchira local as his vice-presidential mate, and* vice versa." However, the respondents interviewed expressed different perceptions of Abkhazia's informal politics. In their opinion, instead of real clans,[44] there are just clientelist networks based on family, friendship or business interests. A former high-ranking politician and state servant stated that in Abkhazia "[t]*here are powerful lobby groups connected to the members of the government. They are comprised mostly of businessmen, but not always. Clans as such do not exist. Of course, family members always help each other, but the lobby groups I am speaking about, are just lobby groups, nothing more, they are not based on blood ties."*[45] Abkhazia's informal politics does not seem to be a single-pyramid one. More clientelist groups compete. In the words of a civil society leader, "[t]*here is an extensive corruption throughout the society based on friendship and kinship ties. But it is not a centralized system. You simply need some acquaintances in order to make things go faster."*[46]

The situation, however, seems to be more complex on the regional and local level in both de facto states. One respondent from Nagorno-Karabakh explained that in the villages, the role of kinship-based networks is much more important than in towns: *"Local 'clans' dominate the life in rural areas. In a village, four to five*

---

[40]One respondent called influencing of judges the "telephone right".

[41]Interview No 8.

[42]Interview No 9.

[43]Interview No 9.

[44]There is a tendency of some of the authors to label all well-organized clientelist networks in the post-Soviet area as clans. Nevertheless, the clan is more an anthropological than a political concept. Collins (2004, 2006), Horák (2010, 2012) or Schatz (2004, 2005) described clan politics in Central Asia; however, it can be a far-fetched attempt to apply the concept outside this region.

[45]Interview No 11.

[46]Interview No 15.

greater families control everything. It is their members who are elected to the council of elders and become the mayors."[47]

Important informal practices are connected with the electoral process and electoral behaviour of the population. As explained by a Karabakhi journalist: "*Significant part of the population is employed in the state sector. We also have a compulsory military service, a people's army, so practically all men are also soldiers. And people who are in the army or work for the government are inclined to vote for the pro-government parties.*"[48] Moreover, there seems to be a direct corruption present in the electoral process in Nagorno-Karabakh: "*People vote for money. They receive cash, or somebody pays their debts. And people often get into debts on their electricity or gas bills. However, these things have started when Sahakyan became the President, they had not been common before.*"[49]

In Abkhazia in the areas inhabited by the ethnic Abkhaz, the election campaign seems to be relatively fair. A local politician claimed that "[i]*t is not possible to commit a major electoral fraud* [because Abkhazia] *is a small country, we know each other, and such a thing would be easily revealed.*"[50] Moreover, it seems that people in Abkhazia "*are used to a kind of election campaign in which candidates personally approach their voters. A candidate who does not lead the campaign personally has no chance. Both Beslan Butba and Raul Khajimba once employed 'polittekhnologi' from Moscow, but their attempts failed. People did not vote for them.*"[51] On the local and regional level, the entire electoral process seems to have a far more grass-roots character. "*A lot of young and competent people are pushed by their friends and neighbours to stand as candidates for local or regional 'soviets'. The campaign is not money-consuming, they can manage even without party's support; everything goes on the basis of friendship or family relations. Candidate's friends and family members act in support of the candidate and try to convince their acquaintances to vote for him/her.*"[52]

Whereas the post of the President of Abkhazia is reserved for an ethnic Abkhaz, in each Parliamentary elections, some MPs representing other ethnic groups are elected. Their numbers, however, are significantly lower than the number of ethnic Abkhaz MPs and do not correspond to the actual share of ethnically non-Abkhaz population in the country. The way the ethnically non-Abkhaz MPs used to be elected resembles consociational practices, however, informal ones. "*Before 2012, there were 'gentlemen's agreements' between the ethnic communities. Gagra and Gulrypsh used to be districts reserved for the Armenian, and Gal(i) for the Megrelian MPs.*"[53] "*The ethnic Abkhaz did not stand as candidates* [in these

---

[47]Interview No 1.
[48]Interview No 6.
[49]Interview No 8.
[50]Interview No 13.
[51]Interview No 14.
[52]Interview No 13.
[53]Interview No 15.

districts] *in order that ethnically non-Abkhaz MPs could be elected. Two Russians, two or three Armenians and some Megrels used to sit in the Parliament.*"[54] *"In selected electoral districts, the ethnic Abkhaz used to vote for ethnic Armenians, and the Armenians used to repay them in the same manner in remaining districts. However, a few years ago, seats in the Parliament became interesting from the economic point of view, or due to the parliamentary immunity. Elections have become more competitive and the gentlemen's agreements have faded away.*"[55]

Still, some ethnically non-Abkhaz MPs can be found in the Parliament, but they are mostly Armenians. This ethnic community seems to be well organized and *"unlike Russians or Turks, they do not divide their votes between more candidates, but agree on one candidate, for whom they all vote"*.[56] Megrels, who also live in Georgia and consider themselves to be Georgians (at least in the political meaning of the word) (Kopečková 2012, 113), were largely enfranchised during Bagapsh's and Ankvab's administrations; however, Khajimba has reversed the process and most of the Megrels were deprived of their voting rights. Those who still have the right to vote cast their ballots for *"those who promise them better integration"*[57] or at least to *"someone, be it ethnic Abkhaz, who is from the Gal(i) region."*[58] One respondent even claimed that *"the Megrels, who are the most vulnerable part of the population"*, are intimidated by criminal groups who use their votes in order to enter the Parliament.[59]

The patron states, i.e. Russia and Armenia, also have an informal influence on Abkhazia's or Nagorno-Karabakh's politics, respectively. Although it is almost impossible to be an anti-Russian politician in Abkhazia,[60] Russia seems to prefer those politicians who obligingly comply with Moscow's wishes. This was the case of Raul Khajimba, who was supported by Moscow in 2003, 2009 and 2011 presidential elections. He lost all of them, despite having the aid of the *polittekhnologi* sent from Moscow. In 2014, however, *"the coup d'état* [which ousted President Ankvab and installed Khajimba on his place] *was* [according to the respondent's best knowledge] *organized by Vladislav Surkov from Putin's Presidential Office"*.[61]

The influence of the Armenian Republic in Nagorno-Karabakh is substantial too. Like Russia in case of Abkhazia, Armenia contributes to Nagorno-Karabakh's budget and protects it militarily.[62] Both entities also have harmonized legislations and foreign ministries even officially issued "guidance for cooperation".[63]

---

[54]Interview No 14.
[55]Interview No 12.
[56]Interview No 11.
[57]Interview No 12.
[58]Interview No 11.
[59]Interview No 12.
[60]Interview No 17.
[61]Interview No 14.
[62]Interview No 10.
[63]Interview No 5.

However, there are also other mechanisms by which the Armenian Republic influences Nagorno-Karabakh's politics. First, "[t]*he Armenian and Karabakhi political elites are intermingled. Former citizens of Nagorno-Karabakh are in Armenia's government, including the President* [Serzh Sargsyan], *and former Armenia's citizens, became ministers or MPs in Nagorno-Karabakh.*"[64] Second, there seem to be certain limits restricting who can become a leading political figure in Nagorno-Karabakh. One of the respondents, who asked for a complete anonymity, revealed that "[t]*o become the President of Nagorno-Karabakh, one has to fulfil two conditions: to have support in Nagorno-Karabakh and have good relations with the President of Armenia.*"

6 Possible Reforms of Political Systems

Possible reforms of political systems in de facto states are a frequent topic of discussions among stakeholders. In the final chapter of this contribution, opinions on some of the discussed reforms are provided. The strong position of the President in both Abkhazia and Nagorno-Karabakh opens the question of a possible shift to parliamentarism. However, for some, the constitutions and the formal divisions of powers are sufficiently well defined. As explained by a former Abkhazian politician, "*the Constitution is not a problem per se. The problem is that we do not respect the Constitution.*"[65] Those, who would imagine a reform, are at the same time relatively sceptic that such a reform can be implemented in practice. In Abkhazia, the reform of the Constitution has been demanded by almost every opposition party or movement. However, "*always, when the opposition comes to power, they fill the posts with their people and realize that current institutions serve well those who are in power. Thus, all the constitutional reforms were forsaken.*"[66]

In Abkhazia, however, it is not the presidential system as such, but the majoritarian electoral system and the weak self-government, which are considered by the respondents as the most problematic issues. Some respondents were confident that proportional or at least mixed electoral system "*will lead to a system of real political parties*".[67] On the contrary, others showed certain scepticism: "*I used to support the idea of mixed electoral system. However, after* [Khajimba's] *coup, I am not convinced anymore. First, we need political parties, we need to change our political culture. Mixed electoral system will not save us. Maybe, if we reform the self-government, if we enable people to directly elect mayors, if we provide the mayors with competences and financial resources enough to be able to solve local and regional problems on their own, and, finally, adopt a new law on political*

---

[64]Interview No 1.
[65]Interview No 16.
[66]Interview No 14.
[67]Interview No 14.

parties and build political parties from the ground, we can, step by step, change the nature of the parties and the political culture."[68]

In Nagorno-Karabakh, during the research in October 2015, the Dashnaks and the *Azat Hayrenik* clearly supported the transition to parliamentarism. Whereas *"the Dashnaks have always been for the parliamentary system, because it is a tradition from the First Armenian Republic* [dominated by the Dashnaks],"[69] *Azat Hayerenik*, despite its declarations, was suspected by opposition parties of supporting the idea of parliamentarism for purely opportunistic reasons. *"Perhaps, they* [Azat Hayrenik] *like the provision that there is not a limit of the two consecutive terms for becoming the Prime Minister, as there is for becoming the President."*[70] There was also a strong belief that Nagorno-Karabakh would follow the example of the Armenian Republic, which, indeed, 2 months after the field research in Nagorno-Karabakh was concluded, decided in a referendum on a transition to parliamentarism. A Karabakhi civil society leader explained: *"I am afraid, that if the Armenian Republic changes its constitution, Nagorno-Karabakh will change it too. But I think it is not a good solution. Both constitutions,* [of the Armenian Republic and Nagorno-Karabakh], *are good constitutions, the problem is that they are not fully respected. In Nagorno-Karabakh, it is the President and the Prime Minister, who support the change of the constitution, but they do it because they are corrupt, and they are afraid that a new presidential administration would reveal their crimes. This is the reason why they want to remain in power forever and they think parliamentarism will make it possible."*[71] However, there were even opponents of the ruling Karabakhi regime who supported the shift to parliamentarism, such as a Yerevan-based journalist, originally from Nagorno-Karabakh. *"I support the change* [to parliamentarism], *because in presidentialism, everything is dependent on the decision of one person. And this is not good. Decisions have to be discussed, and not made according to someone's personal interests."*[72]

The discussion about the constitutional reform in Nagorno-Karabakh, however, gained a new dimension after heavy clashes between Karabakhi and Azerbaijani units on the line of contact in April 2016 (so-called Four-Day War), which claimed about 350 casualties including civilians (US Department of State 2016). President Sahakyan and both ruling parties including their leaders, Prime Minister Harutyunyan and Speaker of the Parliament Ghulyan, changed their opinions and started to argue for strengthening presidential competences, which would provide for better security and defensive capacity of Nagorno-Karabakh, whereas the Dashnaks, the *Sharzhum-88* and the *Azgayin Veracnund* opposed the changes (Sargsyan 2016). The final version of the draft was not yet available in times of writing; however, the Armenian media speculated that the mandate of present-day

---

[68]Interview No 16.
[69]Interview No 2.
[70]Interview No 1.
[71]Interview No 8.
[72]Interview No 9.

President Sahakyan would be extended by three years to 2020 in order to cover the transition period (Григорян 2016). In this context, the opposition expressed concerns that the drafted constitutional changes will "*ensure the continued dominance of the ruling political elite*" (Sargsyan 2016, 3).

Regarding the electoral system, respondents in Nagorno-Karabakh divided into two groups. Whereas the first group supports further reforms and the transition to a proportional system, the second group points out that the mixed electoral system has its advantages. The arguments of the first group are that proportional electoral system is more democratic, although they also have concerns if such a reform can help to change the character of the regime. "*If the reform [of the electoral system] is intended seriously, then it can help the democratisation of Nagorno-Karabakh. In proportional system, there would be more competition and the role of the parties would increase. But if we do not change our culture of electoral behaviour and people will continue to cast ballots to those who will pay them, nothing will change.*"[73] The second group argues that mixed system enables independents to run, and that in Nagorno-Karabakh, there are many competent people who would never enter any political party. Some argued that "*representatives of the regions should be elected in single-mandate districts, whereas the remaining MPs should be elected on party lists.*"[74]

Finally, the local self-government in Nagorno-Karabakh is viewed as a sector which needs a reform in any case. This reform, however, should focus more on the financial and budgetary aspects than on the shape of the elected bodies. An opposition MP expressed opinion that the self-governing communities should initiate such a process. "*I proposed to them [the heads of the communities] to establish a union of self-governing communities in order to support their demands for more tax revenues and a larger budget, but it went unheard*".[75] Regional self-government seems to be out of discussion, at least unless the Karabakh conflict is solved: "*In our situation, the regional self-government is pointless and ineffective. The head of regional administration is also the military commander of the region and s/he must be the part of 'vertikala vlasti'. When the conflict is solved, then we can discuss the establishing of regional self-government*".[76]

7 Conclusion

Both Abkhazia and Nagorno-Karabakh have democratized in the past decade. However, their political institutions, despite the democratic façade, are far from being democratic inside. The chapter has demonstrated the complex structure of

---

[73]Interview No 8.
[74]Interview No 4.
[75]Interview No 1.
[76]Interview No 4.

selected political institutions and, above all, granted local stakeholders a room for commenting on their political institutions. On some points, the respondents were very critical and it was possible to identify certain prevailing perceptions of some of the institutions.

Though both the concerned de facto states have different types of constitutions, Abkhazia, a presidential model with simultaneously elected President and Vice-President, and Nagorno-Karabakh, a semi-presidential model with the Prime Minister formally responsible to the National Assembly, both the countries show apparent signs of super-presidentialism, in which presidents dominate over the legislative, the judiciary and the self-government. There seem to be two reasons for the de facto super-presidential systems. First, there is a negative experience with the parliamentarism, which was, technically, the system of government in the Soviet Union. Second, the armed conflicts which led to the separation of both Abkhazia and Nagorno-Karabakh produced strong leaders, for whom the constitutions were tailored.

In both Abkhazia and Nagorno-Karabakh, the discussion on possible constitutional reform is underway. However, whereas in Abkhazia the discussion focuses primarily on the elections (see later), in Nagorno-Karabakh it concentrates on the competences of the President and the Prime Minister and their relations to the National Assembly. The Karabakhi society is divided into supporters of parliamentarism and presidentialism (or semi-presidentialism). Whereas supporters of parliamentarism point to the Armenian tradition of the parliamentary form of government and its "more democratic character", supporters of presidentialism regard parliamentarism as inefficient form of government, a kind of luxury Nagorno-Karabakh simply cannot afford, as the entity is endangered by possible Azerbaijani military offensive. Interestingly, in Abkhazia, which is under Russia's protection, the respondents ruled out the possibility of war with Georgia and did not think about the models of government in terms of efficiency in the case of war. The Karabakhi opposition watches the intentions of the ruling parties, which initially after the example of the Republic of Armenia considered a shift to parliamentarism, and later after the "Four-Day War" turned to favour presidentialism, with a growing distrust. There is a widespread opinion in Nagorno-Karabakh that the drafted change of the constitution is to extend the presidential term and to ensure the dominance of the ruling elite.

The system of political parties in both Abkhazia and Nagorno-Karabakh is underdeveloped, and the parties as such are relatively weak. This state has more reasons; however, only three of them are the same in the both compared cases. First, the strong presidencies and weak legislatures naturally weaken the institution of the political party. Second, both Abkhazia and Nagorno-Karabakh are single-issue regimes, for which protecting the (de facto) national independence is their *raison d'être*. Thus, the opposition political parties hesitate to undermine the ruling regimes in order not to endanger the "unity" of the nation. Third, political parties are based on strong personalities and clientelist relations rather than ideologies and programmes. This makes unstable not only the individual political parties, as they suffer from personal conflicts, but also the whole system of political parties, as the parties easily move from the government to the opposition and back.

Though political parties in Nagorno-Karabakh and Abkhazia share a lot of similarities, the Karabakhi party system seems to be more developed than the Abkhazian one. First, in Abkhazia, there has always been the first-past-the-post electoral system and the grass-roots method of nominating the candidates. This has further weakened the position of political parties at the expense of civil society organizations and the so-called sociopolitical movements, which entered the parliament and some of them later re-registered as political parties. The problem is that these parties still largely represent only specific groups of population, such as the war veterans. In Nagorno-Karabakh, the electoral system changed to the mixed one a decade ago, and since that time, the number of parliamentary seats assigned by the proportional voting has been increasing, thus strengthening the role of political parties. Also, the fact that the Armenians have a long tradition of political partisanship dating back to the nineteenth century, apparently contributed to less amorphous political parties than in Abkhazia.

The weakness of political parties and the need for an electoral reform was often mentioned by the respondents as one of the most pressing problems of Abkhazia's political system. After long discussions and several postponements, it seemed that Abkhazia would finally introduce mixed electoral system in 2016;[77] however, this reform is apparently on a side track as the opposition parties are preoccupied with challenging President Khajimba, who came to power after the *coup d'état* in 2014 (Dzutsati 2016; Fuller, 2016). However, even if such a reform is adopted, only forthcoming years would show if such a move is sufficient to increase the relevance of political parties.

The self-government in Abkhazia and Nagorno-Karabakh is heavily dependent on the executive. However, only one cause is the same in the both compared cases —the lack of financial resources which limits the autonomy of the self-governing bodies. Abkhazia and Nagorno-Karabakh are comparable in the area and population, but it is only Abkhazia which has two-level system of self-government, i.e. on the regional and local (municipal) levels. In Nagorno-Karabakh, it is only the municipalities which enjoy self-governing status, whereas the regions are units for administrative and, due to the risk of war with Azerbaijan, also military purposes. On the other hand, Karabakhi mayors are directly elected and thus less dependent on the central government than mayors in Abkhazia, who are in fact selected by the President. Despite certain differences in the systems of self-government in the both compared de facto states, respondents agreed on one more thing: the self-government is inefficient not only because of certain legal and financial difficulties, but also because of lack of public awareness of the self-governing bodies' competences.

The informal political institutions play a crucial role in the both de facto states. The most important informal institution is clientelism on the state level and clannish politics on the local level. Furthermore, informal practices are also typical for the electoral process. In Abkhazia, respondents stressed that candidates have to

---

[77]Interview No. 14.

personally approach the voters. While such practices were valued and appreciated by the respondents, the already mentioned low relevance of political parties, which goes hand in hand with the grass-roots character of the campaigning, was paradoxically seen as problematic. In Nagorno-Karabakh, apparently because of the slightly more developed political parties and the mixed electoral system, the electoral process is less grass-root and respondents often mentioned vote buying as a serious problem. On the contrary, in Abkhazia, the intimidation of voters or vote buying was seen as home only to ethnically distinct regions. The ethnicity, indeed, plays a great role in the electoral process in Abkhazia. Whereas gentlemen's agreements between ethnic communities on whom to support in the elections have reportedly faded away, at least the Armenians still mobilize around one or two candidates and are able to push them to the parliament.

References

Bakke, K. M., O'Loughlin, J., Toal, G., & Ward, M. D. (2014). Convincing state-builders? Disaggregating internal legitimacy in Abkhazia. *International Studies Quarterly, 58*(3), 591–607.
Berg, E., & Mölder, M. (2012). Who is entitled to 'earn sovereignty'? Legitimacy and regime support in Abkhazia and Nagorno-Karabakh. *Nations and Nationalism, 18*(3), 527–545.
Berg, E., & Pegg, S. (2016, May). Scrutinizing a policy of 'engagement without recognition': US requests for diplomatic actions with de facto states. *Foreign Policy Analysis*, Early View. https://doi.org/10.1093/fpa/orw044. Accessed April 25, 2017.
Biernacki, P., & Waldorf, D. (1981). Snowball sampling: Problems and techniques of chain referral sampling. *Sociological Methods & Research, 10*(2), 141–163.
Carothers, T. (2002). The end of the transition paradigm. *Journal of Democracy, 13*(1), 5–21.
Caspersen, N. (2008). From Kosovo to Karabakh: International responses to de facto states. *Südosteuropa, 56*(1), 58–83.
Caspersen, N. (2009). Playing the recognition game: External actors and de facto states. *The International Spectator, 44*(4), 47–60.
Collins, K. (2004). The logic of clan politics: Evidence from the Central Asian trajectories. *World Politics, 56*(2), 224–261.
Collins, K. (2006). *Clan politics and regime transition in Central Asia*. New York: Cambridge University Press.
Constitution of the Nagorno-Karabakh Republic (non-official translation). (2006). The office of the NKR president. http://www.president.nkr.am/en/constitution/fullText. Accessed January 25, 2016.
Croissant, M. P. (1998). *The Armenia-Azerbaijan conflict. Causes and implications*. Praeger: Westport and London.
De Waal, T. (2003). *Black garden: Armenia and Azerbaijan through peace and war*. London, New York: New York University Press.
Diamond, L. (2002). Thinking about hybrid regimes. *Journal of Democracy, 13*(2), 21–35.
Dzutsati, V. (2016). Abkhazia's president faces public campaign calling for his resignation. *Eurasia Daily Monitor 13*(72).
Elgie, R. (2007). What is semi-presidentialism and where is it found? In R. Elgie & S. Moestrup (Eds.), *Semi-presidentialism outside Europe: A comparative study* (pp. 1–13). Abingdon, New York: Routledge.
Fish, M. S. (1997). The pitfalls of Russian superpresidentialism. *Current History, 96*(612), 326–330.

Flick, U. (2009). *An introduction to qualitative research*. London: SAGE Publications.
Fuller, L. (2016). *Composition of new Abkhaz government unlikely to mollify opposition*. Radio Free Europe/Radio Liberty. http://www.rferl.org/content/abkhazia-cabinet-opposition/27955060.html. Accessed September 9, 2016.
Francis, C. (2011). *Conflict resolution and status: The case of Georgia and Abkhazia (1989–2008)*. Brussels: ASP/VUBPress/UPA.
Freedom House. (2015). *Freedom in the world comparative and historical data. Individual territory ratings and status*. FIW 1973–2015. Washington: Freedom House. https://freedomhouse.org/sites/default/files/Individual%20Territory%20Ratings%20and%20Status%2C%201973-2015%20%28final%29.xls. Accessed January 25, 2016.
Gerrits, A. W. M., & Bader, M. (2016). Russian Patronage over Abkhazia and South Ossetia: Implications for conflict resolution. *East European Politics, 32*(3), 297–313.
Goetz, L. (2015). Nagorno-Karabakh: European dreams. Open Democracy. https://www.opendemocracy.net/can-europe-make-it/lucas-goetz/nagornokarabakh-european-dreams. Accessed January 25, 2016.
Hale, H. E. (2015). *Patronal politics*. New York: Cambridge University Press.
Hoch, T., Baar, V., & Kopeček, V. (2010). Podmínky demokratizace v de facto státech: případová studie Abcházie. *Středoevropské politické studie, 12*(4), 285–300.
Hoch, T., & Souleimanov, E. (2013). Russia's role in the peace process in Abkhazia. In M. Malek (Ed.), *Ausgewählte sicherheits politische Fragenim Südkaukasus* (pp. 21–51). Wien: Bundesministerium für Landesverteidigung und Sport.
Horák, S. (2010). Changes in the political elite in post-Soviet Turkmenistan. *China and Eurasia Forum Quarterly, 8*(3), 27–46.
Horák, S. (2012). The elite in post-Soviet and post-Niyazow Turkmenistan: Does political culture form a leader? *Demokratizatsiya: The Journal of Post-Soviet Democratization, 20*(4), 371–385.
Ishiyama, J. T., & Kennedy, R. (2001). Superpresidentialism and political party development in Russia, Ukraine, Armenia and Kyrgyzstan. *Europe-Asia Studies, 53*(8), 1177–1191.
Kitschelt, H., Mansfeldova, Z., Markowski, R., & Tóka, G. (1999). *Post-communist party systems. Competition, representation and inter-party cooperation*. Cambridge: Cambridge University Press.
Kolstø, P. (2006). The sustainability and future of unrecognized quasi-states. *Journal of Peace Research, 43*(6), 723–740.
Kolstø, P., & Blakkisrud, H. (2012). De facto states and democracy: The case of Nagorno-Karabakh. *Communist and Post-Communist Studies, 45*(1–2), 141–151.
Kopeček, V., Hoch, T., & Baar, V. (2016). De facto states and democracy: The case of Abkhazia. *Bulletin of Geography. Socio-Economic Series, 32*, 85–104.
Kopečková, L. (2012). Language policy in Georgia with focus on non-Georgian minorities. *The Annual of Language & Politics and Politics of Identity, 6*(1). http://alppi.vedeckecasopisy.cz/publicFiles/00165.pdf. Accessed January 25, 2016.
Krylov, A. (2002). The special features of forming a multiparty system in Abkhazia. *Central Asia and the Caucasus, 3*(2). http://www.ca-c.org/journal/eng-02-2002/07.kriprimen.shtml. Accessed January 25, 2016.
Lauth, H.-J. (2000). Informal institutions and democracy. *Democratization, 7*(4), 21–50.
Levitsky, S., & Way, L. A. (2010). *Competitive authoritarianism: Hybrid regimes after the cold war*. Cambridge: Cambridge University Press.
Lynch, D. (2004). *Engaging Eurasia's separatist states: Unresolved conflicts and de facto states*. Washington: United States Institute of Peace Press.
Matsuzato, K. (2008). From belligerent to multi-ethnic democracy: Domestic politics in unrecognized states after ceasefires. *Eurasian Review, 1*, 95–119.
Miller, A. H., Erb, G., Reisinger, W. M., & Hesli, V. L. (2000). Emerging party systems in post-soviet societies: Fact or fiction? *The Journal of Politics, 62*(2), 455–490.
Morlino, L. (2009). Are there hybrid regimes? Or are they just an optical illusion? *European Political Science Review, 1*(2), 273–296.

NKR USA. (2005). *Nagorno-Karabakh Republic Artsakh. State building: Progress toward freedom, democracy and economic development*. Washington: Office of the Nagorno-Karabakh Republic in the USA. http://www.nkrusa.org/nk_conflict/assets/nkr-state-building.pdf. Accessed January 25, 2016.

Noy, C. (2008). Sampling knowledge: The hermeneutics of snowball sampling in qualitative research. *International Journal of Social Research Methodology, 11*(4), 327–344.

Ó Beacháin, D. Ó. (2012). The dynamics of electoral politics in Abkhazia. *Communist and Post-Communist Studies, 45*(1–2), 165–174.

Pegg, S. (1998). *International society and the de facto state*. Aldershot: Ashgate Publishing.

Popescu, N. (2006). *Outsourcing de facto statehood: Russia and the secessionist entities in Georgia and Moldova*. CEPS policy brief no. 109. Brussels: Centre for European Policy Studies. http://www.ceeol.com/aspx/getdocument.aspx?logid=5&id=adf0c7e85b4349a1b60d17cf295ee0a7. Accessed January 25, 2016.

RFE/RL. (2012). *Karabakh voters faced with choice between stagnation and change*. Radio Free Europe/Radio Liberty. http://www.rferl.org/content/karabakh-voters-faced-with-choice-between-stagnation-and-change/24646763.html. Accessed January 25, 2016.

Riegl, M. (2010). Terminologie kvazistátů. *Acta Politologica, 2*(1), 57–71.

Sargsyan, A. (2016). *An assessment of proposed constitutional changes in Nagorno-Karabakh*. RSC guest analysis no. 5. Yerevan: Regional Studies Center. http://regional-studies.org/images/pr/2016/august/23/RSC_Guest_Analysis_5_Alvard_Sargsyan_8.16.pdf. Accessed September 9, 2016.

Schatz, E. (2004). *Modern clan politics: The power of "blood" in Kazakhstan and beyond*. Washington: University of Washington Press.

Schatz, E. (2005). Reconceptualizing clans: Kinship networks and statehood in Kazakhstan. *Nationalities Papers, 33*(2), 231–254.

Skakov, A. (2005). Abkhazia at a crossroads: On the domestic political situation in the Republic of Abkhazia. *Iran & the Caucasus, 9*(1), 159–185.

Smolnik, F. (2012). Political rule and violent conflict: Elections as 'institutional mutation' in Nagorno-Karabakh. *Communist and Post-Communist Studies, 4*(1–2), 153–163.

Souleimanov, E. (2013). *Understanding ethnopolitical conflict: Karabakh, South Ossetia, and Abkhazia wars reconsidered*. Basingstoke, New York: Palgrave Macmillan.

Toal, G., & O'Loughlin, J. (2013). Land for peace in Nagorny-Karabakh? Political geographies and public attitudes inside a contested de facto state. *Territory, Politics, Governance, 1*(2), 158–182.

Trier, T., Lohm, H., & Szakonyi, D. (2010). *Under siege: Inter-ethnic relations in Abkhazia*. New York: Columbia University Press.

US Department of State. (2016). *Background briefing on the Nagorno-Karabakh conflict*. Press release|Special briefing. US Department of State. http://www.state.gov/r/pa/prs/ps/2016/05/257263.htm. Accessed September 9, 2016.

Von Steinsdorff, S. (2012). Incomplete state building: Incomplete democracy? How to interpret internal political development in the post-Soviet de facto states. *Communist and Post-Communist Studies, 45*(1–2), 201–206.

Von Steinsdorff, S., & Fruhstorfer, A. (2012). Post-Soviet de facto states in search of internal and external legitimacy. Introduction. *Communist and Post-Communist Studies, 45*(1–2), 117–121.

Wilson, A. (2005). *Virtual politics: Faking democracy in the post-soviet world*. New Haven, London: Yale University Press.

Абхазия-Информ [Abkhazia-Inform]. (2015, September 25). Республиканскую политическую партию Народный фронт Абхазии за справедливостьи развитиевозглавили четыресо председателя [Four Co-Chairs Lead the Republican Political Party National Front of Abkhazia for Justice and Development]. http://abkhazinform.com/item/2192-respublikanskuyu-politicheskuyu-partiyu-narodnyj-front-abkhazii-za-spravedlivost-i-razvitie-vozglavili-chetyre-sopredsedatelya. Accessed January 25, 2016.

Апсныпресс [Apsnypress]. (2013, June 27). Общественная организация ветеранов отечественной войны народа Абхазии « Амцахара » преобразована в политическую партию [Socio-political Organization of Veterans of the Patriotic War of the Abkhazian Nation "Amtsakhara" Transformed into a Political Party]. http://www.apsnypress.info/news/obshchestvennaya-organizatsiya-veteranov-otechestvennoy-voyny-naroda-abkhazii-amtsakhara-preobrazova/. Accessed January 25, 2016.

Григорян, Алвард [Grigoryan, Alvard]. (2016, July 28). Эксперты считают изменение конституции Нагорного Карабаха возможным только после всенародного референдума [Experts Think that Change of Nagorno-Karabakh's Constitution is Possible Only after a National Referendum]. *Кавказский узел* [Kavkazskiy Uzel]. http://www.kavkaz-uzel.eu/articles/284857/. Accessed September 9, 2016.

Закон Республики Абхазия об управлении административно-территориальных единицах Республики Абхазия [Law of the Republic of Abkhazia on Administration of Administrative-territorial Units of the Republic of Abkhazia] No. 375-с—XIII, 1997. http://presidentofabkhazia.org/upload/iblock/447/Закон_об__управлении_в_административно-территориальных_единицах_Республики_Абхазия_2015_03_31_13_14_08_048. Accessed January 25, 2016.

Закон Республики Абхазияовы борах в органы местного самоуправления [Law of the Republic of Abkhazia on Elections to the Bodies of Local Self-government] № 1549-с-XIV, 2006. http://presidentofabkhazia.org/upload/iblock/428/Закон__о_выборах_в_органы_местного_самоуправления_2015_03_31_18_45_28_954.pdf. Accessed January 25, 2015.

Конституция Республики Абхазия (си змнени ямиот 30 Апреля 2014) [Constitution of the Republic of Abkhazia (as amended by 30 April 2014)] No. 3494-с-V, 2014. http://presidentofabkhazia.org/upload/iblock/9b1Конституция_Республики_Абхазия_2015_03_31_13_14_23_110.pdf. Accessed January 25, 2016.

Кучуберия, Анжела [Kuchuberia, Anzhela]. (2007, September 26). "В Абхазии создана новая политическ аяпартия [New Political Party Founded in Abkhazia]." *Кавказский узел* [Kavkazskiy Uzel], http://www.kavkaz-uzel.ru/articles/124112/. Accessed January 25, 2016.

Кучуберия, Анжела [Kuchuberia, Anzhela]. (2008, January 30). "Партия экономического развития и Народная партия Абхазии договорились сотрудничать [Party of Economic Development and Peoples' Party of Abkhazia Agreed on Co-operation]." Кавказский узел [Kavkazskiy Uzel]. http://www.kavkaz-uzel.ru/articles/133378/. Accessed January 25, 2016.

Interviews

Interview No 1, with an opposition MP, Stepanakert/Khankendy, de facto Nagorno-Karabakh, 19 October 2015.
Interview No 2, with a Dashnak MP, Stepanakert, Nagorno-Karabakh, 19 October, 2015.
Interview No 3, with an opposition MP, Stepanakert/Khankendy, de facto Nagorno-Karabakh, 19 October 2015.
Interview No 4, with a former high-ranked Karabakhi politician, a civil society leader in present, Stepanakert/Khankendy, de facto Nagorno-Karabakh, 20 October 2015.
Interview No 5, with a high-ranked Karabakhi diplomat, Stepanakert/Khankendy, de facto Nagorno-Karabakh, 21 October 2015.
Interview No 6, with a Karabakhi journalist, civil society leader and former politician, Yerevan, Armenia, 26 October 2015.
Interview No 7, with an independent Armenian journalist, Yerevan, Armenia, 26 October 2015.
Interview No 8, with a Karabakhi civil society leader, Stepanakert/Khankendy, de facto Nagorno-Karabakh, 27 October 2015.
Interview No 9, with an independent Karabakhi journalist, Yerevan, Armenia, 27 October 2015.
Interview No 10, with an Armenian political analyst, Yerevan, Armenia, 16 October 2015.
Interview No 11, with a former Abkhazian politician and high-ranked state servant, Sukhum(i), de facto Abkhazia, 31 August 2015.

Interview No 12, with an Abkhazian civil society leader, Sukhum(i), de facto Abkhazia, 1 September 2015.

Interview No 13, with an Abkhazian local politician, Sukhum(i), de facto Abkhazia, 3 August, 2015.

Interview No 14, with an Abkhazian journalist and former politician, Sukhum(i), de facto Abkhazia, 3 September 2015.

Interview No 15, with an Abkhazian civil society leader and member of the ethnic Armenian community, Sukhum(i), de facto Abkhazia, 4 September 2015.

Interview No 16, with an Abkhazian civil society leader and former politician, Sukhum(i), de facto Abkhazia, 7 September 2015.

Interview No 17, with an independent Abkhazian journalist, Sukhum(i), de facto Abkhazia, 20 October 2009.

Interview No 18, with a representative of the *Amtsakhara*, Sukhum(i), de facto Abkhazia, 7 September 2015.

Author Biography

Vincenc Kopeček holds Ph.D. in political and cultural geography and works as an Assistant Professor at the Department of Human Geography, University of Ostrava, Czechia. In his research, he focuses on ethnic conflicts, de facto states, political regimes and informal political institutions in the South Caucasus. He has published in Europe-Asia Studies, Problems of Post-Communism, the Annual of Language and Politics and Politics of Identity and Bulletin of Geography Socio-Economic Series and is an author of a Czech language monograph. He is a member of the Central Eurasian Studies Society and a member of the editorial board of the Czech Journal of International Relations.

Iran's Problems with Territorial Non-state Actors: A Case Study of Sistan and Balochistan

Robert Czulda

The main goal of this contribution is to analyse Iran's ongoing internal security problem that is related to a clearly defined geographical factor—the Sistan and Balochistan province, which has been affected by a violent conflict between the Balochi insurgents and Iranian security forces. This conflict generates not only instability for Iran but also forces political and military decision makers to devote significant resources to neutralizing the problem. The main research questions are as follows: (1) What is the scope (local, national or international) of the ongoing conflict in Sistan and Balochistan? and (2) Can it inspire insurgents in other parts of Iran to rise up against the central authorities? To answer these questions and to accomplish the main research objective, the paper is divided into several parts. The first part will be devoted to the role and influence of geographical factors on Iran's development, as well as on foreign and security policy from the historical perspective. This section is necessary to understand the genesis of the current problems with several centrifugal tendencies (including in Sistan and Balochistan) that the central authorities are experiencing. The second part of the paper will focus on current links between geography and Iran's security and defence, while the third will be devoted to the case study of Sistan and Balochistan, including both the local and wider impacts of the conflict.

This chapter is dedicated to the Charles University Research Development Schemes, programme PROGRES Q18—Social sciences: from multidisciplinary to interdisciplinary.

R. Czulda (✉)
University of Lodz, Lodz, Poland
e-mail: rczulda@uni.lodz.pl

© Springer International Publishing AG 2017
M. Riegl and B. Doboš (eds.), *Unrecognized States and Secession in the 21st Century*, DOI 10.1007/978-3-319-56913-0_8

1 Iran and Geography—A Historical Dimension

Iran is a good example of a state heavily affected by geographical factors—both positively and negatively, both currently and in the past. On the one hand, Iran's location at the crossroads of several important regions, such as Europe, the Caucasus, Central Asia and the Middle East (the Levant), is very beneficial.[1] Iran (known as Persia until 1935) borders politically, militarily and economically important areas, such as the Caspian Sea, the Persian Gulf and the Gulf of Oman. Such an excellent location, with a moderate and favourable climate when compared to many neighbouring states, for example Afghanistan, Iraq or Saudi Arabia, gave Persia an opportunity to develop and then expand its power in several directions. Cyrus II of Persia (who reigned between 559–530 BC) founded the great Achaemenid Empire, conquering parts of Southwest Asia, most of Central Asia, the Caucasus and Babylon. His son, Cambyses II (reigning between 530–522 BC) continued his legacy and conquered Egypt and Cyrenaica, while Darius I (reigning between 522–486 BC) transformed Persia. The empire was, by then, also controlling parts of the Balkans, most of the Black Sea's coastal regions, the Caucasus and other lands stretching as far as the Indus Valley to the east and Libya to the west—making it, undoubtedly, one of the most powerful and the greatest empires in history.

Iran's topography gave the country security. Surrounded on three sides by mountains and by water on the fourth, with a wasteland at its centre, Iran was extremely difficult to conquer, as it was relatively easy to block strategic points and stop the advancing troops, fatigued by crossing a difficult terrain. However, the geography also had (and still has) a negative impact on Iran's economic and social development, and thus on Iran's national power and security as well. Due to its variable climate, Iran's economic and social growth was diverse and unequal. A rugged and highly mountainous terrain resulted in the fact that Iran's shape was "a bowl, with a high outer rim surrounding an irregular and lower, but not low-lying, interior" (Fisher 1968, p. 5), making it unable to enjoy harmonious and equitable development. The centralization of a state authority over remote provinces was a challenging task, too—the landform had prevented the development of a road network in many areas of Persia. Thus, until the twentieth century, many populated areas tended to be relatively isolated from one another. This brought about, with consequences felt even now, the creation of many local communities and separatist movements that are intractable to the decisions made by the central government.

It would be a mistake to underestimate the impact of geography on Iran's political history. As Graham E. Fuller put it, "in Iran history itself is in part a product of classical geopolitical factors" (Fuller 1991, p. 2). No other statement about the issue could be more true. In subsequent centuries, the geographical

---

[1]Thanks to these trade routes, the city of Tabriz was established. It "has at several periods functioned as the capital of a wide territory, which has sometimes included not only Iran but even lands beyond" (Fisher 1968, p. 13).

location of Iran ceased to be a blessing and became a curse. Persia's proximity to the Arab world changed its destiny, which was ultimately to be conquered by the Arabs (633–654). It led to the end of the Sasanian Empire and the replacement of the Zoroastrian religion by Islam. As Marek Kęskrawiec put it, "the new faith arrived from the Arabian desert, on which earlier the Zoroastrian rulers of Persia didn't want to even look at. Their conquests always spared this bleak, half-dead land with poor, sparse and backward population" (Kęskrawiec 2010, p. 115). That same factor, i.e. geographical proximity to larger and much stronger entities, such as Russia, later led to a series of destructive wars (1722–1723, 1796, 1804–1813 and 1826–1828). These conflicts ultimately weakened Persia and resulted in it losing sovereignty over some of its territories, including the Caucasus. The same problem occurred in its relations with the powerful Ottoman Empire and the United Kingdom, which waged several wars against Persia that was weak, corrupted and mired in internal chaos (1722–1727, 1730–1735, 1743–1746, 1775–1776, 1821–1823 with the Ottoman Empire and 1856–1857 with the United Kingdom, respectively). In the end, Persia became so weak that these empires were able to meddle in Iran's internal affairs with impunity. Thus, a constant fear of foreign interference formed the basis of Iranian mentality and nationalism.

The significance of Iran's geography was confirmed further in later years and decades. As Lord Curzon, the British Secretary of State for Foreign Affairs, said in 1919, Persia should not be left without external control due to "her geographical position"—"we cannot permit the existence, close to the frontiers of our Indian Empire of a hotbed of misrule, enemy intrigue, financial chaos, and political disorder" (Katouzian 2006, p. 107). The same manner of thinking was prevalent in 1941, when Iran lost its neutrality due to its geostrategic significance—its proximity to Soviet oil fields in the Caucasus, and the need to open transit routes from the British Empire to the Soviet Union led to Iran being attacked by Soviet and British troops (Stewart 1988, p. 28). During the Cold War, Iran's geographical position placed the country between two spheres of influence of two superpowers: the United States and the Soviet Union. While for the former Iran was the best candidate to play the role of a "regional policeman", for the latter it was a doorway to the Persian Gulf and the Levant.

2 Current Impact of Geography on Iran

Iran, the 17th largest country in the world (1,684,000 km^2),[2] is still affected by geographical factors that remain ambiguous or even double-edged in nature—on the one hand, they strengthen its position in the region and the world, but on the other hand, they expose Iran to serious threats and challenges. From the former

---

[2]Its territory is larger than the combined territories of France, Germany, the Netherlands, Belgium, Spain and Portugal.

perspective, not only should its advantageous location be underlined (at the crossroad of important trade routes, Iran can serve, at least potentially, as a broker in many trade deals), but also its access to the most important natural resources in the world. In the past, those assets were Iran's curse (as in the previously mentioned aggression in 1941, and that of 1953, when the British and the Americans removed the democratically elected Prime Minister Mohammad Mosaddegh in order to keep their control over Iranian oil). Currently, it is estimated that Iran has the fourth largest reserves of oil (9%) and the second largest reserves of natural gas (16%) in the world.

Topography is still relevant, as a mountainous terrain would make any external aggression more difficult to carry out, despite modern technology. The small size of the Persian Gulf (just 21 nautical miles wide at its narrowest part) results in a small operational space, which would cause the US Navy problems in strategic manoeuvres. Aircraft carriers would have to operate from the Oman Gulf. More importantly, the northern parts of the Persian Gulf have many small rock islands, which would not only impede the movements of large units, but also make it possible for small Iranian units (including midget submarines) to hide. This would enable the Iranians to mitigate their technological weakness. The water's high salt content also hinders the ability to use passive sonar to locate other ships without being detected.

From a security perspective, however, geographical factors (mainly location) are simultaneously disadvantageous for this country. Due to its large size and mountainous nature, Iran is unable to create an integrated radar picture of its territory (hundreds of ground-based radar stations and surface-to-air missile batteries would be needed to achieve this). In addition to this, Iran is bordered by unstable neighbours, such as Afghanistan and Pakistan (borders that are 935 and 972 km long, respectively). Such a geographical proximity to these two countries, one a de facto failed state (Afghanistan) and one that is failing (Pakistan), causes many problems and threats. One such problem is illegal migration; it is estimated that Iran hosts up to three million Afghans, and the number is on the rise. Another is drug smuggling and, in this case, as Trita Parsi notes, "the geography is clearly working against" Iran (Al Arabiya News 2015). The country has been at the frontline of the open war against narcotics: it is estimated that Iran is responsible for 80% of the opium and 25% of the heroin intercepted worldwide.[3] Due to its geographical location, Iran is one of the most important routes for drug trafficking—from Afghanistan directly, or via Pakistan, drugs are being smuggled into Iran and then to the Persian Gulf states, Turkey or the Caucasus. This problem, however, exacts a high price from Iran—it is estimated that approximately 2.2 million Iranians are addicted to drugs.

Iran's geographical location intensifies the country's sense of alienation and, therefore, its sense of anxiety and insecurity. The Iranians, mainly Shia Muslims, are located within the Sunni-dominated world and perceived by the Sunni majority

---

[3]Data provided by the Iranian Embassy in Warsaw, Poland (December 2011).

as religious renegades. What is more, the majority of Iranians are not Arabs and they have a distant or even a hostile attitude towards Arabs (and vice versa). At the same time, Iran has a justified and understandable sense of being surrounded by allies of the United States—Turkey, Pakistan and Saudi Arabia. Iran shares its western borders with Turkey, which is a member of the hostile (from the Iranian point of view) NATO. The north is also challenging because of the unstable Kurdistan region, the Caucasus (Armenia, pro-Western and pro-Israeli Azerbaijan, pro-Western Georgia) and the Caspian Sea, which is affected by significant territorial claims. Iran's western neighbour is Iraq, ruled until 2003 by unpredictable Saddam Hussein who attacked Iran in 1980. The country continues to generate sectarian violence and instability, which might affect the Khuzestan province with its large Arab community. This area, which is "extremely low-lying and flat", plays a major role in Iran's security: it is the country's main granary and the location of its major oil reserves (Fisher 1968, p. 33).

One of the most important threats and challenges related to geographical factors faced by Iran is that of having many centrifugal tendencies, which can be identified as situations in which an element (or a number of elements) begins, for some reason, to see its position within the system as unfavourable. As a result, it decides to initiate an attempt to withdraw from the system, which might result in either a peaceful or violent struggle for more rights, recognition, autonomy or even full independence. As mentioned earlier, Iran has had many problems with separatist movements throughout its history. Military campaigns in the early 1920s, when several rebel groupings were crushed, include those in the forests of Gilan (northern Iran), where insurgents against the central government emerged; in Khorasan (near the border with Afghanistan), where self-styled autonomous authorities were established; in Kurdistan, where local tribes rebelled against the Qajar dynasty; or in Khuzestan, where an autonomous Arab emirate was dissolved. In the 1930s, the Iranian army was again involved in restoring order and in forcing several tribes to accept the central authorities. They fought with Qashqai Kurds, Bakhtiaris and Lurs. Carina Jahani explained that "in Iran during the Pahlavi era all attempts at strengthening local customs, traditions, and cultures were viewed as opposition to the nation and as threats to the territorial integrity of Iran" (Jahani 2014, p. 287).

Without any exaggeration, it can be said that the ethnic-based conflicts that have exploded periodically (including in the early 1980s, when Iran was immersed in chaos resulting from the Islamic Revolution) have been a major source of threat to Iran's internal stability and national cohesion. Conflicts in different parts of Iran with different scopes and scales have continued since then, including in Khuzestan (Arab separatism), Iranian Azerbaijan (Azeri separatism), Kurdistan and Khorasan (Kurdish separatism), Sistan and Balochistan (Balochi separatism) as well as in Golestan and South Khorasan (Turkmen separatism). Although the Iranian constitution of 1979 secures, according to Article 15, linguistic rights ("the use of regional and tribal languages in the press and mass media, as well as for teaching of their literature in schools, is allowed in addition to Persian"), there is a feeling of discrimination among Iranian ethnic subgroups. As Alam Saleh points out, "the ethnic regions are poorer, relatively speaking, than the Persian parts of Iran. Ethnic subgroups believe that the state intentionally deprives ethnic regions and keeps their occupants in poverty so as to aid its successful control of the deprived groups" (Saleh 2013, p. 144).This description applies to several regions of Iran but the most extreme example is currently Sistan and Balochistan in south-eastern Iran.

3 Sistan and Balochistan—The Local Dimension

An example of the impact of a non-state actor on Iran's current internal security and stability is an ongoing, low-intensity and yet violent conflict between Iranian security forces and several Sunni militant groups in the rugged Sistan and Balochistan province. The province is in south-eastern Iran, lying along the Gulf of Oman near the border with Pakistan and Afghanistan, with a total population of approximately three million people. It is mainly inhabited by the Baloch people (approximately 1.8 million people living in this region, and 2% of the country's population), who live in various countries, including Pakistan (approximately 7.3 million) and Afghanistan (350,000). The Baloch people might feel alienated in Iran for three reasons. First, while the majority of Iranians are Shia Muslims, the Baloch people are predominantly Sunnis (approximately 10 million Sunni Iranians live in the country). Second, they do not belong to the Persian ethnic group. Third, the Baloch people speak their own Baloch language. At least some members of the group feel that, in Iran, they are discriminated against in terms of religion, politics and the economy, which only makes their antipathy towards the central government in Tehran and their feeling of otherness stronger. Baloch nationalism is deeply rooted in the history of Balochistan—the people identify themselves "as part of an ancient tradition separate from that of Iran's Persian ethnicity" (Al Jazeera 2009)[4] and as a nation that is distinct from its neighbour's history.

The Baloch independent movement was ultimately crushed by the United Kingdom and Persia; therefore, in the late-19th century, the region was divided between the United Kingdom, Persia and Afghanistan. After these events had taken place, the Baloch people became "engulfed in the dark shadows of despair, frustration, and a growing sense of total defeat and helplessness" (Dashti 2012, p. 299). The final show of armed resistance was broken by the Iranian army in 1928, when Iran finally gained political control over the region. The last hopes of freedom were dashed in early 1929, when the Baloch chief Dust Mohammad Khan was arrested and executed. Since this moment, the Baloch people started to engage in clandestine political activities, challenging central authorities and hoping to achieve sovereignty. Violence returned to the region in 1979, when the fights between the Sunni Balochs and Shia Sistanis "escalated into gun battles […] that left nearly one hundred dead and injured […] Snipers targeted revolutionary militiamen and Pasdaran soldiers sent to protect the city while other Balochs attacked patrolling

---

[4]For further analysis, see Dashti (2012) and Wirsing (2008).

army tanks and armoured personnel carriers. Iran declared a state of emergency in the region and sent more troops into Balochistan before calming the situation" (Ward 2009, p. 233).

Beik Mohammadi calls Sistan and Balochistan "geographically isolated", as well as "one of the most deprived regions in Iran," for several reasons, including its significant distance from Tehran and other developed cities, the lack of precipitation, the desert climate, a severe shortage of crop land, soil salinity and the lack of drinking water (Mohammadi 2006, pp. 493, 501–503). Such an opinion is not exaggerated; while northern Sistan is a desert, southern Balochistan is a vast mountainous area. Both regions, considered by some as "the closest thing to Mars on Earth" (Zurutuza 2011), are characterized by very hot climate and semi-arid land with a low level of rainfall. The province is considered to be one of the less developed regions, with significant social and economic problems such as illiteracy, unemployment and poverty—70% of the local population is believed to live below the poverty line (its per capita income is the lowest in Iran) and 66% of the province's population has no access to drinking water.[5] Due to its distance from urban centres, the province does not have any significant industry,[6] while its geographical location has enabled the local population (then and now) to resist central authorities and remain more affiliated to Balochs in Pakistan and Afghanistan than to other Iranian citizens.

At the same time, the region of Sistan and Balochistan has been heavily affected by the problems generated by the neighbouring countries of Afghanistan and Pakistan, such as the above-mentioned organized crime and illegal migration. According to official Iranian statistics, almost 4000 Iranian security force members have died in the region over the past 34 years (Press TV 2015a). Due to these security implications, the economy suffers—a small, Iranian private initiative does not see a reason for investing in such an unstable, undeveloped and dangerous region. The government in Tehran blames the local population for this situation; authorities sometimes accuse it of drug dealing, kidnapping and clandestine cooperation with Pakistan, which has been battling its own Balochi separatist insurgency for decades. According to available statistics, Balochs have accounted for at least 20% of executions in Iran since 2006 (Farooq 2013). Those who are convicted are considered by Tehran as "bandits linked to groups hostile to the state" (Esfandiari 2013).

Local discontent is obvious. This was proven officially in 2015 when the region was visited by the Iranian President Hasan Rouhani, who addressed Balochi issues by making a statement that "all Iranians are equal" and "there is no such thing as a second-rate citizen" in Iran (IRNA 2014). Regarding religion, at least some Balochi people argue that not only do they not have Sunni mosques but also that "Sunni

---

[5]Such numbers were officially confirmed by Hamidreza Pashang, Member of the Iranian Parliament from the Sistan and Balochistan province (Payvand Iran News 2015).

[6]From the economic point of view, the most strategically important area is the Chabahar port, with its free-trade zone. India is interested in investing there, as it would give the country access to Afghanistan while bypassing Pakistan (Tasnim News Agency 2015a).

worshippers must listen to sermons by imams appointed by Shia rulers in faraway Tehran, a reminder that they cannot choose their own religious leaders or run their own religious school".[7]

The most recent phase of the armed struggle started in 2005, when the local insurgents joined the fight that had been carried on by their kin in Pakistan for many years. In that year, the motorcade of the then Iranian President, Mahmoud Ahmadinejad, was ambushed. A few months later, Balochi insurgents killed 21 civilians in a road blockade. In 2007, a car bomb killed 18 members of Iran's Islamic Revolutionary Guards Corps, while, in 2009, a suicide bomber killed 43 people, including General Noor Ali Shooshtari (Deputy Commander of the IRGC's ground forces) and several other high-ranking military officials, wounding 150 others. In response, Tehran initiated a broad operation and additional police and military units were deployed to the province. Intelligence officers started a hunting operation to find and apprehend the leaders of the resistance. Finally, in February 2010, the leader of the armed resistance, Abdolmalek Rigi, was captured. The then 27-year-old Balochi explained that the main reason behind the armed campaign was his personal traumatic experience, as well as a conviction of the discrimination and injustice perpetrated by the authorities. His main goal was, according to his own statement, to protect the local population from a "despotic religious government". Tehran has a different opinion; the insurgents are considered by Iran as either "terrorists" or "the armed bandits" (FARS News Agency 2015). Such clear-cut labels seem understandable, since local fighters attack Iranian border posts, trains, infrastructure, buildings or even Shia mosques, which are considered symbols of the Shia oppression and dominance (an explosion in 2009 killed 25 people, and a 2010 twin suicide-bomb attack left 27 dead).

During the first phase, the most important group fighting the central government was Jundallah ("*Soldiers of God*"), established in 2003. The majority of Jundallah's members were recruited from Sunni religious communities and from the tribe of Abdolmalek Rigi. Its declared goal was not the independence of a state, either secular or religious, but the fight for the rights of Sunnis in Iran (Hersh 2008). After the group was destroyed in 2011 by Iranian forces, its remaining members established Jaishul-Adl ("*Army of Justice*"), which has been continuing the armed tradition of its predecessors. According to the group's own statement, it is fighting for Baloch religious and national rights (Hussain 2013). The first attack by this group took place in October 2013, when 14 Iranian border guards were killed and six more injured. In the official statement, the group explained that "this successful operation is an answer to the violent crimes" of the IRGC in the "Islamic land of Syria and is also an answer for oppression and crimes the regime has committed against the oppressed Sunnis of Iran" (Karami 2013).

Several major attacks have occurred since then, including the murder of an Iranian prosecutor in November 2013 and an audacious attack in February 2014

---

[7]This is the opinion of Hassan Amini, the dissident Sunni cleric now living in Iran's Kurdistan (Bozorgmehr 2015).

when five Iranian border guards were kidnapped and taken into Pakistan (four were freed and one was killed) (Press TV 2015b). The best illustration of the scale of the problem, as well as of the determination and power of local armed cells, is an attack carried out by Jaishul-Adl—which remains lightly armed infantry without any heavy weaponry—in September 2014, on a border base. In response, Iran announced that it would deploy its military aircraft to Sistan and Balochistan in night operations to "counter outlaws and terrorist groups" (Tasnim News Agency 2014). The Iranian military also responded with a series of armed incursions into Pakistani territory, as well as with a reported shelling of Balochi villages in Pakistan.

4 Sistan and Balochistan—International and National Dimensions

As of late 2015, the situation in Sistan and Balochistan has seemed relatively stable. After a surge in the previous years, the current level of violence is moderately low.[8] However, this conflict should not be underestimated or neglected; the situation might change very soon. By destroying the Jundallah group, the central authorities in Tehran have neutralized only the most obvious and painful symptoms of social discontent, and not its root causes. Nor would the physical destruction of Jaishul-Adl change the situation—it would soon be replaced by a new group that, as many examples in history show, is likely to be even more violent and ruthless.[9]

The Iranian authorities have been failing to deliver what the people need. However, an imminent shift in Tehran's approach towards its minorities is unlikely. Some high hopes have been associated in this regard—with Hassan Rouhani, who was elected president in 2013. Rouhani, considered by the majority of Iranians and experts as a moderate conservative, enjoyed substantial support from minority groups, including those in Kurdistan and Sistan and Balochistan,[10] as he promised more political, social and economic justice, as well as the dominance of dialogue

---

[8]In October 2015, two people, a policeman and a civilian, were killed in a shooting attack by "armed bandits" (Press TV 2015c). In the same month, security forces freed two hostages abducted by "armed terrorists" (MEHR News Agency 2015). However, it is impossible, given the available information, to determine whether it was an incident related to Balochi separatists (political violence) or just organized crime. The last major clash related unambiguously to politics occurred in April 2015, when eight members of the Iranian security forces were killed in a cross-border ambush. The attack was subsequently claimed by Jaishul-Adl.

[9]Such a scenario occurred in December 2013, when two groups operating in Sistan and Balochistan, known as Harakat al-Ansar and Hizbul-Furqan, merged and jointly established the more radical Ansar al-Furqan ("*Partisans of the Criterion*"). This is an anti-governmental group with a basis in radical (Salafism) Sunni ideology with reported ties to the al-Nusra Front. Harakat al-Ansar was established in 2012 by former members of Jundallah.

[10]Rouhani won 73.3% of the votes in Sistan and Balochistan, and 70.8% in Kurdistan (Al Jazeera 2014).

over confrontation in solving internal issues. During his presidential campaign, he pledged to solve the issue of freedom to teach and publish in ethnic languages. He also stressed the need to improve regional cooperation (Maleki 2013). So far, he has failed to improve the situation.

A positive breakthrough is required because the conflict also has a wider dimension. It not only involves a relatively large number of security forces and financial resources, which cannot be used elsewhere, but also threatens economic projects, including the multinational (Iran–Pakistan–India, now Iran–Pakistan–China) LNG gas pipeline. Iran has already finished its part in the project but remains afraid of attacks on the network, similar to the massive campaign of attacks on a gas pipeline in Pakistan (mainly in Balochistan's districts such as Jaffarabad, Naseerabad, Sohbat Pur and Dera Bugti). Between 2010 and 2014, local insurgents in Pakistan have carried out more than 100 attacks on gas pipelines and approximately 45 attacks on the railway network (Dawn 2015). In January 2015, the Iranian Ministry of Interior announced it would not issue its permission for the construction of an oil pipeline in the province due to security concerns (Radio Zamaneh 2015). The same problem hampers the potential involvement of Iran in the multi-billion CPEC (*China-Pakistan Economic Corridor*) project.

The conflict has a heavy impact on the relations between Iran and Pakistan which, although both signed a security agreement in February 2013 on the joint prevention and combat of organized crime, as well as fighting terrorism, are already strained. Pakistan is a secular and Sunni-dominated state that is considered by Iran as an ally of not only the United States but also of Saudi Arabia, which is a more direct regional competitor. Incursions of Iranian security forces into Pakistani territory, as well as artillery shelling, have triggered protests among politicians in Islamabad, while Iran simultaneously accuses its eastern neighbour of failing to stop the Balochi insurgents from carrying out cross-border attacks on Iranian soil and of providing them with a safe haven (IHS Jane's 360, 2014). In March 2014, bilateral relations became strained once more when the Iranian authorities deported some Pakistani families from Sistan and Balochistan, despite the fact that they possessed all of the required travel documents.

Despite the low scale of current violence, the conflict poses a real threat to Iran's internal stability and security. A fear that unhappy Balochi people would become exposed to radical Sunni Islam and then join the Islamic State *en masse* is rejected by some as being highly unlikely.[11] Such a threat, however, cannot be fully discounted. Regarding Balochistan in Pakistan, Frederic Grare warns that "Islamization is currently experiencing a qualitative change […] Radicalization is on the rise and sectarian groups have stepped up their activities in the region. The number of sectarian killings has increased almost exponentially over the past few years in a province traditionally known for its deeply entrenched secularism"

---

[11]It is important to mention, however, that Ali Shamkhani (Secretary of the Supreme National Security Council, born in Ahvaz in a family of Iranian-Arab origins) confirmed that at least 22 Sunni Iranians were arrested while trying to cross the border and join the Islamic State. He also confirmed that its flag was raised in western Iran at least once (Bozorgmehr 2015).

(Grare 2013). Hoshang Noraiee adds that "religion in Balochistan has thus become stronger and more radicalized in the past 25 years" (Noraiee 2008: 361–362).

Of course, Balochi fighters cannot capture Tehran, as they have limited capabilities and interest in expanding their operations beyond their own region. Cooperation between Baloch fighters and, for instance, Kurdish fighters, is also unlikely. IHS Jane's names several reasons for this, including geographical separation and the fact that Iranian security forces could interrupt any transfer of militants or resources. It also points out that although the groups have some common interests, their strategic goals are different—insurgents in Sistan and Balochistan fight for greater freedom of the Balochi and Sunni people, while those in Kurdistan fight for Kurdish autonomy/independence. Fighters in Khuzestan are interested in the emancipation of the Arabs (IHS Jane's 360 2014).

What Balochi fighters can achieve is to trigger a lethal snowball, a chain of unintended consequences, which is dangerous for the Shia-dominated authorities. Other regions, where people do not perceive themselves to be minorities but as nations (Saleh 2013, pp. 149–150), might feel inspired and become willing to follow the Balochi example of engaging in more active armed resistance. This situation applies to Khuzestan, where Arab separatists (ASMLA—*Arab Struggle Movement for the Liberation of Ahvaz*, founded in 1999) are still active. It is sufficient to mention in this regard a 4-day riot in 2005 which left at least 50 dead; a series of bombings in Ahvaz in 2005 and 2006, leaving more than 25 dead and 220 injured; and several armed attacks in 2015, also on police checkpoints, in which a number of security forces members were killed.[12] Some unrest might also plague Iran's northern parts, where Azeri separatism remains a problem and the concept of the "Great Azerbaijan" is still alive in some circles. Such a scenario might seem unlikely for now but the same was said first of Yugoslavia and later of Libya and Syria—despite ethnic differences, the countries all looked stable and solid but, ultimately, they all ended up mired in the chaos of sectarian violence. Major socio-political changes, as shown by the example of the Arab Spring, sometimes begin with an inconspicuous spark.

The risk of armed struggle for more rights is more likely in countries such as Iran, where: (1) there are strong ethnic divisions; (2) democratic and peaceful ways of defusing tensions are undeveloped; (3) the system of government is centralized, with poor or even non-existent real power vested in the local authorities and (4) civic society is weak or non-existent. In such a situation, the government uses force not only because it is a traditional way of solving social unrest in the Middle East but also because authorities are uncertain about their own long-term legitimacy among the people. According to Alam Saleh, that is the case in Iran: "Tehran's reliance on the securitization of ethnic tensions, and its method of dealing with the

---

[12]Iran claims that there are no major security threats within the country. For example, in June 2015, the Iranian Intelligence Minister, Mahmoud Alavi, said that "despite the fact that security problems mainly occur along countries' borders and that there is much insecurity in Iran's neighbouring countries […] there is full and exemplary security across the country and along our borders" (Tasnim News Agency 2015b).

issue through coercive measures, has led to a greater intensification of societal insecurity and, as a result, to an undermining of Iran's territorial integrity" (Saleh 2013, p. 166). At the same time, the authorities are unable to offer the society a modern national identity, attractive not only to the Persians but also to other ethnic groups, which would be at the same time compatible with the foundations of the Islamic Republic and contrary to pre-1979 Iran.

A strong feeling of collective injustice might make such a scenario more plausible. An example of such negative feelings of the local community (or at least a part of it) is not only the insurgency in Sistan and Balochistan but also an open letter written by Sunni activists to the Iranian Supreme Leader Ali Khamenei in October 2012 (Mohammadi 2014). In June 2015, a similar opinion was expressed by Hamidreza Pashang, Iranian Member of Parliament for Sistan and Balochistan, who said openly that: "The underdevelopment of the province is due to discrimination, neglect and marginalization of the province" (Payvand Iran News 2015). As Alam Saleh explains, "the more the state ignores ethnic expectations, the more frustrated the deprived groups become" (Saleh 2013, p. 146). Iranian officials argue that such accusations are not true; for example, the Intelligence Minister Mahmoud Alavi rejected these claims by saying that "Iran has never discriminated between Shias and Sunnis" and that "we are all brothers and Iranians" (Tehran Times 2015). In fact, people do not have to be discriminated against, because even a perceived exclusion can create a sense of injustice and alienation. Such negative sentiments towards the central authorities and feelings of injustice might be intentionally fuelled by external groups who can exacerbate resentments. In the case of Iran, such foreign interference is even easier to achieve due to the transnational character of minority groups.[13] Rainer Bauböck agrees with such an opinion: "a national minority that is not granted an adequate form of self-government may welcome external forces for protection of their rights through bilateral agreement" (Bauböck 2007, p. 101).

5 Final Remarks

Iran argues that its problem with the minorities is not a real, socio-political problem but, rather it is artificial hype fuelled by external and hostile forces that wish to destabilize the internal situation. Tehran claims that those groups are "under the command and support of the spy agencies of the arrogant and colonial powers" (FARS News Agency 2015). The Basij group (Iran's popular militia) went even further and officially accused "America's bloody regime" of supporting terrorists who committed "the crime against humanity" by attacking civilian targets (FARS News Agency 2013). Although it seems highly plausible that external powers,

---

[13]This strategy was used by, for example, Iraq during the 1980s, when it supported the Balochi Autonomist Movement fighting the central authorities.

including the United States (at least during the administration of President George W. Bush) and Israel, but also Saudi Arabia, are or were involved in supporting these groups,[14] it would be a mistake to consider these local insurgents as lacking ideology, as mercenaries fighting only for financial gain. Even if they have been supported by external powers, there are some internal reasons for the social unrest and for the support these groups receive from local communities. The continuation of the Iranian government's current policy (i.e., the lack of economic and social reforms) might lead in the future to an alliance between secular and religious groups, but also to deeper cooperation between communities in Iran and their countrymen in the Kurdistan of Syria, Iraq and Turkey, as well as in the Balochistan in Pakistan. This would make the situation more difficult and complex.

Is there any solution to the problem presented here? If the failure to meet (either intentionally or not) the political, social, economic and cultural demands and aspirations of minorities is a simple path leading to armed protest and violence against the government and therefore to internal instability, as we can witness now, then perhaps the opposite policy is the best strategy for avoiding it. Unfortunately, there is no simple solution—any concessions in social or cultural liberties given to the minorities would be considered not as a gesture of conciliation and goodwill but as a sign of weakness that would encourage other ethnic groups (but also political, anti-governmental groups) to act. This is what happened to Shah Mohammad Reza Pahlavi, whose concessions were considered in the late 1970s as a sign of weakness and ultimately encouraged the people to overthrow him.

References

Al Arabiya News. (2015, May 21). *Inside Iran: Millions continue to battle drug addiction.* http://english.alarabiya.net/en/perspective/features/2015/05/21/Inside-Iran-Millions-continue-battle-drug-addiction.html. Accessed November 1, 2015.

Al Jazeera. (2009, October 19). *In depth: Sistan-Baluchestan.* http://www.aljazeera.com/focus/2009/10/20091018135453355456.html. Accessed November 1, 2015.

Bauböck, R. (2007). Political boundaries in a multilevel democracy. In S. Benhabib & I. Shapiro (Eds.), *Identities, affiliations and allegiances.* Cambridge: Cambridge University Press.

Bozorgmehr, N. (2015, January 1). Fears grow over Iran's disgruntled sunni muslims. *Financial Times.* http://www.ft.com/intl/cms/s/0/3a246c0a-86d7-11e4-8a51-00144feabdc0.html. Accessed November 1, 2015.

---

[14]In 2013, the "Foreign Policy" journal wrote that Israel's Mossad posed as US agents and tried to recruit Jundallah's members for a covert war against Iran (Perry 2012). This claim has never been officially either confirmed or denied. The same applies to Abdolmalek Rigi's public confession, aired by Iranian TV, in which he said that he had met Western agents who promised him weapons and assistance. Iran's Intelligence Minister, Heydar Moslehi, added that Rigi also met several European intelligence representatives during his stay in Afghanistan. Some Iranian media also accused Qatar and Saudi Arabia.

Dashti, N. (2012). *The Baloch and Balochistan: A historical account from the beginning to the fall of the Baloch State*. Bloomington: Trafford Publishing.
Dawn. (2015, February 3). Attack on gas pipeline. http://www.dawn.com/news/1161115. Accessed November 1, 2015.
Esfandiari, G. (2013, November 7). *Violence returns to Iran's Sistan-Baluchistan province*. Radio Free Europe—Radio Liberty. http://www.rferl.org/content/violence-sistan-baluchistan/25161200.html. Accessed November 1, 2015.
Farooq, U. (2013, December 5). The battle for Sistan-Baluchistan. *The Wall Street Journal—India*. http://blogs.wsj.com/indiarealtime/2013/12/05/the-battle-for-sistan-baluchistan. Accessed November 1, 2015.
FARS News Agency. (2013, October 27). *Shahadatemarzabananekeshvar be pasokhnakhahadmand* (Martyrs of our country border gourd will not go unanswered). http://farsnews.com/newstext.php?nn=13920805001013. Accessed November 1, 2015.
FARS News Agency. (2015, February 6). *Iran arrests 3 terrorists along southeastern borders*. http://english.farsnews.com/newstext.aspx?nn=13931117000511. Accessed November 1, 2015.
Fisher, W. B. (1968). *The Cambridge history of Iran. The land of Iran*. Cambridge: Cambridge University Press.
Fuller, G. E. (1991). *The "Center of the Universe": The geopolitics of Iran*. Boulder: Westview Press.
Grare, F. (April 11, 2013). *Balochistan: The state versus the nation*. Carnegie Endowment for International Peace. http://carnegieendowment.org/publications/?fa=51488. Accessed November 1, 2015.
Hersh, S. M. (2008, July 7). Preparing the battleground. *The New Yorker*. http://www.newyorker.com/magazine/2008/07/07/preparing-the-battlefield. Accessed November 1, 2015.
HIS Jane's 360. (2014, December 10). *Increasing frequency of Jaish al-Adl attacks in Iran raises risk of Iranian-Pakistani border incidents*. http://www.janes.com/article/46912/increasing-frequency-of-jaish-al-adl-attacks-in-iran-raises-risk-of-iranian-pakistani-border-incidents. Accessed November 1, 2015.
Hussain, S. (2013, December 11). The other Jihad. *The News International*. http://www.thenews.com.pk/Todays-News-9-219446-The-other-jihad. Accessed November 1, 2015.
IRNA. (2014, 15 April). *President Rouhani: There is no second-class citizen in Iran's system*. http://www.irna.ir/en/News/2672767/Politic/President_Rouhani__There_is_no_second-class_citizen_in_Iran%CB%88s_system. Accessed November 1, 2015.
Jahani, C. (2014). The Baluch as an ethnic group in the Persian Gulf Region. In L. G. Potter (Ed.), *The Persian Gulf in modern times. People, ports, and history*. New York: Palgrave Macmillan.
Karami, A. (October 27, 2013). Sunni group takes credit for attack that killed 14 Iranians. *Iran Pulse*. http://iranpulse.al-monitor.com/index.php/2013/10/3123/sunni-group-takes-credit-for-attack-that-killed-14-iranians. Accessed November 1, 2015.
Katouzian, H. (2006). *State and society in Iran. The eclipse of the Qajars and the emergence of the Pahlavis*. London: I.B. Tauris.
Kęskrawiec, M. (2010). *Czwarty pożar Teheranu*. WAB: Warszawa.
Maleki, A. (2013, July 14). *Rouhani Stresses Regionalism in Iranian foreign policy*. Baloch Media. http://www.balochonline.com/en/rouhani-stresses-regionalism-in-iranian-foreign-policy.html. Accessed November 2, 2015.
MEHR News Agency. (2015, October 19). *Intelligence forces save hostages in SE Iran*. http://en.mehrnews.com/news/111205/Intelligence-forces-save-hostages-in-SE-Iran. Accessed November 2, 2015.
Mohammadi, B. (2006). Population, poverty and environment in Sistan and Beluchestan. In A. Mohammad, A. Munir, & S. H. Siddiqui (Eds.), *Environment, agriculture and poverty in developing countries* (Vol. III). New Delhi: Concept Publishing Company.

Mohammadi, F. (2014, March 9). *Iranian Sunnis complain of discrimination*. Al Jazeera. http://www.aljazeera.com/indepth/features/2014/03/iranian-sunnis-complain-discrimination-2014397125688907.html. Accessed November 2, 2015.

Noraeiee, H. (2008). Change and continuity: Power and religion in Iranian Baluchistan. In: C. Jahani, A. Korn, & P. Titus (Ed.), The Baloch and others: Linguistic, historical and socio-political perspectives on pluralism in Baluchistan. Wiesbaden: Reichert.

Payvand Iran News. (2015, June 14). *Sistan Baluchistan MP lists distressing stats about province*. http://www.payvand.com/news/15/jun/1132.html. Accessed November 1, 2015.

Perry, M. (2012, January 13). False flag. *Foreign Policy*. http://foreignpolicy.com/2012/01/13/false-flag. Accessed November 1 2015.

Press TV. (2015a, April 11). *Iran seizes almost 500 tonnes of narcotics in one year: Police*. http://www.presstv.ir/Detail/2015/04/11/405765/490-tonnes-of-drugs-seized-in-Iran. Accessed November 1, 2015.

Press TV. (2015b, March 22). *Body of dead Iranian border guard returns home*. http://presstv.com/Detail/2015/03/22/402963/Iran-dead-guards-body-returns-home. Accessed November 1, 2015.

Press TV. (2015c, October 6). *Armed bandits shoot two dead in southeastern Iran*. http://www.presstv.ir/Detail/2015/10/06/432200/Iran-SistanandBaluchestan-Iranshahr-bandits-Ali-Moradi-Pakistan. Accessed November 2, 2015.

Radio Zamaneh. (2015, January 15). *Fears of bandits discourages pipeline construction*. http://archive.radiozamaneh.com/english/content/fears-bandits-discourages-pipeline-construction. Accessed November 1, 2015.

Saleh, A. (2013). *Ethnic identity and the state in Iran*. New York: Palgrave Macmillan.

Stewart, R. A. (1988). *Sunrise at Abadan. The British and Soviet invasion of Iran, 1941*. New York: Greenwood Publishing Group.

Tasnim News Agency. (2014, October 23). Iran's military to conduct nightly flights over southeast borders. http://www.tasnimnews.com/en/news/2014/10/23/537701/iran-apos-s-military-to-conduct-nightly-flights-over-southeast-borders. Accessed November 1, 2015.

Tasnim News Agency. (2015a, October 18). *Indian PM to consider Iran's Chabahar investment proposals soon: Minister*. http://www.tasnimnews.com/en/news/2015/10/18/892370/indian-pm-to-consider-iran-s-chabahar-investment-proposals-soon-minister. Accessed November 1, 2015.

Tasnim News Agency. (2015b, June 13). *Iranian borders fully secure: Intelligence minister*. http://www.tasnimnews.com/en/news/2015/06/13/768494/iranian-borders-fully-secure-intelligence-minister. Accessed November 1, 2015.

Tehran Times. (2015, October 21). *Iran has never discriminated between shias and sunnis*. http://www.tehrantimes.com/Index_view.asp?code=250251. Accessed November 2, 2015.

Ward, S. R. (2009). *Immortal. A military history of Iran and its armed forces*. Washington, DC: Georgetown University Press.

Wirsing, R. (2008). *Baloch nationalism and the geopolitics of energy resources: The changing context of separatism in Pakistan*. Carlisle: Strategic Studies Institute.

Zurutuza, K. (2011, May 16). Inside Iran's most secretive region. *The Diplomat*. http://thediplomat.com/2011/05/inside-irans-most-secretive-region. Accessed November 1, 2015.

Author Biography

Robert Czulda is a specialist in contemporary international security; defence and arms issues, Assistant Professor (Adjunct) at the Department of Theory of Foreign and Security Policy (Katedra Teorii Polityki Zagranicznej i Bezpieczeństwa) at the University of Lodz (Uniwersytet Łódzki), alumni of the Young Leaders Dialogue of the US Department of State (2010–2011), fellow of the Lanckoroński Foundation in London (2014), visiting lecturer at universities in Lithuania, Iran, Ireland, Turkey and Slovakia, as well as the National Cheng-chi University in Taipei, within the framework of the Taiwan Fellowship programme (2013). Works as a freelance journalist in Poland and Germany.

Kurdistan Region's Quest for Independent Statehood: Trapped in Internal and Geopolitical Rivalries

Martin Riegl, Bohumil Doboš, Jakub Landovský and Shmuel Bar

As the sectarian violence in Syria and Iraq continues, the entire Sykes-Picot Agreement architecture is on its 100-year anniversary about to crumble. This event manifests an important geopolitical phenomenon. It is self-evident that what has been lost is not only governmental but more importantly territorial legitimacy (Clapham 2005) of both central governments in Baghdad and Damascus, as perceived by the citizens of both countries. While the state borders drawn a century ago are becoming blurred due to internal conflicts and activities of armed and aggressive non-state territorial actors like Daesh, new internal boundaries still uncharted on the political map of Iraq are consolidating in practice.

The aim of this text is not to deal with the factors leading to disintegration of the present-day Syria or Iraq, but to analyze the impact of geopolitical interests of key players on the future status of the Kurdistan Region (KR). The text thus analyzes a recent discussion on the reappraisal of relations between the central government in Baghdad and the Kurdistan Regional Government (KRG), which has been representing a de facto state in making since 1991, and reflects the role of an internal as well as geopolitical situation in the region on the future status of the KR. The authors argue that, although the KR meets the requirements for the remedial theory of secession and fulfills the criteria of effective statehood (based on the Montevideo Convention on the Rights and Duties of States), the final decision on the status of KR will be determined by broader interests of geopolitical actors (Turkey, Iran,

---

This chapter is dedicated to the Charles University Research Development Schemes, program PROGRES Q18—Social sciences: from multidisciplinary to interdisciplinary.

M. Riegl · B. Doboš (✉) · J. Landovský
Faculty of Social Sciences, Institute of Political Studies,
Charles University, Prague, Czech Republic
e-mail: bohumil.dobos@gmail.com

S. Bar
Institute of Policy and Strategy, Herzliya, Israel

Israel, USA, EU and Russia). The theoretical framework used to analyze the case of contemporary KR follows the contribution presented by two of the authors of this study earlier in the book. We explain the final status settlement by the (super) powers' involvement in the conflict. The analysis is thus rooted in the previously presented "modified (super)power rule" theoretical framework.

While the attitude and actions of the two neighboring states of Turkey and Iran will be decisive for maintaining KR's de facto independence and economic survival, the US position coordinated with the EU will determine KR's government ability to seek external legitimacy (Pegg and Kolstø 2014). Washington and Brussels are decisive for collective recognition as analyzed by Rich (1993) in case of the dissolution of SFRY and USSR. In addition, there is Russia and Israel with their own geopolitical interests in the region, which in the latter case side with KR's aspirations. All three regional powers' positions toward KR's independence claim will reflect their concerns about internal and external threats stemming from the internal situation (Kurdish minorities on their sovereign territory) and external threats stemming from the long-term animosities among Turkey, Iran, Israel but also Iraq.

KR's independence outlook is even further complicated by its internal situation. First of all, Erbil and Sulaymaniyah provinces follow different geopolitical orientations, and second, the parent state enjoys widespread international support which significantly reduces the KR's prospects for independence. Moreover, key external players simultaneously provide active support both to the de facto state as well as to the central government. This creates unique geopolitical conditions for the prospective secession of the KR. To paraphrase R. Rich's and M. Fabry's conclusion, the current recognition regime after the dissolution of SFRY, USSR and the secession of Kosovo is less coherent and predictable as it is neither based on criteria of effectiveness nor on moral-legal entitlement to independent statehood. This observation is particularly apposite in the case of KR.

1 Post-cold War Geopolitics

The post-Cold War international developments have challenged some of the basic principles on which the bipolar geopolitical order functioned. Not only have the power shifts caused tectonic movements in the distribution of global power, but there has also been an increasingly important systemic change taking place. This change reflects the issues that are inherent to the frozen political map of the world with borders in many parts of the world drawn imprecisely or arbitrarily. As the new entities try to escape the trap of undesired statehood and establish their own political entity, they remain trapped in the "middle" and are, consequently, challenging the binary nature of modern geopolitics (state/no state) and the institution of state itself (Walter et al. 2014, 18). Despite the fact that many authors label these units illegal or pathological (Berg and Kuusk 2010; Pegg and Kolstø 2014; McConnell 2009), they often provide a more effective political organization than their recognized parent states are able to provide.[1] The research on the secessionist attempts has different priorities, focusing on the character of parent, patron states and their position in an international system (Geldenhuys 2009); the internal and external legitimacy of unrecognized entities (Pegg and Kolstø 2014); the legitimization strategy of de facto states' elites (Caspersen 2011; Lynch 2004); legality, and legitimacy of the attempts to fragment political map by the bids for independence (Walter et al. 2014); the international community approach (Lynch 2004), etc. While successful attempts at unilateral secession are far outnumbered by unsuccessful ones (Crawford 2006), even forcefully and brutally suppressed attempts at secession did not discourage break-away regions to give up their quests for sovereign statehood. For example, the case of Biafra did not prevent the secession of Bangladesh (Fabry 2010). We can thus identify the cases ranging from full international recognition (Bangladesh, Eritrea, South Sudan), through the cases like the delayed successful secession from colonial power (Equatorial Guinea), secessionist entities that have received wide international recognition, their self-determination claims have been widely accepted as legitimate but are still de facto and de iure parts of their parent states (Palestine or the Western Sahara), or entities that have obtained a de facto independence and varying degrees of international recognition (Kosovo, Somaliland, or Abkhazia), to entities that have been re-incorporated into their parent states forcefully (Katanga, Biafra, or Cabinda).

Obviously, the dozens of the post-1945 secessionist attempts led to extremely variable outcomes that cannot be explained by legality, moral justification (normative stand), nor by coherent application of the regulative rules for international recognition. It is clear that the outcome of secession is determined by external politics (Horowitz 2000). Neither meeting the criteria of effectiveness nor fulfilling normative criteria guarantees that an entity will gain collective recognition. As pointed out by Walter von Ungern-Sternberg and Abushov (2014), the international community has failed to define a clear set of recognition criteria (both normative and procedural) in case of the successful secession of Bangladesh and Kosovo; however, this does not mean that the secession outcome is not a completely random process.

As noted in the contribution dedicated to the conceptualization of the (super) power rule, the outcome of the secession/recognition process is largely determined by the (super)power intervention (Sterio 2013). As previously remarked, effective (super)power support is a sufficient condition for the de facto outcome of the secessionist attempt, while the support and lack of active opposition is a necessary condition for de iure recognition of the entity. To evaluate the scenarios of KR's future status, we must take into consideration these factors.

Secession will not be successful if the parent state enjoys strong and effective support from the patron state that is able to project its power effectively enough to deny the secessionist entity a de facto independence or collective recognition by the international community. The theoretical framework applied is based on an

---

[1] See for example Kopeček et al. (2016).

understanding that chances of secessionist entities to gain external legitimacy are de facto decided by the role of (super)power(s) in the region, and their international acceptance and recognition is based both on the role of the patron state and the normative criteria. In the following analysis, we will first focus on five sectors that are usually connected to the issue of the outcome of secession—analysis of the internal situation in the parent state; geopolitical position of the parent state; origins and legitimacy of secessionist claims; analysis of the parent state's reaction to the claims; and international approach toward the secession. Consequently, we will focus on the issue of (super)power support as a key variable in the secession outcome.

2 Quest for Independence Within an Artificial Geopolitical Construct

The geopolitical order established by the Sykes-Picot Agreement (officially the Asia Minor Agreement) between the governments of the United Kingdom and France created, among others, to a large extent artificial states of Iraq and Syria by establishing spheres of influence in the Middle East. This geopolitical order has been waning in the Middle East of today.[2] Lack of territorial legitimacy of Iraqi state has already been confirmed by King Fasail I, according to whom Iraq as a territorial unit made no sense.[3] Therefore, one might argue that the fragility of present-day Iraq is rooted in the very artificiality of the geopolitical order established in the second decade of 20th century, and the fall of Saddam Hussein's regime has just unraveled its virtually non-existing territorial but also governmental legitimacy, having been further deepened by the oppressive nature of Hussein's regime. *"George W. Bush administration assumption that toppling Saddam would lead to stability rather than chaos when the U.S. military 'shocked and awed' its way to Baghdad* (Khedery 2015)" was proven wrong.

Despite the enormous resources which the United States and the West in general invested in the state-building and nation-building process in Iraq, the continuing sectarian violence and the rise of the violent non-state territorial actor Daesh

---

[2]As noted by Ali Khedery, *"(s)ince the founding of modern Iraq in 1920, the country has rarely witnessed extended peace and stability ... After the Allied victory in World War I and the collapse of the Ottoman Empire, however, the Treaty of Sèvres created new and artificial borders to divide the spoils. France assumed a mandate over the Levant, and the British were determined to carve out a sphere of influence in oil-rich Mesopotamia, installing a descendant of the Prophet Muhammad, Faisal bin al-Hussein, as Iraq's first monarch in 1921* (Khedery 2015)."

[3]*"With my heart filled with sadness, I have to say that it is my belief that there is no Iraqi people inside Iraq. There are only diverse groups with no national sentiments. They are filled with superstitious and false religious traditions with no common grounds between them. They easily accept rumours and are prone to chaos, prepared always to revolt against any government* (Khedery 2015)."

unravel the inability of the central government to project state authority throughout its territory. According to the Fragile States Index, Iraq ranks 12th among the least stable countries (the overall score is 114.5 out of 120) (Failed State Index 2015). The situation on the ground is further exacerbated by the economic conditions. On February 11th PM Haider al-Abadi announced that, *"Iraqi oil revenues have fallen to just 15% of the revenues we had two years ago. This is a major decline and we therefore have great difficulties* (France24 2016)."

Central government's inability to maintain its territorial integrity and fulfill basic state functions can serve as a justification for KR to secede under the conditions of the volatility of the parent state. The KRG[4] has managed to build relatively strong institutions which are far from perfect, but still in a sharp contrast to the collapse of the Iraqi forces which weakened Baghdad's position toward KRG. Considering the costs of the US involvement in Iraq which between 2003 and 2012 climbed to 1.7 trillion USD (Trotta 2013) and the fear of destabilization, the crucial question is whether the administration in Washington will *"accept the fractious reality on the ground, abandon its fixation with artificial borders, and start allowing the various parts of Iraq and Syria to embark on the journey to self-determination* (Khedery 2015)." Such a decision would presuppose a dramatic change in the US foreign policy toward the central government in Baghdad, which has been based on a strong adherence to Iraqi territorial integrity since 2003.

3 Uneasy Relations and Case for Remedial Secession

The history of violent cohabitation of the Kurds with the other nations in Iraq offers many just causes for remedial secession. The non-ratified Treaty of Sèvres which envisaged a local and territorially based autonomy for the Kurdish people living east of the Euphrates (Treaty of Sèvres 1924, art. 62) and even future independence (Treaty of Sèvres 1924, art. 64), depending on the decision of the Council of League of Nations, was for decades the last Kurdish chance for real autonomy. However, the subsequent Treaty of Lausanne signed in 1923 did not contain any provisions on the autonomy for the Kurds.

Nevertheless, the Kurds have never given up their prospect for self-determination. Already in 1931, *"it became known that the Anglo-Iraqi treaty contained no minority guarantees, and Kurdish revolt broke out (...)* (Sluglett 2011, 539–540)." Cohabitation of the Kurds with other groups within a single state was marked by other eruptions of violence which occurred between 1961 and 1975, and throughout the 1980s. Under various regimes in Baghdad, the Kurds experienced forced removals, destruction of villages, harsh oppression, mass deportations and

---

[4]*"The Kurdistan Regional Government refers to the Kurdish self-government that has administered the Kurdish region in northern Iraq since 1992 ... and consists of the three provinces of Irbil, Sulaymaniyah, and Dohuk* (Gunter 2014, 167)."

killings, and chemical attacks. The violence against the Kurds culminated in an infamous al-Anfal campaign, which resulted in the death of 6000 civilians (Sluglett 2011, 539–540). Referring to the atrocities committed during the Anfal campaign is an integral part of the President M. Barzani's narrative (Presidency KRD) when it comes to the right of Kurdish people to decide their fate in a referendum. However, the game changer for the de facto independence of KR was the spontaneous uprising in the Kurdish area following the defeat of the Iraqi ground forces in 1991, which resulted in a displacement of 1.5 million Kurdish refugees (Sluglett 2011, 540–541). "The side" effect of the UNSC Resolution 688 adopted on April 5, 1991, in which UN SC confirmed its respect to territorial integrity and sovereignty of the parent state, was the establishment of the de facto independent KR comprising Dohuk, Erbil and Sulaymaniyah provinces through the declaration of no-fly zone over northern Iraq enforced by the US-led coalition. The adoption of the above-mentioned Resolution 688 was clearly motivated by humanitarian concerns.[5] The al-Anfal campaign, which has caused the deaths of tens of thousands Kurds, would be by itself a just cause for remedial secession. The Kurdish perception of the intercommunal relations is best described by M. Barzani's words: *"The Shia fear past repression, the Sunnis fear future repression, and we Kurds fear both* (Khedery 2015)."

Following decades of discussions on the normative criteria for secession, a set of normative criteria that justifies secessionist attempts in general was adopted in the academia. D. Geldenhuys provides a rather exhaustive list of just causes for secession in his analysis of contested states, incorporating among others genocide, cultural extinction, oppression, or deliberate and systematic discrimination (Geldenhuys 2009, 40–42). The list of the just causes offers a clear picture that KR might be considered a model case for remedial secession due to the history of past injustices. From the point of normative aspects of secession, it is obvious that KR meets conditions, which are generally accepted as a just cause for secession (history of oppression, democratic governance, the right to external self-determination as a last resort option, inability of the central government to protect security interests of the region, etc.). Furthermore, the KR has been able to build, although far from perfect, a viable democratic political system, economy, and security apparatus, which stands in a sharp contrast to the inability of the central government to provide its citizens with basic security. This fact by itself can be used as a legitimate reason for secession. However, as D. Geldenhuys noted, there is no guarantee that the

---

[5]*"Gravely concerned by the repression of the Iraqi civilian population in many parts of Iraq, including most recently in Kurdish-populated, which led to a massive flow of refugees towards and across international frontiers and to cross-border incursions which threaten international peace and security in the region .... Condemns the repression of the Iraqi civilian population in many parts of Iraq, including most recently in Kurdish-populated areas, the consequences of which threaten international peace and security in the region. Requests the Security-General to pursue his humanitarian efforts in Iraq and to report forthwith, if appropriate on the basis of a further mission to the region, on the plight of the civilian Iraqi population, and in particular to the Kurdish population, suffering from the repression in all its forms inflicted by the Iraqi authorities* (UN 1991)."

international community will follow the rules, however vague they might be (Geldenhuys 2009, 42). The KR's claims might also be challenged by pointing at the forceful removal of the regime that was responsible for the atrocities committed in the past and the strong support of the international community for the territorial integrity of the fragile central government, motivated by the fear of intermittent fragmentation in the region. The factors discussed in the theoretical section are presented in Table 1.

4 KR—Truly Effective De Facto State?

The KR region is often portrayed as an island of stability in the region, but it also experienced a bloody conflict between the Kurdistan Democratic Party (KDP) and Patriotic Union of Kurdistan (PUK), which broke out in 1994. Since then, the KR region has been divided by internal borders and checkpoints.[6] Nonetheless, the state institutions are centralized and, most importantly, the unity of institutions is reflected in the now-unified Peshmerga forces. The main pillar of KR's internal stability dates back to 1998 US-negotiated peace treaty, which ended the conflict between feuding KDP and PUK parties. In the agreement, M. Barzani (Kurdistan Democratic Party) and J. Talabani (Patriotic Union of Kurdistan) agreed to share power and revenues, to deny the territorial basis in northern Iraq to PKK and access to the Iraqi army, and to divide KR into two areas of control. At the same time, the US pledged to protect the Kurdish people from an Iraqi intervention by force. In the same year, the US adopted Iraq Liberation Act of 1998 (US Congress 1998) which explicitly denied legitimacy of S. Hussein's regime and provided a legal framework for assistance to democratic movements, including the KDP and PUK (US Congress 1998). The Washington agreement allowed KR to consolidate their de facto state which cooperated in a very significant manner with the US-led coalition during the 2003 invasion of Iraq, but also bolstered internal lines of division between Erbil and Sulaymaniyah. An important milestone for KR's politics was a power sharing agreement in 2007 (Cordesman and Khazai 2014). Under the new government and 2009 constitution for the KR,[7] M. Barzani is the President (directly elected in 2009) and Q. Talabani, the son of the former president of Iraq J. Talabani, is the vice prime minister.

This territorial division[8] based on clan cleavage is a direct threat to the internal stability, especially in the conditions of the postponed direct presidential elections accompanied by violent protests in the PUK-controlled areas, following the expiration of Barzani's presidential term and of the planned referendum on the future

---

[6]For the issue of division of Kurdish population and political power, see Thorton (2015).

[7]When the Kurdish parliament unilaterally approved a new constitution for the KRG in June 2009, Baghdad denounced the move as tantamount to secession (Gunter 2014, p. 167).

[8]KR comprises three governorates of Dohuk, Erbil, and Sulaymaniyah.

Table 1 Kurdistan and secession

Name	Parent state	Effectiveness of secessionist entity	Effectiveness of parent state	Normative claims	Support for secession	Support for parent state
Kurdistan region	Iraq	Stable	Collapsed	Historical, effectiveness, violent oppression, self-determination	Israel	Wide international support

status of KR. PUK has been voicing its strong criticism about both issues, and the situation has been further exacerbated by the deteriorating economic situation due to collapse of the crude oil price, which ended the era of prosperity. The economic conditions severely threaten the effectiveness of the de facto state institutions, which face the Daesh threat along the 1000-km-long frontline. The KRG is not only virtually independent in the sphere of politics and economics, but even conducts its independent foreign policy (including visa regime). KRG has so far opened 13 delegations worldwide (including the USA, EU, Iran) and hosts dozens international offices (including USA, EU, Russia, Turkey) (KRG 2016a, b).

The ties between Baghdad and Erbil were further loosened by the decision of the central government to cut the annual financial allocations approved under the constitution of 2014, according to which the Kurds were supposed to receive 17%[9] of the Iraqi national budget (Gunter 2014, 169). De facto division might be further strengthened by the eventual collapse of the Mosul Dam, which would completely change the demography of Iraq.

Concerning the area of security, the Peshmerga troops are officially a part of Iraqi security forces, but in fact guarantee the de facto independence of the KR. The fact that cannot be ignored is that "the boundary" between the central government and the KR is much shorter than "the boundary" between Da´esh and the KR. As of the beginning of the year 2016, delayed salary payments (3–4-month delays) to Peshmerga forces have seriously threatened the viability of the force. Yet another danger is the political tension over a planned referendum.[10] President Barzani's repeated calls for referendum on independence [first announced in July 2014 (Nashashibi 2016)] are in PUK leaders' eyes Barzani's strategy to distract attention from the political and economic problems. Internal cleavages might burst out once

---

[9]According to the KRG, since 2005 KR has never received the full 17% of its share of the federal budget; in fact, the funds received have never exceeded 11.4%. In addition to that, the federal government has cut the KRG's share of the federal budget since February 2014. According to an agreement signed between Erbil and Baghdad on December 2, 2014, in addition to the budget of the Kurdistan Region, Baghdad should send 100 billion Iraqi dinars from the sovereign expenditures to the Peshmerga every month, but that agreement has never been implemented (KRG 2016c).

[10]In January 2005, unofficial referendum booths were set up alongside the regular polling stations for the Iraqi elections. Out of the two million Kurds who voted in the unofficial referendum, 90% chose independence (Sluglett 2011, p. 541).

the common enemy, Daesh, has been defeated. PUK, additionally, plays an important role in the central government as the current president of Iraq Fuad Masum was the first prime minister of the KRG and currently is the second Kurdish president of Iraq succeeding Jalal Talabani. Both Talabani and Masum belonged to the founding fathers of PUK in 1975 and still maintain close contacts.

While the KR proves its effectiveness, a potential secession of the oil-rich region, which produces a disproportionate share of economic resources, could undermine and weaken the parent state's economy. The issue of conditions that may justify not allowing a secession has been raised during the 1980s discussion between Beran (1984) and Birch (1984) on a normative theory of secession. The economic argument is, however, being challenged by the central government's decision to freeze KR's share of the national budget in 2014.

5 KR Amidst Geopolitical Rivalries

Independence has been the ultimate goal of the Iraqi Kurds for decades. Yet this ambition is on a collision course with the concerns of the neighboring states with regard to the implications of the independent KR for their own territorial integrity. Although the KR has proved its effectiveness since 1991, its economic survival and internal stability rest in the hands of external geopolitical agents. Not only due to the KRG's profilation as a reliable ally of the West, the stance of the USA and the EU is about to determine a future de iure status of the KR. Both are the only geopolitical agents able to secure collective recognition (conditional or not) within the international community, as demonstrated during the dissolution of USSR and SFRY and in case of the secession of Kosovo. Besides the importance of the USA and the EU for the de iure status of KR, both players do provide a (limited) military support (small arms, ammunition, training within the Kurdistan Training Coordination Centre) to the KRG. The USA practically enabled establishment of the de facto independent KR through the imposition of no-fly zone over northern Iraq. However, the administration in Washington faces a strategic dilemma which has its roots in the 2003 invasion of Iraq. Even when leaving aside the resources invested in the recovery of Iraq, both G.W. Bush and B. Obama expressed a strong adherence to the concept of the territorial integrity of Iraq. In this regard, the timeframe is also important, and the Kurds are aware that the current US administration will do nothing that may irritate Turkish R. Erdogan at this point, but they are preparing the stage for the next administration.

At the same time, the KRG shows a strong pro-western orientation and the Peshmerga force represents the most formidable troops on the ground fighting Daesh. A unilateral declaration of independence of KR may plunge the whole region into spiral of chaos. Moreover, uncoordinated and one-sided international recognition of KR can alienate Turkey—a US crucial regional ally—and trigger irredentist tendencies.

Another external player, which is geographically present in the region, is Israel, the only country in the region openly supporting KR's independence quest. Their close political and economic relations date back to the 1960s. The limits of an open cooperation lie in the Kurdish people's hostility toward Israel, but still the KDP under M. Barzani has continued to maintain silent communication with Jerusalem (Berman 2016, 5). *"The Israeli strategic interests lie in expectation that Iraqi Kurdistan, if and when it gains full independence, will be a reliable ally, a Western-oriented democratic state with common enemies (Berman 2016, 9)."* The government in Tel Aviv has so far been the only one which declares its open support to the Kurdish claim for independent statehood and its right to external self-determination.[11] In this regard, it is important to point at a policy called "the Periphery Strategy" that was based on the assumption that the neighboring Arab countries were not ripe for peace, so Israel reached out to minorities and periphery Middle Eastern countries. This was the basis of Israel's outreach to the Kurds, Ethiopia, South Sudan, Oman, Morocco, etc. Today, this policy is being revived and the Kurds are a critical part of it (Bengio 2016).

The Syrian Kurds already announced their plan to open the foreign office in the Russian Federation with the consent of the Kremlin (Solomon 2016). Although Russia by itself cannot guarantee collective recognition as the cases of Abkhazia and South Ossetia showed, *"unification of parts of Syrian Kurdistan with Russian backing would help Iraqi Kurdistan achieve independence and allow Russia to weaken a position of Ankara in the region* (Bar 2016)." The general Moscow approach toward the de facto states shows strong reluctance to the recognition of such entities, the only examples of granting recognition being Abkhazia and South Ossetia. On the other hand, the Kremlin refused to recognize even the Russia-backed break-away regions of Transnistria or Nagorno-Karabakh.[12]

Important regional players—Turkey and Iran—are generally hostile to KR's independence despite the strong mutual economic ties and other forms of cooperation. Due to their geographic proximity, they have not only broader geopolitical interests in the region and specifically in influencing the Baghdad government, but also particular interests in Erbil and Sulaymaniyah provinces. Both neighboring countries are vital for economic viability but also for internal stability of the KR. Turkey has been important for the KR as the transit country for its oil exports, which are crucial for the economic viability of the land-locked KR. The cooperation has already materialized in building a pipeline between the two entities, which is equally important to Turkey, being completely dependent on the import of strategic resources. Furthermore, Turkey is the KR's largest trading partner, including the construction and energy sector (Fidan 2015).

Ankara's security interests in the region stem from the long-term PKK's military presence on the KR's territory, from which it also launches attacks on Turkey. To

---

[11]Prime Minister Benjamin Netanjahu followed with the clearest declaration of Israeli support, telling a Tel Aviv conference that Israel should "support the Kurdish aspiration for independence (Berman 2016, p. 9)."

[12]As noted by M. Fabry, *"Russia's recognition of Abkhazia and South Ossetia in the aftermath of Western recognition of Kosovo demonstrates that even precedent-sensitive foreign policy justifications may not achieve their desired effect if they are not accepted by major powers* (Fabry 2010, p. 224)."

counter PKK's activities, the Turkish forces had by the end of 2015 entered KR's territory without the permission of the Shiite-led central government in Baghdad backed by Iran. Although Ankara maintains strong and cooperative relations with KRG, it is unlikely to extend them to the international recognition of the KR, which might be perceived as a potential de-stabilizing and threatening irredentist factor for its own population and territorial integrity. The Justice and Development Party (AKP) in Turkey has adopted a strategy based on the integration of the KR into the Turkish economy in order to take advantage of its huge oil and gas resources and thus reduce Turkey's dependence on Russian supplies. This might have been misunderstood by President Barzani during his visit to Turkey on December 9, 2015, when he met Turkey's president and prime minister and KR's "national" flag was used by the flag protocol (KRP 2015). Such a step can be explained not only as a diplomatic courtesy, but also as a signal or show of force toward the Shiite-dominated government in Baghdad that enjoys a wide Russian support.

Iran's footprints in the region date back to 1988 when Teheran played a major role in saving the lives of thousands of people who had fled the gas attacks (Berman 2016, 4). Moreover, Iran was involved in the internal conflict within the KR in the 1990s when it supported the PUK party against its rival the KDP (Berman 2016, 4). Iran's role in the KR is not motivated solely by its economic interests[13] (Turkey still holds the upper hand in the economic sector of the KR), but it is true that the Iranian export dominates, mostly due to its geographic position, the Sulaymaniyah Province which features a diverse "geopolitical" orientation within the KR. It is also the only country which opened a delegation in Sulaymaniyah (KRG 2016a). Iran exerts its political influence within the KR through the PUK party and new anti-corruption party Gorran (Change)[14], which has split from the PUK party. However, the political influence of Gorran has been significantly reduced. President Barzani oscillates between the strategic necessity to improve relations with Iran and its interference in internal affairs of the KR. On the other side, the long-term interest of Iran has been to downgrade the role of Turkey and the West in the region. As Gunter argues, *"Premature Kurdish independence that would be seen as destroying Iraq would be opposed not only by the United States but also by all the KRG's regional neighbours (*Gunter 2014, 171)." The historical experience with secessionist claims of the Kurds within their own territory and declaration of independence of the Republic of Mahabad (a short-lived Kurdish state backed up by the USSR) inevitably play an important role in Teheran's strategic calculations. KR's independence might trigger secessionist trends among Iran's Kurds, whose region is contiguous to Iraqi Kurdistan, leading possibly to the conflicts between Turkey and

---

[13]Trade between Iran and the Kurdistan Region Explorer increased from bilateral trade worth 100 million USD in 2000, to 4 billion USD annually on the eve of the IS invasion in 2014 (Berman 2016, p. 5).

[14]PUK leaders, including the former Iraqi President Jalal Talabani, visit Iran regularly and maintain close ties with Iranian officials. The growing ties with Gorran have reinforced Iran's political influence (Berman 2016, p. 5).

Iran. Table 2 covers the interests of different external actors and Table 3 their position toward different Iraqi actors.[15]

Table 2 Strategic position of external geopolitical agents

Name	Strategic necessity	Preferred status quo	Alliance/links
USA	Maintain strategic allies/not to alienate Turkey	Territorial integrity of Iraq/de facto independence of KR	Iraq/KR
EU	Maintain strategic allies/prevent chaos in the region	Territorial integrity of Iraq	Iraq/KR
Turkey	To combat PKK/contain the influence of Iran and Russia	Territorial integrity of Iraq/de facto independence of KR	KR (Erbil)
Iran	To back the central government/diminish the influence of the West, Turkey and Israel	Territorial integrity of Iraq	Iraq/KR (Sulaymaniyah)
Israel	To contain Iran/gain strategic ally	Self-determination of KR	KR (Erbil)
Russia	To diminish the influence of the West and Turkey	Territorial integrity of Iraq	No strong ties

Table 3 External geopolitical players' approach toward the central and regional government

Name	Iraq—central government	KR—Erbil	KR—Sulaymaniyah
USA	Active support—full-spectrum assistance	Active support—limited military assistance	Limited military assistance
EU	Active support—full-spectrum assistance	Active support—limited military and humanitarian assistance	Limited military assistance
Turkey	Conflict over presence of the Turkish troops in northern Iraq (Dohuk governorate)	Active support—economic and military cooperation	Neutral
Iran	Active support—full spectrum of assistance	Active support—limited military assistance	Active support—military and economic cooperation
Israel	No diplomatic relations	Active support—covert political and military cooperation	N/A
Russia	Active support	N/A	N/A

---

[15] According to unofficial reports, government of Hungary is ready to officially recognize the KR's bid for statehood.

6 Conclusion—Analysis of KR's Independence Prospects

President Barzani's plan to conduct the referendum on independence once again raises the question on the basic rules of the current recognition regime and criteria for legal/legitimate entitlement to independent statehood. As noted by R. Rich already in 1993, recognition has been a major political question for centuries (Rich 1993, 55). Moreover, the question of recognition of states has become less predictable and more a matter of political discretion as a result of the recent recognition practices (Rich 1993, 63). This observation has been confirmed by the secession of Kosovo, which revealed the fact that policy of recognition has suffered from an inconsistent approach of the international community. Thus, the current recognition regime neither adheres to the de facto self-determination/recognition regime nor to the contemporary self-determination/recognition regime and continues to be based on ad hoc approach, and—as concluded by M. Fabry—the contemporary recognition practice is not sustainable (Fabry 2010). Similarly to M. Sterio, M. Fabry has also stressed the role of major powers for the contemporary recognition regime (Fabry 2010, 224) which has suffered from unpredictability. This, however, does not make the prospect of KR for independence clearer as both de facto state's and central government's institutions enjoy widespread and active international support. This significantly reduces the probability that any major power will accept the KR's quest for de iure independence, but at the same time, it is likely that these powers will support KR's de facto independence.

KRG is thus stuck in a tricky geopolitical situation. It claims to be entitled to self-determination, remedial secession, and it has also been able to have established democratic de facto statehood since 1991. Furthermore, it has widely benefited from economic and political engagement with the international community, which perceives the KR as a potentially reliable and democratic ally. On the other side, the prospect of de iure independent KR raises serious concerns about the entire geopolitical architecture of the region, not only among regional powers which host substantial and potentially irredentist Kurdish minorities and whose geopolitical interests are antagonistic, but also in the eyes of the USA or the EU. The situation is even more complicated by the internal division of the KR, when the provinces of Erbil and Sulaymaniyah follow different economic and geopolitical orientations toward Turkey and Iran, respectively. Both provinces are even divided over the issue of independence referendum, which the PUK party perceives as a part of internal political struggle.

Applying the modified (super)power rule, we can observe that despite the fact that the KR fulfills the condition of human rights abuses, weakness of the parent state, and comparative internal effectiveness, it is unable to harbor sufficient support for the international recognition. What will be decisive for the future of the KR is the fact that independence claims are being raised under unique geopolitical conditions and rivalries. First, the oppressive regime responsible for past injustices has been forcefully removed, which at least relatively weakens justification of secession as the last resort option under remedial secession. Second, the international community perceives both the central government in Baghdad and the regional government in Erbil as legitimate and allied; however, their ultimate goals (territorial integrity vs. external self-determination) are mutually incompatible. This creates a unique situation, when the international community provides extensive support to the territorial integrity of the central government but also to the de facto institutions of the KR, the existence of which was enabled by the imposition of the no-fly zone in 1991 by the decision of the UN SC. Although the KRG enjoys various levels of support (diplomatic, economic, and military), no external player except for Israel is ready, due to domestic or foreign-policy priorities, to support its claim to independence.

The KR's quest for sovereignty is thus questioned by competing, conflicting, and complex geopolitical interests of external players who have stakes both in preserving territorial integrity of Iraq, but also in preserving the de facto institutions of the KR. Under the given geopolitical conditions, the only feasible solution for the KRG seems to be a political dialogue on the future status quo with the central government, its neighbors, the USA and the EU. However, major European countries as well as the USA openly support the principle of territorial integrity. If there is any chance for an independent KR, it rests on the process of mutually agreed or negotiated secession, or a broader geopolitical deal established by the external powers that would be consequently forced upon the Iraqi government.

References

Bar, S. (2016, February 7). *Middle East strategic outlook*. Gatestone Institute. http://www.gatestoneinstitute.org/7380/middle-east-strategic-outlook-february. Accessed February 8, 2016.

Ben Solomon, A. (2016, February 9). Analysis: Russia, US compete to ally with Kurds in ISIS fight. *The Jerusalem Post*. http://www.jpost.com/Middle-East/ANALYSIS-Russia-US-compete-to-ally-with-Kurds-in-ISIS-fight-444316. Accessed May 4, 2016.

Bengio, O. (2016, March 18). Israel and the Kurds: Love by proxy. *The American Interest*. http://www.the-american-interest.com/2016/03/18/israel-and-the-kurds-love-by-proxy/. Accessed May 26, 2016.

Beran, H. (1984). A liberal theory of secession. *Political Studies, 32*, 21–31.

Berg, E., & Kuusk, E. (2010). What makes sovereignty a relative concept? An empirical approach to international society. *Political Geography, 29*(1), 40–49.

Berman, L. (2016). The Iranian penetration of Iraqi Kurdistan. *Jerusalem Center for Public Affairs, 16*(3). http://jcpa.org/article/the-iranian-penetration-of-iraqi-kurdistan/. Accessed May 25, 2016.

Birch, A. H. (1984). Another liberal theory of secession. *Political Studies, 32*, 596–602.

Caspersen, N. (2011). *Unrecognized states: The struggle for sovereignty in the modern international system*. Malden: Polity Press.

Clapham, C. (2005). *Africa and the international system: The politics of state survival*. Cambridge: Cambridge University Press.

Cordesman, A. H., & Khazai, S. (2014). *Iraq in crisis*. Lanham, Boulder, New York, Toronto and Plymouth: Rowman and Littlefield.

Crawford, J. (2006). *The creation of states in international law*. Oxford: Clarendon Press.

Fabry, M. (2010). *Recognizing States: International society and the establishment of new states since 1776.* Oxford University Press.
Fidan, C. B. (2015, February). *Turkey: The Kurdistan region's largest trading partner.* Invest in Group. http://investingroup.org/analysis/195/turkey-the-kurdistan-regions-largest-trading-partner-kurdistan/. Accessed February 15, 2016.
Fragile State Index. (2015). http://fsi.fundforpeace.org/. Accessed January 20, 2016.
France24. (2016, February 11). *Iraq oil revenues now at just 15% of level two years ago: PM.* http://www.france24.com/en/20160211-iraq-oil-revenues-now-just-15-level-two-years-ago-pm. Accessed July 16, 2016.
Geldenhyus, D. (2009). *Contested states in world politics.* London: Palgrave Macmillan.
Gunter, M. M. (2014). Unrecognized de facto states in world politics: The kurds. *Brown Journal of World Affairs, 20*(2), 147–164.
Horowitz, D. L. (2000). *Ethnic groups in conflict.* Berkeley: University Press California.
Khedery, A. (September 22, 2015). Iraq in pieces: Breaking up to stay together, *Foreign Affairs.* https://www.foreignaffairs.com/articles/iraq/2015-09-22/iraq-pieces. Accessed July 16, 2016.
Kopeček, V., Hoch, T., & Baar, V. (2016). Conflict transformation and civil society: The case of Nagorno-Karabakh. *Europe-Asia Studies, 68*(3), 441–459.
KRG. (2016a, May 4). *Department of foreign relations.* KRG offices abroad. http://dfr.gov.krd/p/p.aspx?p=40&l=12&s=020100&r=364. Accessed May 4, 2016.
KRG. (2016b, May 4). *Current international offices in the Kurdistan region.* Department of Foreign Relations. http://dfr.gov.krd/p/p.aspx?p=37. Accessed May 4, 2016.
KRG. (2016c, February 17). *Official KRG response to statements made by prime minister of Iraq, Haider al-Abadi.* http://cabinet.gov.krd/a/d.aspx?s=040000&l=12&a=54240. Accessed May 4, 2016.
KRP. (2015, December 9). *President Barzani meets with Turkey's president and prime minister.* http://www.presidency.krd/english/articledisplay.aspx?id=KlfOYxWQSGc=. Accessed February 15, 2016.
Lynch, D. (2004). *Engaging Eurasia's separatist states: Unresolved conflicts and de facto states.* Washington: United States Institute of Peace Press.
McConnell, F. (2009). De facto, displaced, tacit: The sovereign articulations of the Tibetan government-in-exile. *Political Geography, 28*(6), 343–352.
Nashashibi, S. (2016, May 4). Barzani's gamble may unsettle the entire region. *The National.* http://www.thenational.ae/opinion/comment/barzanis-gamble-may-unsettle-the-entire-region. Accessed May 4, 2016.
Pegg, S., & Kolstø, P. (2014). Somaliland: Dynamics of internal legitimacy and (lack of) external sovereignty. *Geoforum, 66,* 193–202.
Rich, R. (1993). Recognition of states: The collapse of Yugoslavia and the Soviet Union. Symposium: Recent developments in the practice of state recognition. *European Journal of International Relations, 4*(1), 36–65.
S/RES/0688. (1991, April 5). *United nations.* http://fas.org/news/un/iraq/sres/sres0688.htm. Accessed February 15, 2016.
Sluglett, P. (2011). Case study 19: Kurdistan: A suspended secession from Iraq. In A. Pavkovič & P. Radan (Eds.), *The Ashgate research companion to secession* (pp. 539–543). Farnham: Ashgate.
Sterio, M. (2013). On the right to external self-determination: "Selfistans," secession, and the great powers' rule. *Minnesota Journal of International Law, 19*(1), 137–176.
The Treaty of Sèvres, The Treaties of Peace 1919–1923, Vol. II. (1924). *Carnegie endowment for international peace,* 1924. http://wwi.lib.byu.edu/index.php/Section_I,_Articles_1_-_260. Accessed February 12, 2016.
Thornton, R. (2015). Problems with the Kurds as proxies against Islamic State: Insights from the siege of Kobane. *Small Wars and Insurgencies, 26*(6), 865–885.

Trotta, D. (2013, March 14) Iraq war costs U.S. more than $2 trillion: study. *Reuters*. http://www.reuters.com/article/us-iraq-war-anniversary-idUSBRE92D0PG20130314. Accessed August 18, 2016.

US Congress. (1998, October 31). *Iraq liberation act of 1998*. https://www.gpo.gov/fdsys/pkg/PLAW-105publ338/html/PLAW-105publ338.htm. Accessed January 10, 2016.

Walter, C., von Ungern-Sternberg, A., & Abushov, K. (2014). *Self-determination and secession in international law*. Oxford: Oxford University Press.

Author Biographies

Martin Riegl was born in 1980. He currently lectures at the Institute of Political Studies of Faculty of Social Sciences, Charles University. He graduated in 2010 at Faculty of Social Sciences, Charles University (program Political Science), where successfully finished doctoral studies in the field of Political Geography. Since 2008, he has been lecturing at the Department of Political Science (FSS, UK). His academic research is focused on the institution of the sovereign state, geopolitics of political disintegration, secession, unrecognized states, and state failure, and actively participated at scientific conferences and workshops in the Czech Republic, Slovakia, Germany, Belgium, Poland, United Kingdom, Taiwan, etc.

Bohumil Doboš is a Ph.D. student at the Institute of Political Studies, Faculty of Social Sciences, Charles University. His research interest lies in areas of post-Westphalian geopolitics, New Middle Age theory, geopolitical anomalies, geopolitics of violent non-state actors, and astropolitics. He is also a coordinator of the Geopolitical Studies Research Centre at the same institute and employee at the Ministry of Defence of the Czech republic—Defence Policy and Strategy Division.

Jakub Landovský was born in 1976. He currently works as assistant professor at Faculty of Social Sciences of Charles University. He was Fulbright visiting researcher at Oregon State University, consultant for both UNDP and Czech Ministry of Foreign Affairs. He worked as an adviser to the Chairman of Foreign Affairs Committee of the Parliament of the Czech Republic and directed the Middle East Water Project for Forum 2000 foundation. His research interests include security environment, geopolitics of freshwater, resources international water law and international relations. Actively participates at security conferences abroad.

Shmuel Bar holds a Ph.D. in history of the Middle East from Tel-Aviv University. Dr. Bar is a senior research fellow at the Samuel Neaman Institute for National Policy Studies at the Technion in Haifa, Israel, and a veteran of Israel's intelligence community. He served for thirty years in the Israeli government, first in the IDF Intelligence and then in the Israeli Office of the Prime Minister. He specializes in the ideology and operational codes of Islamic fundamentalist movements and particularly of the Jihadi movement that later evolved into al-Qaeda. During this period he also served as First Secretary at the Israeli Embassy in The Hague, Netherlands. Since 2002, he was Director of Studies at the Institute of Policy and Strategy in Herzliya, Israel and on the steering team of the prestigious annual "Herzliya Conference". He is also an adjunct Senior Fellow at the Hudson Institute and has been Distinguished Visiting Fellow at the Hoover Institution at Stanford University.

Bougainville: From Conflict to Independence Under the Law?

Vladimír Baar

The conflict between separatist structures in the northern area of the Solomon Islands, the largest part of which is formed by the island of Bougainville,[1] and the government of Papua New Guinea is generally not known to the same extent as other conflicts of a similar type. However, there is an assumption that in the next few years, it can come to the center of attention just like it happened with South Sudan in the first decade of the twenty-first century. Similar to its case, a peace treaty was signed after a long period of combat and contained a commitment to hold a referendum on independence and respect its outcome. The peace treaty of 2001, mentioned above, guarantees holding a referendum on a full independence.[2] Part of the agreement was a clause specifying the conditions under which the first referendum can be held, no earlier than 10 years and no later than 15 years after the election of the first autonomous Bougainville government,[3] i.e., in 2015 at the earliest. According to the recent reports from the area, the referendum will be held at the end of the agreed period. For now, Bougainville remains an autonomous

---

This chapter is dedicated to the Charles University Research Development Schemes, program PROGRES Q18—Social sciences: from multidisciplinary to interdisciplinary.

---

[1]As the name of the island of Bougainville is used for the name of the entire administrative region, which was originally a district, then a province and now is an autonomous region, the name Bougainville is used in this work meaning the entire administrative unit with the official name Autonomous Region of Bougainville, abbreviated ARB. For the island itself, the appellation "the island of Bougainville" will be used.
[2]Connell (2005, p. 193).
[3]Such a government was established only in 2005, and thus, the earliest date for the referendum is the year 2015.

V. Baar (✉)
University of Ostrava, Ostrava, Czechia
e-mail: Vladimir.baar@osu.cz

region, whose status and self-governance model is similar to, for example, the one of Aceh, Indonesia (Connell 2005, p. 216).

1 The Roots and the Course of the Conflict

For the island of Bougainville, 1964 was a crucial year; vast deposits of copper and gold were discovered in its mountainous southern part. The site of discovery and later a mine, Panguna, played a key role in the development of the Bougainville conflict. Mine management was taken over by an Australian mining company, Bougainville Copper Limited (BCL), the main investor of which was the company Conzinc Riotinto of Australia.[4] Australian miners, who realized that their government is committed to the United Nations to bring the entrusted territory to independence, approached local residents with this objective in mind. Therefore, they pledged to create jobs and fund scholarships for university students without future employment with BCL being a condition. The joint territorial administration of Papua New Guinea at that time won a right to a 20% shareholding of the mine. Other shares were offered to Bougainvilleans, and some of them were bought by religious organizations. BCL leaders assumed that if labor and social facilities were created for the people of the trust territory, the mine and the company's assets would not be nationalized after eventual declaration of independence (Braithwaite et al. 2010, p. 47). In the early seventies, however, the representatives of the colonial administration faced criticism from the residents of Bougainville that the conditions negotiated with the BCL were disadvantageous. As reported by Braithwaite, *We will see that by contemporary standards, the BCL deal was a very good one for the PNG state, but miserly to local landowners* (Braithwaite et al. 2010, p. 53).

Thus, it comes as no surprise that the Bougainville politicians started considering a possible independent development of their rich island. Already in August 1968 at a meeting of Bougainvillean university students in Port Moresby, an association was formed under an interesting name of Mungkas Association,[5] which had placed the referendum on the secession of the island as its objective.[6] In July 1969, another

---

[4]This company is a subsidiary of the Rio Tinto-Zinc Corporation, established in 1962 by a merger of Rio Tinto Company with the Australian company Consolidated Zinc; BCL is now a separate part of Rio Tinto Copper Group, one of the five primary offshoots of the British–Australian corporation Rio Tinto Group.

[5]*Mungkas* is a Terei term for people with black color of skin (*Blackskins*), which was to symbolize the specific of Bougainville as distinct from people with "red" color of skin (*Redskins*) from the mountains of Papua.

[6]For more see http://fandlnews.wordpress.com/about-bougainville/history-of-bougainville/.

movement formed in Kieta, called *Napidakoe Navitu*[7] and presided by Paul Lapun. The movement was very active and already in March used the monthly journal *Bougainville News* to hold an unofficial referendum on independence. Sixteen thousands of leaflets were distributed with a question whether people agree with the separation of the island and about 11,000 returned with a positive response (Griffin 1982, p. 131). At the end of 1972, the future Prime Minister Leo Hannett even went to negotiate on connection possibilities with the then British Solomon Islands (Laracy 1991, p. 55),[8] but was rejected. Later, in February 1973, Hannett initiated the establishment of the Bougainville Special Political Committee (BSPC), which was described by Griffin as *ethnonational entity* (Griffin 1982, p. 137). In a way, he was right, because within a few months, the BSPC managed to raise a strong interest among the people in the possibility of independence. In July, Hannett announced an intention to create the government of the Bougainville District and exactly a year later Bougainville Interim Provincial Government (BIPG) was established with Alexis Sarei in its head. During 1974, the then prime minister of the autonomous government of Papua New Guinea Michael Somare tried to counter the danger by making various concessions. He agreed with the creation of an interim provincial government and subsequently proposed new arrangement proceeds for the profit from the mine. The money from its profits should have flowed directly to Bougainville, in the amount of 5%, compared to 1.25% that went to landowners.

Despite these responsive measures, BIPG voted in May 1975 for secession from Papua New Guinea, and for changing its name to the North Solomons, and two weeks before the prepared declaration of independence of Papua New Guinea, on September 1, 1975, the interim provincial government led by Alexis Sarei unilaterally declared the Republic of the North Solomons. This move, however, was neither recognized by Papua New Guinea nor did it receive the recognition of sovereignty from the member states of the United Nations. The uncompromising attitude of the rebels forced the government of PNG to seek help of its former administrator Australia. Australia sent troops to the area, which pacified the situation. Consequently, talks between the PNG government and the rebels started, and in less than a year, a solution was reached with an agreement being signed, guaranteeing a certain degree of autonomy to the North Solomon Islands. This led to the calming of the situation and reintegration of the separatist republic into PNG on August 9, 1976, with the status of province. However, the situation worsened over

---

[7]For more information, see Griffin (1982); the expression *navitu* means unity in Naasioi, *Napidakoe* was composed from the first syllables or letters—**Na**asioi (an area around Kieta), Pirung (a term used for all the people of islands and coastal areas), Damara (area surrounding Panguna), Koromira (another area name), Evo (area name); the association still exists.

[8]It can be concluded that for local politicians, even the idea of irredentism was not too distant. It is questionable whether the British would reject their quest if they also directly ruled Papua and New Guinea. However, with regard to Australian interests, resp. interests of the Australian–British BCL, they apparently did not want to unnecessarily provoke their ally Australia.

the coming years in connection with the activities of BCL (Braithwaite et al. 2010, p. 68).

In 1978, local landowners, mostly members of the ethno-linguistic community of Naasioi, organized into Panguna Landowners Association (PLA). Their activities to improve the situation, however, were very insufficient. An increasing dissatisfaction, a sense of injustice, and abuse led in 1987 to the first violent actions, which later became the basis of the civil war. Members of the generation frustrated not only by the BCL, but also by the policy of their predecessors, founded New Panguna Landowners Association (NPLA) in the same year. Subsequently, they occupied the offices of the original association and declared themselves a new board of directors. Francis Ona, a prominent member of the original managing board of PLA, became the leader of this group of the dissatisfied. At the same time, they presented a set of extreme requirements, which was so unrealistic, that the BCL did not take it seriously and resolutely rejected it. NPLA had demanded a compensation of 10 billion in the local kina currency for environmental damage, as well as 50% of the profit of BCL and a guarantee that the ownership of BCL would be transferred to Bougainville over the next five years (Braithwaite et al. 2010).

Between 1987 and 1988, NPLA organized public demonstrations, some of which resulted in violent attacks against BCL and its assets. Not only the landowners were involved in these attacks, but some young miners who felt discriminated by the BCL also participated. In November 1988, the rebels destroyed electricity pylons and some of the equipment of the mine. This led to a violent reaction on the part of the state police, which became the impetus for Ona to form his own armed forces called Bougainville Revolutionary Army (BRA). Creating BRA is seen by scholars as a crucial milestone of the subsequent 10-year armed conflict.

In March 1989, the government sent first military troops to Bougainville to stop spreading violence and attacks against government buildings. The rebels responded to this act with large-scale attacks. Subsequently, in May, BCL management stopped mining and evacuated its employees. In June 1989, the PNG government declared a state of emergency on Bougainville, which signaled the end of autonomy, but at the same time, the Prime Minister Namaliu offered a "peace package" to the people of Bougainville. The prime minister of the province of the North Solomons, Joseph Kabui, responded by demanding a very broad autonomy for the province and the establishment of a special committee for its preparation. Naasioi John Bika was appointed to lead the committee; however, on 11th September, he was murdered by the members of BRA. This incident happened one day before Bika's flight to Port Moresby, where he was to sign a peace agreement which also included an increase in the profits from mining to 10%—half of which was to be received by the provincial government, and half by the landowners (Braithwaite et al. 2010). According to Regan, NPLA primarily demanded reopening of the mine, while their aim was to force BCL to a new settlement for redistribution of profits to local landowners. However, most of the disappointed supporters of BRA and its members insisted on a complete closure of the mine and the expulsion of all

"Redskins" as well as Australians from Bougainville, which in turn significantly radicalized the approach of the management of BRA (Regan 2007).

Violence between government troops (PNGDF—Papua New Guinea Defence Force) and the rebels further escalated; soldiers and policemen often treated the insurgents with brutality and they also did not spare the civilians suspected of supporting them. In January 1990, PNGDF launched an operation aptly called *Operation Footloose*, which meant the actual outbreak of war between government troops and the Bougainville revolutionary army. The aim of the architects of this military action was to compel BRA to agree to peace negotiations from a position of strength; however, as it later turned out, not only was BRA not defeated, but in a few weeks, it also taught PNGDF a hard military lesson.

The BRA leaders took advantage of the new situation immediately and tried to take power into their own hands. On May 17, 1990, independence was proclaimed anew, under the name Republic of Me'ekamui, and Bougainville Interim Government (BIG) was formed. It was led by the self-proclaimed President Francis Ona, with Joseph Kabuias as his deputy and Sam Kauona as the defense minister. Again, Bougainville did not achieve any recognition. Reaction to this act was, on the other hand, an absolute sea and air blockade maintained by Papua New Guinea for the following 8 months (Regan 2007). At the same time, the PNG government withdrew all state employees from the region, with the intention to leave Bougainville in a state of utter chaos. Therefore, prior to its departure from the region, the government ordered the release of all prisoners, which led to an increase in criminality in the area and subsequent involvement of criminal groups in the ongoing violence.

The island's economy at that time was going through a deep crisis. Harvests of export crops fell dramatically and the population returned to subsistence farming. For this reason, there was a meeting between the representatives of the Papua New Guinea government and BRA (headed by Joseph Kabui) in the Solomon capital of Honiara, which took place on January 23, 1991, to sign a declaration on peace and reconciliation, known as *The Honiara Declaration*.[9] However, Francis Ona and his followers refused to respect the declaration and continued in the occupation of Panguna.

After the elections in 1992, the new government of PNG favored a military solution to the problem with the target of regaining control over the area of the Panguna mine. The government sought aid in Australia, which had previously supported the Papua New Guinea cabinet with a sum of AUD 52 mil. However, after surveying the situation, the Australian officials concluded that solution cannot be reached by military means. They realized that BRA does not have a single control center, but is controlled by a series of autonomous cells. It was not possible to destroy one center without the others continuing the fight. Total destruction of BRA would not be possible without huge civilian casualties, which was a factor of

---

[9]For the full text, see Uppsala Conflict Data Program (2001).

consideration for democratic Australia. Therefore, Australia along with New Zealand offered to play the role of peacemakers.

In the middle of 1994, Julius Chan became the prime minister of PNG; he was determined to solve the conflict peacefully. In September 1994, the talks between BRA and government representatives of Papua New Guinea commenced. This peace conference was again hosted by Honiara. The moderate faction of BRA (without Francis Ona and his radical wing), which was present at the conference, agreed with a ceasefire and future negotiations about the political status of Bougainville. On November 25, 1994, the *Mirigini Charter*[10] was signed in Waigani. Papua New Guinea committed itself to the creation of the Bougainville Transitional Government (BTG), which was, since April 1995, presided by a member of BIG, Theodore Miriung. Three seats reserved for the radical wing of BRA remained unoccupied—Francis Ona, Joseph Kabui, and Sam Kauona refused to join the government. However, at the turn of 1995 and 1996, the representatives of BTG and BIG attended a joint meeting in Australia.

This fact further strengthened the government's suspicion considering the close relations of BTG and the insurgents. When they returned, in January 1996, PNGDF troops launched an attack, which led to the death of BTG Prime Minister, Theodore Miriung. This failure caused a subsequent breach of all peace treaties and triggered another chain of violence.

PNGDF's incapability to defeat BRA made Prime Minister Chan radically change his opinion on the solution to the conflict. In May, he ordered[11] the liquidation of the rebels by any means—to search for and kill, liquidate the civilians supporting the rebels, destroy their gardens and homes, etc.[12] Since the results were not satisfying, in January 1997, the government secretly hired South African mercenaries with the help of a British military agency. They were to perform a devastating operation against BRA and take over the Panguna mine. The operation had its distinctive name *Operasen Rausim Kwik*, which in Tok Pisin means *get rid of them quickly*. PNGDF commander Brigadier General Jerry Singirok surprisingly refused to cooperate with these mercenaries and his vigorous performance urged the prime minister to resign. The whole affair, known as the *Sandline Affair*,[13] resulted in the downfall of the government, and Chan and two other members of government were put to trial (Rajakulendran 2003).

It became clear after this affair that a new approach is required and another phase of peace-making attempts must commence. The role of mediator was taken up by

---

[10]Named after the Mirigini ship, on which the charter was signed.

[11]Order 2133 PNG Defence Force 21/5/96.

[12]It is literarily stated at http://www.eco-action.org/dod/no8/boug.html: *Search for the rebels and kill them... Any civilians who are suspected of harbouring the BRA must be killed without question... Get the rebels out. Do not leave any of them, but wipe them out... Destroy all food—gardens, houses and any shelter found in the jungle, clean it up... Any civilian found to be an ordinary civilian is to be forced into care centres. If anyone is disorderly they must be beaten.*

[13]The name is derived from the name of the private military agency *Sandline International*, which is based in Britain, but hires primarily African mercenaries.

New Zealand, owing to which a consensus was reached on the creation of a regional monitoring group created from the representatives of New Zealand, Australia, Vanuatu, Tonga, and Fiji.

Subsequently, meetings of leaders were organized to discuss a gradual withdrawal of security units of Papua New Guinea from Bougainville and its future political status, establishment of Bougainville Reconciliation Government (BRG), and placement of the UN Observer Mission (UNPOB—United Nations Political Office in Bougainville), which was to cooperate with a smaller regional observer mission of the four Pacific countries mentioned above.

Other conditions for the implementation of the peace deal were confirmed by signing *Arawa Agreement* on April 30, 1998.[14] The treaty divided the former allies Ona and Kabui. While Kabui as a signatory to the contract went north to Buka to participate in the preparation of the BRG, Ona stayed in Arawa and on May 23, 1998, confirmed the independence of the Republic Me'ekamui. He was reelected president and BIG and continued under his leadership. This further complicated the situation.

Two years later, a new man entered the political scene of Bougainville—Noah Misingku, a poor Papuan man who made his fortune by operating a financial system, known as U-Vistract, for the initiation of which he had borrowed 200 PGK.[15] According to the experts, the U-Vistract was based on a so-called pyramidal effect that soon brought huge profits—some PGK 350 mil. (USD 160 mil.). Because his "business" was not perceived favorably by the banks and the authorities, he decided to take advantage of the situation when there was still a group of rebels around Francis Ona on Bougainville and prepared to return to the island. On April 21, 2000, he called a large gathering of his followers to a stadium at Port Moresby and had himself crowned a ruler *of the kingdom Papa'ala*.[16] Then, he went to the Solomon Islands and from here to Bougainville to the village of Tonu, where he had a palace built. He later met with Francis Ona, whom he financially supported and recognized as the leader in the struggle for independence.

In the course of 1998, when BRA and BIG actively participated in the peace negotiations, the radical wing of BRA with Francis Ona as a leader formed militant Me'ekamui Defence Forces (MDF), which according to Ona were better suited to guard the implementation of the requirements needed to achieve complete independence of the Bougainville Island. The platform of this formation was the southeastern part of the island of Bougainville. The surroundings of the Panguna mine were proclaimed by the MDF as inaccessible Me'ekamui Peace Zone (MPZ), also known as *No Go Zone*. Apart from other uses, this place still serves as a store for illegal weapons. The rebels use the road blocks in order to maintain control over these territories and to enrich themselves at the expense of the motorists who need

---

[14]See the full text at http://publicinternationallawandpolicygroup.org/wp-content/uploads/2011/10/Lincoln-Agreement-on-Peace-Security-and-Development-of-Bougainville-Annex-1998.pdf.

[15]PGK is international code for kina—currency of Papua New Guinea.

[16]Papa'ala is the name of the highest deity in the myths of Bougainville and also a name of an area surrounding the village of Tonu, where his messenger secretly lives among people.

to pass through. These inaccessible areas are completely closed off to foreigners. The one who earns the most on the series of road blocks is Noah Musingku, the self-proclaimed king of Papa´ala and Me'ekamui. The police of Papua New Guinea have, however, never arrested him. At present, a self-proclaimed general, Chris Uma, who provides security to Musingku, is the leader of MDF.[17]

By the end of 2000, the Australian foreign minister, Alexander Downer, visited Papua New Guinea and Bougainville. He presented there his proposal on a conditioned postponed referendum on the political future of Bougainville. An agreement regulating the referendum on independence, *Agreed Principles on Referendum*,[18] signed on January 26, 2001. An essential step in the peace building process was *The Bougainville Peace Agreement*,[19] which was signed on August 30, 2001, in Arawa. It combined three former agreements: on the issue of referendum determining the political future of Bougainville, the plan of disarmament, and the agreements about the rules of autonomous administration. Francis Ona was not involved in any of the previous negotiations or peace agreements. The preparation of the Constitution of the Autonomous Region of Bougainville in early 2004 (but approved only on 12th November) caused his negative response. On the day of the 4th anniversary of the declaration of independence of Me'ekamui in May 2004, he changed the republican status of the country to a monarchy crowning himself king under the name of Francis Peii I.[20] This act, although again not recognized by anyone, gave Francis Ona a strong influence on the island until his death caused by malaria on July 24, 2005. He himself attributed to his influence a very low turnout for the elections to Bougainville parliament, which took place in June 2005 under the auspices of New Zealand. Joseph Kubui, a former ally of Ona, came out from these elections as the first president of the Autonomous Region of Bougainville (ARB) and also the prime minister of Autonomous Bougainville Government (ABG). The election turnout was only 9% (8844) of the approximately 100 thousand potential voters. It was thus possible to deduce from these figures that the people did not support autonomy within PNG, but a complete independence, which Ona had demanded. President Kabui was elected with just 5099 votes (59.75%). The future presidents of ARB failed at this stage—Momis received 2669 votes (31.27%) and Tanis only 459 (5.38%).

Although Kabui won, the sheer number of votes by which he gained the highest office in the province significantly limited his prestige. Moreover, he adopted some unpopular measures, after which he came under a strong political pressure that excessively strained his health, and in June 2008, he died of a heart attack. Despite the criticism, which cost him his life, a state funeral was held for him, because the

---

[17] See Islands Business (2010).

[18] See full text at http://ips.cap.anu.edu.au/ssgm/resource_documents/bougainville/PDF/AgreedPrinciplesonReferendum-26Jan01-1.pdf.

[19] See full text at http://ips.cap.anu.edu.au/ssgm/resource_documents/bougainville/PDF/BougainvillePeaceAgreement29Aug01.pdf.

[20] The word *peii* itself means in Naasioi a ruler or a king.

PNG government was well aware that without his pragmatic approach, the conflict would not have been resolved. In the new elections, in which 14 candidates participated, a duel was expected between Sam Akoitai (supporter of autonomy) and Sam Kauonou (a supporter of independence). Surprisingly, however, another supporter of independence, James Tanis, who in the first presidential election of 2005 had not even reached five hundred votes, won dramatically. However, his government was limited to the remaining period of the mandate of Kabui. In mid-2010, another peaceful election took place, the results of which changed 90% of the political representation of Bougainville. John Momis was elected president, a pragmatic politician involved in politics since 1972, when he was first elected to the provincial parliament of Bougainville at the age of 30. He easily won these elections against six other candidates with the overall gain of 52.35% of the vote (43,047), while his biggest rival, incumbent President James Tanis won only less than 20.92% of the vote (17,205 votes). His resounding victory was seen as a sign of support of the voters for the preservation of broad autonomy and the remaining within Papua New Guinea, as Tanis acted as an advocate of secession and full independence. As his main priorities, Momis announced in particular the fight against political corruption and the disposal of large quantities of weapons and arsenal that remained among people since the conflict ended. Although initially he tried to convince people about the high costs associated with the referendum on independence, in the second half of his mandate, he stood up clearly for its implementation. He visited the area under the control of rebels occupying the Panguna mine, whose leaders had expressed their support to him. Thanks to them, he won the last elections in 2015 against eight opponents convincingly with a higher number of votes than in 2010.[21] He then promised that the referendum would be held by the end of his term of office (at the turn of the year 2019/20).

Ono's policy of full independence is being continued today by Musingku. He let himself be crowned as "King David Peii II," the only ruler of Twin Kingdoms of Papa'ala and Me'ekamui. Although he initially rejected the legitimacy of the ARB and ABG, after the first election his efforts to establish good relations with these structures were apparent, which culminated this year in an open support of the ARB government in the presidential election in order to achieve the referendum for independence.

2 The Conflict in a Regional Context

The conflict on Bougainville is known as being the worst, which has taken place in Oceania since the Second World War.[22] The number of lives that have been lost in connection with this conflict is estimated at 15–20 thousand. Taking into account the

---

[21]For more see http://bougainvillenews.com/category/elections-2015/.

[22]In terms of conflicts, Oceania is the calmest of the macro-regions of the world, if any conflicts did arise (e.g., on Vanuatu, Fiji, and the Solomon Islands), casualty figures were slight.

total population, which during the years 1989–1997 varied between 150 and 200 thousand people, it is clear that in Oceanian conditions, it is a confrontation with a strong local impact (Wolfers 2006, p. 10). However, in the global context, with respect to the conflicts in Africa and Asia with millions of casualties, this conflict is perceived quite differently. PRIO/UCDP database[23] defines it as an international armed conflict of less intensity and the COSIMO[24] database refers to it only as a crisis, a tense situation when at least one party inclines to armed incidents. Despite its marginalization on the global scale, it is undisputed that the case of Bougainville has significantly interfered with the events at the regional level of Oceania and has forced the local regional powers, Australia and New Zealand, to an intensive engagement.

Although Oceania is not at the center of political attention of the world media, the events of the past three decades suggest that the westernmost part of the Melanesia region is relatively unstable, which its most significant players in Australia, New Zealand, and possibly Papua New Guinea will have to face. The main role in finding the solution to the conflict fell to Australia, which was the former administrator of Papua New Guinea and the most important political actor in the region, significantly interfering in the events and undeniably supporting the government of Papua New Guinea financially and militarily. This support resulted from a fear that practically accomplished separatist tendencies within the PNG could lead to a balkanization in a broader dimension, especially in Melanesia, which is adjacent by its territorial waters to Australia. Australia has, in this case, got into an ambivalent and unenviable position. On the one hand, it is a mature democratic state with an emphasis on human rights, but at the same time, it is also a regional hegemon, whose main objective is the stability of the region.

Although national issues of Melanesian countries are marginal when compared with the problems of a number of African nations, Duncan and Chand labeled Melanesia in 2002 as the *Arc of Instability* (Duncan and Chand 2002) and this term has since been used by other authors.[25] Melanesian arc of instability starts in the west with East Timor,[26] which sought independence from Indonesia for decades, continues with the Southern Moluccas with Christian population, which unsuccessfully tried to separate after the proclamation of independent Indonesia[27] and

---

[23]For more, see http://www.pcr.uu.se/publications/UCDP_pub/UCDP_PRIO_Codebook_v4-2007.pdf.

[24]COnflict SImulated MOdel—database of the Heidelberg Institute for International Conflict Research records information on political conflicts between 1945 and today.

[25]e.g. May (2003) or Connell (2006).

[26]As a former Portuguese colony, East Timor should have been de-colonized, but in 1975 it was forcibly annexed by Indonesia. The Timorese resisted and they finally managed to gain independence with the support of the UN in 2002.

[27]The population of the South Moluccan islands is predominantly Christian and, therefore, tried to separate from predominantly Muslim Indonesia as the Republic of South Moluccas in 1950. But the insurgents were defeated and thousands of people fled to the Netherlands, where there is still their government in exile. Directly on the islands, there are also movements seeking independence. Indonesia has attempted to resolve the situation by separating the predominantly Muslim islands, and in 1999, it established a new province of North Maluku (*Maluku Utara*).

West Papua, which failed to decolonize as an independent state.[28] Even half a century after the original connection to Indonesia, the efforts to secede have not ceased. Indeed, within the Pacific Islands Forum, the Solomon Islands enforce the right of West Papua to separate and intend to initiate in the UN a reintegration of the region onto the list of areas intended for decolonization.[29]

The arc continues with the island of Bougainville, across the Solomon Islands, where at the beginning of the twenty-first century riots broke out among some ethnic groups,[30] Fiji, where the differences between native Fijians and descendants of Indian immigrants culminated in several state coups,[31] but also in the attempt of a remote island of Rotuma for separation,[32] Vanuatu, which had to deal with the separatist tendencies of some islands[33] to New Caledonia, where, like in Fiji, disagreements between the original Kanaks and descendants of immigrants led to an attempt of a unilateral declaration of independence.[34] In 2003, it was reported[35] that a similar autonomy, that had been won by Bougainville, was also demanded by the province of East New Britain. It was rejected by PNG government; however, the same request appeared again a few years later.[36] It is not a new call—the province demanded autonomy, similarly to Bougainville, even before the declaration of

---

[28]In 1963, West Papua was, under pressure from the UN, handed to Indonesia, against the will of local Papuans. Indonesia has been trying since the beginning to resettle Muslim residents from the overpopulated islands into this province; now there is almost half a million of them living there.

[29]For more, see http://pacific.scoop.co.nz/2015/09/solomon-islands-advocates-for-west-papua-at-pif/.

[30]Local problems did not result in separatist attempts, but the armed struggles considerably destabilized the society and the government had to ask for foreign aid. See e.g. Chand (2002) or Kabutaulaka (2000).

[31]The problem is still alive; Fiji has even been excluded from the Commonwealth due to human rights violations. See e.g. Teaiwa (2000) or Durutalo (2008).

[32]This attempt in the year 1987 was a reaction to the proclamation of the Republic in Fiji following the coup and the abolition of the monarchy, respectively a personal union with Britain. The initiative came from the Mölmahao clan in the district of Noa'tau, which proclaimed its own republic Rotuma, claiming that Rotuma had never been a part of Fiji, but accepted the protection of the British Crown on May 13, 1881, seven years after Fiji had become a British colony. The rebellion was soon suppressed and Rotuma gained a certain degree of autonomy. At present, only 2000 people live on Rotuma with another 10,000 Rotumans living on different islands of Fiji.

[33]Separatist attempts appeared like in PNG before the declaration of independence. From 1975 to 1980, the island of Tanna proclaimed independence, later, along with other islands under the name of Tafea, Malekula Island as the Republic Vemerana and later N'Makiaute and northern islands as the Federation of Na-Griamel. Behind a majority of these experiments, there were attempts of foreign companies to gain economic clout. At present, the Na-Griamel movement remains active, but its goal is not a secession of the island, but a preservation of traditions.

[34]For details, see Cechová (2012).

[35]For more, see http://dir.groups.yahoo.com/group/PNGSA/message/912?var=1 or http://pidp.org/archive/2004/May/05-10-01.htm.

[36]For more, see http://garamut.wordpress.com/2009/01/09/east-new-britains-quest-for-autonomy/ or http://asopa.typepad.com/asopa_people/2011/11/east-new-britain-should-have-autonomy-matane.html.

independence of PNG in 1975. More specifically, the call for autonomy of East New Britain is dealt with in a study by Gelu and Axline (2008, pp. 15–21).

3 Domestic Development of the Province

Although at the beginning of the second secession, there was a split within the separatist movement, and BIG had only a small part of the island around the closed mine under its control, pragmatically minded proponents of independence, among them the future presidents Kabui and Momis, managed to negotiate with the government of PNG a broad autonomy of the province and the promise of the execution of referendum in the period 2015–20. President Momis managed to win the presidential elections with overwhelming support for the second time and to establish contacts with Me'ekamui leaders. These got into political isolation, in which they only ruled Panguna with its surroundings, and most of them lived a normal life in the wider hinterland. For the government of ARB, it would probably not be an issue to liberate this area with the support of the central government of PNG; however, fears of a possible guerrilla war led it to search for a compromise. Before the presidential election, Momis confirmed that if he won the election, he would enforce the referendum on independence. However, he has proposed its execution in 2019, possibly 2020 (in the same period a referendum on independence in New Caledonia should take place). This delay is related to the efforts to reach an agreement on the copper mine and its reopening. It is this mine that should become the economic core of the further development of Bougainville.

If Bougainvilleans expressed their approval in the referendum for independence, which is quite a likely option, another island microstate would be created on the world map. Like other island microstates, Bougainville would be forced to face many challenges, particularly if we take into account the massive destruction of the island during the 10-year violence. In spite of an overtly present tension between immigrants and the local population, the Bougainville province was before 1988 one of the most stably developing regions of Papua New Guinea. Health and education systems were on a fairly good level and, owing to the presence of the copper mine, there was a development of infrastructure (Connell 2005, p. 208). Today, the situation is considerably different and Bougainville faces a difficult task to restructure and re-establish the economic and social development. In 1967, a social anthropologist Burton Benedict created an overview of the major obstacles to the development of small island states. The main barrier is seen in dependence on a few primary agricultural commodities. Due to limited industrialization, these countries are dependent on imports, hence foreign capital. The worst off are the archipelagic states that are due to their territorial fragmentation forced to spend large sums on administration, healthcare provision, and transport of goods between the islands (Benedict 1967).

However, if we look at Bougainville, its position in this regard is not bad in comparison with the existing island microstates. Bougainville has a potential to develop a relatively diversified economy that is not dependent on one or two commodities. Today, Bougainville is the main producer of cocoa within Papua New Guinea. However, in this case, it is not a monoculture farming, because another export commodity is copra, another alternative is represented by coffee, nuts, vanilla, and other spices.

The advantage of Bougainville is its good geographic location, because it is not too far from its potential business partners, namely Papua New Guinea and Australia. This also applies to tourism, which has started to develop successfully. In March 2009, Bougainville Tourism Industry Association was established with a very interesting offer for foreign tourists.[37] Bougainville agriculture is self-sufficient and according to Bourke and Betis, Bougainville has enough land to support its inhabitants (Bourke and Betis 2003). Although Bougainvillean agriculture certainly has a great potential, it is clear that the largest source of potential income of the local economy are minerals. Besides Panguna, findings of other raw materials are expected; geological prospecting, however, needs political stability and of course, financial investment. The reopening itself of the gold-bearing and copper mine Panguna continues to be perceived by all the actors as potentially a very dangerous matter that might trigger violence once again, including armed conflicts.

A considerable support for the resumption of mining in the Panguna mine has been expressed by the current President John Momis. He described the production in Panguna as crucial for starting development on Bougainville. The autonomous government of Bougainville shows the same support for the resumption of mining activities.[38] In May 2011, the Executive Director of BCL Peter Taylor also expressed willingness of the company to set new conditions for the profits of mining for the landowners as well as for the Bougainvillean government[39] and submitted a draft of a new agreement called *Bougainville Copper Agreement* (BCA). This, however, received support neither of the provincial government nor of the landowners. The need to satisfy the interests of owners is clearly confirmed only in the new *Bougainville Mining Act* (BMA) adopted in March 2015. According to this act, the mine shall not be opened without their consent, but it also implies that the BCL may not be interested in reopening the mine for reasons of lower profits and higher costs of putting the mine in operation.[40] It seems that the adoption of the BMA just before the elections has positively affected the majority of owners and will be a key factor to end the blockade of the mine.

It seems that Bougainvilleans are beginning to realize that without the income from mining, it will be very difficult to create and sustain an independent state. Regan also reassures the public that it has been clearly declared by both BCL and

---

[37]For more, see http://www.bougainvilletourism.org.pg/bat.html.

[38]For more, see http://beta.afr.com/p/world/bougainville_mine_could_reopen_by_ZpzTJfLChF0 Q76Xw0Yu1eI.

[39]For more, see http://www.theaustralian.com.au/business/bougainville-president-backs-panguna-mine/story-e6frg8zx-1226058523408.

[40]For more, see http://bougainvillenews.com/category/elections-2015/.

the national government of Papua New Guinea that there is a need for a broad consensus on this issue. The other side of things can be seen in the fact that the costs to restore mining are estimated at USD 300 mil., and after its experience from the late 1980s, BCL will realistically not undergo such risks without having a broad public support. However, the tapped reserves are large enough[41] to ensure that the compromise is eventually achieved.

The opening of the Panguna mine appears to be absolutely crucial. Without the production and sale of copper and gold, an independent Bougainville would find itself in the best case at the level of independent Samoa or Tonga, and thus as a relatively poor country dependent on agricultural products and tourism development. The first one of these is influenced by the vagaries of weather and fluctuating market prices and the other one dependent on political stability and ability to offer quality services. This is certainly not the way for Bougainville, because the ARB has long been able to generate a budget from internal resources amounting to only 10%. President Momis understands it very well and publicly declares that prior to the referendum, all ownership issues and renewed mining must be resolved, disarmament of the remaining militant groups must be completed, and a stable political system and method of governance must be created (Hammond 2012). All this is contained in the program of the new government established after the elections in June 2015. It includes three main goals: unification of the population within the ARB, improving the welfare of all Bougainvilleans by promoting appropriate economic development, and securing Bougainville's future by full implementation of the peace agreement from 2001.[42]

The fact that the situation in ARB has consolidated can be evidenced by the fact that a pluralistic party system has been created there with free access to the registration.[43] Alongside purely regional parties, parties with activities throughout the PNG may also operate there, but their influence is negligible. Thus, similarly to the whole PNG, in ARB new parties formed around the most important politicians. In the last decade, the strongest position has been held by the Bougainville People's Congress (BPC), connected with the personality of the President Kabui. With his death, the influence of this party weakened, which does not mean, however, that the party fell into irrelevance. However, the fact remains that the strongest influence was acquired by a party which was founded in 2005 by the current President Momis under the name New Bougainville Party (NBP). Its program (unequivocal support for the execution of the referendum) is not significantly different from the BPC program, which may in the future lead to a merger between the two entities or their offshoots (this trend is fairly widespread in PNG). Supporters of independence are united in Bougainville Independence Movement (BIM), which was also founded in 2005 by the former President Tanis. The program of this party is already clearly discernible from its name, and because its leader belongs to the younger generation

---

[41]For more, see http://bougainvillecopper.com/news-may-2011.html.

[42]For more, see http://bougainvillenews.com/category/elections-2015/.

[43]For more, see http://pidp.org/archive/2005/April/04-01-04.htm.

of Bougainvillean politicians, it can be expected that it will benefit from the political mistakes or failures of the current NBP presidential party. The weakest support has been garnered by the young Bougainville Labour Party (BLP), which follows the tradition of British laborism and is led by a lawyer Thomas Tamusio. It supports the referendum, but prefers social issues. Beyond the formal structure, there are still forces around the Twin Kingdom of Papa'ala and Me'ekamui.

4 Conclusion

Without a deeper sociological research, it is difficult to predict whether Bougainville will choose the path of an independent existence or autonomy within Papua New Guinea. Developments since Bougainvillean Peace Treaty, which has brought a real peace to the inhabitants, even though it has not solved the problem concerning the Panguna mine, have not been progressing in a linear trajectory. Conversely, the last decade has been full of changes in the mood of the population, which means that in the future years the population may react unexpectedly. The first election in the newly constituted ARB was unexpectedly boycotted by the population, which was explained then by Francis Ona as resistance against remaining within Papua New Guinea. Although the first President Joseph Kabui acted as a supporter of autonomy, he did not hide his intention to build a *Kuwait of the Pacific* out of Bougainville.[44] Even after his death, the locals chose a supporter of independence James Tanis overwhelmingly in the elections. After two years, however, they let him fail in the elections and elected John Momis, who ran with a program of autonomy. The truth is, however, that even he has been a supporter of independence for decades and does not condemn the referendum, he only takes into account the high financial costs associated with it. Besides, he was elected the second time owing to the support he had received from the Me'ekamui rebels. It could be said that sentiments toward full independence dominate in the society of Bougainville.

The analysis has shown that the Bougainvillean conflict primarily has an economic dimension in which the vital role is played by the presence of mineral resources and the unfair distribution of profits, but this was not the primary reason for the outbreak of armed violence. It was not even the environmental devastation caused by BCL, which in connection with mining contaminated the surface waters and caused a degradation of agricultural land. It was the target of criticism in the first stage of the conflict in the years 1975–1976, but it never gave rise to an armed resistance. The actual armed revolt was caused by government intervention in the form of revoking the autonomy and declaration of emergency rule in 1989. Ethno-linguistic specifics of the population of Bougainville were certainly not

---

[44]For more, see http://www.abc.net.au/news/2008-06-17/bougainville-parliament-at-odds-over-resources-deal/2474084?section=world.

essential, although the specifics of local culture and its disruption have contributed to the escalation of the conflict. The existing ethnic kinship with the population of the Solomon Islands, however, is too weak, which has resulted in an almost complete absence of irredentist efforts. They briefly appeared as an alternative in 1973–1975, but were quickly abandoned.

From the geographic, demographic, and economic point of view, it is clear that Bougainville as an independent state would not differ from other small countries in Oceania. Unlike most of them (except New Caledonia,[45] which is also preparing for a referendum on independence), it has significant mineral wealth, which would help to significantly improve the economic situation of the island and the living standards of the population.[46] The decision on whether there will be a new state created on the world map will be known for sure by the end of this decade. And since a referendum on independence in New Caledonia will also be carried out in the same period, it will be interesting to see how the local people decide.

References

Banks, G. (2008). Understanding "resource" conflicts in Papua New Guinea. *Asia Pacific Viewpoint, 49*(1), 23–34.
Benedict, B. (1967). *Problems of smaller territories*. London: University of London.
Bourke, M., & Betitis, T. (2003). Sustainability of agriculture in Bougainville Province, Papua New Guinea, Land Management Group. Canberra: ANU E-Press. http://ips.cap.anu.edu.au/ssgm/lmg/pubs/bourke-betitis-bougainville.pdf. Accessed November 26, 2011.
Braithwaite, J. et al. (2010). Reconciliation and architectures of commitment: Sequencing peace in Bougainville. Canberra: ANU E-Press. http://epress.anu.edu.au/bougainville/pdf/whole.pdf. Accessed April 29, 2011.
Chand, S. (2002). Conflict to crisis in Solomon Islands. *Pacific Economic Bulletin, 17*(1), 154–159.
Connell, J. (2005). Bougainville: The future of an Island microstate. *Journal of Pacific Studies, 28* (2), 192–217.
Connell, J. (2006). "Saving the Solomons": A new geopolitics in the "Arc of instability"? *Geographical Research, 44*(2), 111–122.
Čechová, L. (2012). *Nová Kaledonie v procesu k získání nezávislosti*. Ostrava: Ostravská univerzita.
Duncan, R., & Chand, S. (2002). The economics of the "Arc of Instability". *Asian Pacific Economic Literature, 16*(5), 1–9.
Durutalo, L. D. (2008). Fiji: Party politics in the post independence period. Australian National University. http://epress.anu.edu.au/wp-content/uploads/2011/05/ch0946.pdf. Accessed November 5, 2012.
Gelu, A., & Axline, A. (2008). Options for the restructure of decentralised government in Papua New Guinea. Boroko: National Research Institute. http://www.nri.org.pg/publications/Recent

---

[45]New Caledonia is extremely rich in nickel ore (its reserves are among the largest in the world).
[46]The truth is that even on Nauru with its phosphates, raw materials were abundant, making it the richest state in Oceania. After the reserves had been depleted, the country fell into insignificance. Such a scenario, however, is improbable for Bougainville, where the resource base is much larger.

%20Publications/2010%20Publications/Gelu%20and%20Axeline%20Special%20Publication%20No.50.pdf. Accessed June 20, 2012.

Griffin, J. (1982). Napidakoe Navitu. In R. J. May (Ed.), *Micronationalist movements in Papua New Guinea*. Canberra: Australian National University.

Hale, H. (2008). *The foundations of ethnic politics: Separatism of states and nations in Eurasia and the world*. Cambridge: Cambridge University Press.

Hammond, T. G. (2011). Conflict resolution in a hybrid state: The Bougainville story. *Foreign Policy Journal*. http://www.foreignpolicyjournal.com/2011/04/22/conflict-resolution-in-a-hybrid-state-the-bougainville-story/. Accessed April 23, 2012.

Hammond, T. G. (2012). Resolving hybrid conflicts: The Bougainville story. *Foreign Policy Journal*. http://www.foreignpolicyjournal.com/2012/12/22/resolving-hybrid-conflicts-the-bougainville-story/. Accessed December 27, 2012.

Henderson, J. (1999). Bougainville: The uncertain road to peace. *New Zealand International Review, 24*(3), 10–13.

Islands Business. (2010, May 17). Rebel group backs Bougainville President. http://www.islandsbusiness.com/news/index_dynamic/containerNameToReplace=MiddleMiddle/focusModuleID=130/focusContentID=19420/tableName=mediaRelease/overideSkinName=newsArticle-full.tpl. Accessed September 8, 2011.

Kabutaulaka, T. T. (2000). Beyond ethnicity: Understanding the crisis in the Solomon Islands. Suva: University of South Pacific. http://www.vanuatu.usp.ac.fj/sol_adobe_documents/usp%20only/pacific%20general/Kabataulaka.htm. Accessed June 27, 2012.

Laracy, H. (1991). Bougainville Secessionism. *Journal de la Société des océanistes, 92*(92–93), 53–60.

Matthew, A. (2000). Bougainville and Papua New Guinea: Complexities of secession in a multi-ethnic developing state. *Political Studies, 48*(4), 724–744.

May, R. J. (Ed.). (1982). *Micronationalist movements in Papua New Guinea*. Canberra: Australian National University.

May, R. J. (Ed.). (2003). *"Arc of Instability"? Melanesia in the early 2000s*. Canberra: Australian National University.

Rajakulendran, V. (2003). Australia and New Zealand could play a role to find a Bougainville style solution for Tamils' demand for self-determination in Sri Lanka. http://www.sangam.org/ANALYSIS/Rajakulendran_4_9_03.htm. Accessed 3rd June 2011.

Regan, A. J. (2002). The Bougainville political settlement and the prospects for sustainable peace. *Pacific Economic Bulletin, 17*(1), 114–129.

Regan, A. J. (2007). Development and conflict: The struggle over self-determination in Bougainville. In A. M. Brown (Ed.), *Security and development in the Pacific Islands* (pp. 89–110). Boulder: Lynne Rienner Publisher.

Teaiwa, T. (2000). An analysis of the current political crisis in Fiji. Te Karere Ipurangi—Maori New Online. http://maorinews.com/karere/fiji/teaiwa.htm. Accessed April 10, 2011.

UCDP/PRIO. (2007). Armed conflict dataset codebook. Uppsala, Uppsala Universitet, Department of Peace and Conflict Research. http://www.pcr.uu.se/publications/UCDP_pub/UCDP_PRIO_Codebook_v4-2007.pdf. Accessed April 26, 2011.

Uppsala Conflict Data Program. (2001). The Honiara Declaration. Uppsala Universitet, Department of Peace and Conflict Research. http://www.ucdp.uu.se/gpdatabase/peace/PNG%2019910123.pdf. Accessed July 29, 2011.

Wolfers, E. P. (2006). International peace missions in Bougainville, Papua New Guinea, 1990–2005 Host state perceptions. http://unpan1.un.org/intradoc/groups/public/documents/un/unpan022601.pdf. Accessed February 20, 2011.

Author Biography

Vladimír Baar is a professor of political and cultural geography at the Department of Human Geography and Regional Development, University of Ostrava, Czechia. His research includes ethno-political conflicts, separatism, and irredentism especially in the Post-Soviet area and Oceania.

The Right to Self-determination or Inviolability of Borders in the Horn of Africa? The African Union Approach

Kateřina Rudincová

After the end of the Cold War, several separatist movements emerged in the Horn of Africa. Generally speaking, they pointed out that uti possidetis principle had been applied incorrectly in their cases and that they had been deprived of their right to self-determination and, therefore, they had a right to an independent existence. The independence of Eritrea in 1993 and that of South Sudan in 2011, respectively, can be seen as examples of this approach.

On 9 July 2011, South Sudan declared its independence, which was immediately recognized by the United Nations (UN), the states of international community and the African Union (AU). On the other hand, there are ongoing efforts of Somaliland to achieve international recognition and an increasing number of secessionist movements trying to escape from the conflicts within the boundaries of their parent countries, such as the re-formed Biafran movement, which emerged as a response to the violent attacks of Boko Haram in Nigeria.

There are two very different cases of disintegration processes in the Horn of Africa. On the one hand, there is a de facto state[1] of Somaliland, which has not managed to achieve international recognition yet, even though it meets the three basic criteria for the existence of an independent state set out in the Montevideo Convention, i.e. population, territory and state power (Farley 2010, 805; Hoch and Rudincová 2015). Furthermore, it has managed to build a sufficient capacity to enter

---

This chapter is dedicated to the Charles University Research Development Schemes, programme PROGRES Q18—Social sciences: from multidisciplinary to interdisciplinary.

[1]For various definitions of de facto states, see, e.g. Kolstø (2006), Pegg (1998), Piknerová (2009), Riegl (2010).

K. Rudincová (✉)
Department of Geography, Faculty of Science, Humanities and Education,
Technical University of Liberec, Liberec, Czech Republic
e-mail: katerina.rudincova@tul.cz

into foreign relations with other states and also has built up quite an extensive network of unofficial foreign and economic relations. On the other hand, there is a recently formed state of South Sudan, which was recognized by African countries, the AU and the international community immediately after the declaration of its independence. The AU supported its independence despite the fact that it violates the principle of uti possidetis, since South Sudan had never existed separately, and promoted the right of South Sudanese peoples to self-determination.

Secessionist movements in Africa in general argue by their right to self-determination in order to achieve international recognition. This is the case of both Somaliland and South Sudan, which are the subject of this study. The right to self-determination has been enshrined in a vast number of international documents of global and regional organizations. However, it is limited by the ongoing dedication of international community to the territorial integrity of individual states. Even though the Charter of the Organization of African Unity (OAU) adopted in 1963 called for the self-determination of peoples, it determined the inviolability of existing borders in Africa at the same time. The possibility of emergence of new states in Africa and their possible international recognition has been influenced by the geopolitical factors and, therefore, the approach of the OAU and then the AU to these cases has not been consistent. On the one hand, the African Union supported the peace process in Sudan and its attitude to the possible secession of South Sudan has always been conciliatory. On the other hand, the possibility of Somaliland's independent existence is still being denied by the AU, even though it has managed to achieve relative stability and positive political and security development. Therefore, this study will focus on the comparison of the AU approach to these two cases and will evaluate the factors which led to emergence of independent South Sudan on the one hand and to an ongoing denial of the international recognition for Somaliland on the other.

In this respect, this contribution focuses on the processes of disintegration in the Horn of Africa and possibilities of border revisions, with the emphasis mainly placed on the disintegration of the Somali Republic after the outbreak of civil war in comparison with the territorial disintegration of Sudan. A particular interest has been given to the position of the African Union as an important regional governmental organization. The main question of this article is why there are such different postures of this organization towards these two cases? And which conditions does the separatist movement have to fulfil in order to achieve the support from the AU for its claims?

From the methodological point of view, this contribution is a comparative study (e.g. Lijphart 1971; George and Bennett 2005; Ženka and Kofroň 2012) aimed at determining the stance of the AU towards secessionist claims of Somaliland and South Sudan. These two cases have been selected because of their extreme diversity, yet territorial proximity. The underlying research was conducted at the African Union Commission in Addis Ababa, Ethiopia, in October 2010 and between September and November 2011. During the research stays in Addis Ababa, interviews with the AU Commission officials and an interview with a former Somaliland's foreign minister were carried out. These interviews are supplemented by the interview with the official of the Mission of the EU to the AU conducted in Addis Ababa in October 2010 and by the interview with Prof. Iqbal Jhazbhay, an expert on the issue of international recognition of Somaliland, in November 2011 in Addis Ababa. All the interviews had the character of semi-structured expert interviews which means that respondents were given the opportunity to freely express their opinions and stances.

Concerning the structure of the contribution, the first part of the chapter is dedicated to the examination of theoretical concepts, i.e. the right of peoples to self-determination and the principle of uti possidetis or inviolability of borders in Africa in particular. The second part of the contribution is focused on two case studies, South Sudan and Somaliland, and the concluding part is dedicated to their comparison.

1 The Right to Self-determination in the African Context

The concept of the right to self-determination of peoples originated in the Western political thought and was incorporated into the so-called 14 points after the end of the First World War. In fact, it was a plan how to re-organize Europe and was worked out by the American President Woodrow Wilson. The declaration, which recognized the right to self-determination in connection with the independence of colonial peoples, and therefore putting self-determination in the African context as well, was adopted by the UN General Assembly in 1960 as a part of the Resolution 1514-XV. This resolution states that all peoples have right to freedom, sovereignty and integrity of their territory. According to this resolution, "*all peoples have the right to self-determination; by virtue of that right they freely determine their political status and freely pursue their economic, social and cultural development*" (A/RES/1514 (XV)). Furthermore, the right to self-determination is stressed by the International Covenant on Economic, Social and Cultural Rights, adopted by the UN General Assembly Resolution 2200A (XXI) on 16 December 1966. The same principle was incorporated into the International Covenant on Civil and Political Rights adopted on the same day (A/RES/2200A(XXI)).

In the African context, the right to self-determination of peoples was incorporated into the founding documents of both the Organization of African Unity and the African Union, and into the African Charter of Human and Peoples' Rights (Banjul Charter) as well. The Banjul Charter was adopted at the 18th Assembly of Heads of States and Governments of the OAU in Nairobi in June 1981 and came into force in 1986. This Charter for the first time suggested the OAU's commitment to human rights agenda and its shift from the principle of non-interference to internal matters of individual states. It was adopted in response to the violent regimes in the 1970s, such as Idi Amin's regime in Uganda or Jean-Bédel Bokassa's administration in the Central African Republic. With their removal from power, the African states started to focus on human rights agenda more and they were trying to prevent, even though not successfully and effectively, human rights violations.

Besides individual human rights, the Banjul Charter also incorporated the right to self-determination as a group right, which is stressed in the Articles 19 and 20. Article 20 defines self-determination as the "*right to free colonised or oppressed peoples from the bonds of domination*" (CAB/LEG/67/3). However, the formulation of the unquestionable right of all peoples to self-determination in Article 19 and 20 raises questions whether the self-determination should be understood solely in connection with colonized peoples or whether it applies to all peoples. Certain authors, such as Gittleman (1982), understand the right to self-determination solely in connection with the colonized peoples, and they deny the universal right to self-determination for other African nations. Therefore, they argue that in the post-colonial era, the exercise of this right has to be qualified as secession, which is perceived as mostly unacceptable in the international law (Addo 1988, 184). On the other hand, if these articles apply only to colonial territories and peoples, the enforceability of the Charter would be very limited, since no colonial power has ever been a member of the OAU and, therefore, would not be subject to the African Commission's decision-making. The African Charter is an agreement between sovereign African states and members of the OAU, and for that reason, it is not possible to enforce its effectiveness on the non-members of this organization. On the ground of this fact, the effect of the African Charter should not be limited solely to the colonized peoples (Addo 1988, 185).

Article 20 permits the oppressed peoples to use any means recognized by international community to free themselves. However, as the decision of the African Commission in the case of Katanga (ACHPR Com. 75/92 1995) indicates, any exercise of self-determination can be carried out solely in accordance with the principle of sovereignty and territorial integrity. Independence may be achieved only by an agreement with the parent state or with its consent. Moreover, to achieve justified independence, a denial of participation on the basis of ethnicity or territoriality, and at the same time the violation of human rights to the extent which challenges territorial integrity of a particular state have to be proven (Dersso 2012, 62–63). It follows that the Banjul Charter acknowledges the right of secession only as a last resort, since secession inevitably challenges the current state borders in Africa. Therefore, international organizations including the African Union are not very willing to accept the border changes in the interest of preserving the stability of international system.

2 Uti possidetis or Inviolability of Borders in Africa as Limit to Self-determination

Due to the fact that the boundaries in Africa were established on the basis of various European powers' agreements, they are often viewed as artificial constructs with considerable conflict potential. In fact, all the boundaries are man-made, artificial dividing lines drawn by people; i.e., in this context, the borders in Africa do not make any exception (Touval 1972, 3). However, many African borders consist of straight lines and, according to Herbst (1989, 674–675), up to 44% of African borders trace astronomical lines. The difference between African and European boundaries is that the borders in Africa have only recently been created and their delimitation was mostly a result of decisions made by colonial powers without any regard to the local population. The boundaries in Africa may be perceived as arbitrary or unreasonable for two main reasons: they do not respect local conditions, and they were designed by outside powers. Delimitation of the borders in Africa has often caused division of cultural areas between several states. Therefore, it is surprising that this problem has caused an outbreak of armed conflicts in Africa only on a limited scale (Griffiths 1986, 214). However, the Horn of Africa is one of the regions where the insensitive design of national borders led to separatist and irredentist efforts, as reflected in South Sudan and Somaliland in particular.

Since the newly established states in Africa feared potential separatism and claims of particular nations and ethnic groups to self-determination, the principle of uti possidetis or inviolability of borders inherited from the era of colonialism was enshrined in numerous documents adopted by the OAU. Therefore, the OAU Charter approached the issue of self-determination much more moderately, in contrast to the preceding resolutions adopted by the UN. According to paragraph 3 of the Article III of the OAU Charter, "*respect for the sovereignty and territorial integrity of each State and for its inalienable right to independent existence*" is the crucial principle (OAU Charter 1963). The OAU Charter obliges the member states not to interfere in internal affairs of other states. It also stresses the respect for sovereignty and territorial integrity of each state and its right to an independent existence. At the same time, the OAU Charter appealed to the complete emancipation of all African territories, which were still under the colonial rule at the time of its adoption (OAU Charter 1963). However, the OAU supported emancipation of African territories exclusively within the already existing borders, created in the era of colonialism, and refused to revise colonial boundaries.

During the struggle for independence, it was decided by African leaders that new African states would be created within the already existing colonial borders. Political representations of Morocco and Somalia strictly opposed this agreement, since both of these countries have had their territorial and power claims beyond the borders of defined territories. Delegates from the African countries decided about the inviolability of colonial borders in Africa at the OAU Conference in Cairo in 1964, and it was confirmed by the adoption of the Resolution 16 (1), which deals with the territorial disputes between African states. This resolution declared that "*all Member States pledge themselves to respect the borders existing on their achievement of national independence*" (AHG/Res. 16(I) 1964).

The principle of territorial integrity and respect for state sovereignty was also incorporated into the Constitutive Act of the African Union, adopted in 2000 at the Lomé Summit in Togo and entered into force in 2001. These principles are enshrined in the Article 3 which deals with the objectives of the Union (Constitutive Act of African Union 2000).

By incorporating these clauses into the founding documents and by the adoption of the Resolution 16 (1), the principle of the right of African peoples to self-determination promoted by the UN has been replaced by the doctrine of inviolability of borders in Africa promoted by the OAU and the AU. By this decision, all the efforts to revise inherited borders in Africa became de-legitimate and the separatist and irredentist claims have met with incomprehension. Newly emerged African states were concerned that their territory might be fragmented into smaller political units that would require autonomy or even independence. By adopting resolutions on the inviolability of borders in Africa, they intended to prevent the emergence of separatist movements and outbreak of new independence wars and conflicts. However, exceptions and at the same time precedents occurred in 1993, when Eritrea separated from Ethiopia, and in 2011, respectively, when the referendum on South Sudanese independence was held. Unilateral attempts to achieve independence also occurred, for example, in Somaliland, which declared independence in 1991. The approach of the OAU and later the AU towards the secessions in Africa seems to be ambivalent, since the AU has promoted the formation of independent state in South Sudan and, on the other hand, has railed very critically against the possibility of recognizing the separate existence of Somaliland.[2] The AU approach and arguments it uses to support its policy towards South Sudan and Somaliland are the subject of the following case studies.

3 South Sudan: Secession by Consent

The entire area of Sudan was during the colonial era administered as an Anglo-Egyptian condominium. However, the British policy in southern and northern Sudan differed significantly. The British intended to use southern Sudan as a kind of barrier against the spread of Islam, and therefore, they supported Christian missions sent to the southern Sudan for the purpose of converting locals to Christianity. Use of English at the expense of Arabic was promoted in the south as well and even wearing the traditional Islamic clothing was prohibited (Collins 2008, 35). Britain decided to administer Sudan using the so-called indirect administration, which means that it used local tribal rulers and existing political and social structures. However, due to this policy, British de facto separated "Arab" and "African" population of Sudan and created two distinct political and social entities. The reason for these measures was the attempt to limit the Arab-Islamic influence in the area and to maintain an "African" culture in southern Sudan (Idris 2004, 37–38). As Francis Deng states, the "crisis of national identity" was achieved in Sudan (Deng 1995, 9), since the local inhabitants maintained their ethnic identity and perceived themselves more as Dinka, Nuer or Shilluk than Sudanese. All these factors led to

---

[2]Interview with the Peace and Security Council official, AU Commission, Addis Ababa, 7.10.2010.

the outcome that South Sudan went through a different political and historical development, making it difficult to reunify the two parts of the country into one state (see Rudincová 2015).

Independent Sudan was established in 1956 following a referendum on independence on Egypt and inherited colonial boundaries created by international treaties. The newly formed Sudan was identified as an Arab-Islamic state, and the marginalization of the South occurred almost immediately after gaining independence (Illés 2011, 102). The denial of the right to self-determination of the southern Sudanese ethnic groups led to the outbreak of a long-term civil war in the South. The Sudanese government tried to resolve the rebellion by force at first, but in 1971, it realized that the military solution was impossible and agreed to peace talks with southern rebel groups. One year later, peace agreement between Sudanese government and rebel forces was signed in Addis Ababa and the regional autonomy of South Sudan was recognized (Deng 2010, 35).

The period of peace in Sudan ended when President Jafar Nimairi declared Sudan an Islamic state in 1983 and introduced the Islamic law Sharia across the country. Immediately, opposition groups were created in the southern Sudan. They demanded either the emancipation of the southern Sudanese peoples, as Sudan People Liberation Movement (SPLM), led by John Garang, or complete independence, as wanted by Anyanya II, or Southern Sudan Independence Movement (SSIM) (Prunier and Gisselquist 2003, 105).

During the conflict, there were several attempts initiated mainly from abroad to negotiate peace between the belligerent parties. Nigeria and Intergovernmental Authority on Development (IGAD) chaired by Kenya were the most significant mediators in these negotiations. All of these initiatives, however, failed on key issues, such as setting the boundaries in case of formation of a new state in southern Sudan, or on the conditions of the referendum in the South (Prunier and Gisselquist 2003, 106).

The conflict in Sudan was not limited only to the area of this state, but it indirectly affected all the neighbouring countries, themselves relatively unstable. As a consequence, their own political and security interests were reflected in the Sudanese peace process. For example, Kenya was involved in the peace process, which did not exclude the formation of an independent state in southern Sudan and endorsed the right to self-determination of the southern Sudanese population. On the other hand, Egypt stood up against it and clearly supported unified Sudan (International Crisis Group 2010, 1). Ethiopia, another important regional player, supported South Sudan in its efforts to achieve independence. However, at the same time, Ethiopia maintained good relations with Khartoum and following the secession of Eritrea used Port Sudan, as the secession caused loss of direct access to the sea. Support of South Sudan by Ethiopia stems from the efforts to maintain the balance and security in the Horn of Africa. Any conflict that would once again flare up in Sudan could also spill over to the Ethiopian region of Gambella, which belongs to the most unstable regions in Ethiopia (International Crisis Group 2010, 12–13; Riegl and Doboš 2014, 186–187).

The great success of the peace talks was achieved on 9 January 2005, when the Comprehensive Peace Agreement (CPA) was signed between the Sudanese government and SPLM and ended the long conflict between northern and southern Sudan. In the Article 1.3, the agreement stated that "*the people of South Sudan have the right to self-determination, inter alia, through a referendum to determine their future status*". Based on this statement in the CPA, the people of South Sudan received a six-year transitional period during which the transitional government should have been formed and they should have prepared for a referendum on independence (Deng 2010, 36–37). Due to the prolonged civil war and the feeling of great injustices that was deeply rooted among the inhabitants of southern Sudan, but also due to the location of oil reserves in the southern provinces, it was already a foregone conclusion that if the referendum on independence of the southern Sudan was to be held, the majority of the population would vote in favour of this option. Ideas about a united Sudan would have been acceptable for the residents of the southern provinces only if the new state would be based on strictly secular principles and southern elites would be integrated into state administrative bodies (Kalpakian 2006, 54). However, provisions of the CPA were still designed to "*make unity attractive*" based on the efforts of John Garang to achieve a reformed Sudan and secession was considered the last resort only if the Sudanese government failed to meet the requirements expressed in the peace agreement. Development of the CPA was a result of long-term negotiations, which were supported from abroad, especially from the USA, Great Britain and Norway and regional organizations, for example from IGAD (Intergovernmental Authority on Development) and the African Union. The referendum on independence took place on 11 January 2011, and people of southern Sudan voted 98.8% for independence with a turnout at 97.6% (Southern Sudan Referendum Commission 2011). Consequently, the independent existence of a new state was declared on 9 July 2011. The African Union surprisingly did not prevent the emergence of a new state in the Horn of Africa and, even on the contrary, the representatives of the Peace and Security Department of the AU welcomed the emergence of South Sudan with enthusiasm. South Sudanese independence was immediately recognized by the African Union and its member states, and South Sudan was officially accepted as a 55th member of this organization on 27 July 2011 (Tekle 2011). The main argument, which supported the creation of this state, is that the representation of South Sudan managed to conclude an agreement with a government in the north.[3] Moreover, the status of southern Sudanese nation was determined in a referendum, which was held on the basis of the CPA. Owing to the fact that southern Sudanese people identified themselves as a nation, they decided for independent existence based on the results of a referendum.[4] Therefore, it is possible to deduce that the AU allows the creation of new

---

[3]Interview with the Peace and Security Council official, AU Commission, Addis Ababa, 7.10.2010.

[4]Interview with the Political Affairs Department official, AU Commission, Addis Ababa, 15.11.2011.

states and review of colonial borders solely in the cases when the agreement between the government and separatists has been achieved.[5] The emergence of South Sudan and its right to self-determination were also affected by geopolitical interests of great powers in the region. An important geopolitical and geoeconomic factor of the Sudanese conflict is an oil extraction in southern provinces. The countries, which participated in oil production in southern Sudan, had their own interests in the region. Therefore, they endeavoured to reach safety in order not to jeopardize oilfields and pipelines and at the same time were trying to end the conflict between the central government and the SPLM (El-Tigani 2001, 50–51).

Recognized independence of South Sudan also suggests a changing international policy in Africa, which has become more focused on the issue of human rights, democratization and peaceful conflict resolution. The support of South Sudan by the AU illustrates this new understanding of African politics. Territorial changes are no longer understood solely as the cause of wars and violence, but can be used as a last resort to settle disputes in the cases where other solutions are not possible. However, the AU approach to South Sudan may not be conceived as universal within African international politics, since there is still a considerable emphasis put on the inviolability of colonial borders and on the respect of territorial integrity.

4 Somaliland and Possibilities of Its International Recognition

Another case analysed in this contribution is Somaliland, which has existed as a de facto state since 1991, when the representatives of the Somali National Movement unilaterally declared its independence at the Grand Conference of Northern Nations (*Shirweynaha Beelaha Waqooyi*) on 18 May that year. Its territory corresponds to the former British Protectorate of Somaliland, while the southern regions of Somalia were administered under Italian colonial rule. Both regions went through different historical and political development and gained their independence in 1960. Even before uniting both former colonies into one state, there was a 5-day independent existence of Somaliland, recognized by 35 states (Jhazbhay 2003, 79; Bradbury et al. 2003; Bryden 2003, 342). Just this recognized independence in 1960 is the main argument used by the political representation of Somaliland to justify why the independence of Somaliland should be recognized once again by the international community.[6] Argument of a 5-day independence, however, can only be used as a legal issue, not a political one. The actual states' politics and, therefore,

---

[5]Interview with the Peace and Security Council official, AU Commission, Addis Ababa, 7.10.2010.
[6]Interview with the Somaliland's former Minister of Foreign Affairs, Addis Ababa, 15.10.2010.

their willingness to grant international recognition are influenced by efforts to achieve peace in Somalia, and Somaliland's independence does not fit into this framework.[7]

Legitimization efforts of Somaliland's independence are also based on different colonial past compared to southern Somalia and the fact that Somaliland in fact does not violate the colonial borders, since it only claims such a Somali territory which previously belonged to the British Protectorate of Somaliland and was recognized as an independent state in 1960.[8] The international boundaries of Somaliland are determined in Article 2 of the Somaliland Constitution. It states that *"(t)he territory of the Republic of Somaliland covers the same area as that of the former Somaliland Protectorate and is located between Latitude 8' to 11'30' north of the equator and Longitude 42'45 to 49' East"* (Constitution of the Republic of Somaliland 2001). Therefore, in this case, the principle of uti possidetis, which means the inviolability of boundaries inherited from the colonial past, is respected. Somaliland uses its colonial past as well as the border issue to justify its efforts to achieve its separate existence, since its political representation argues that it does not require anything more than merely maintaining the colonial borders.[9] As noted by the representative of the AU Border Programme, "Somaliland is a victim of the principle of uti possidetis". According to him, Resolution 16 (1) adopted in 1964 did not mean that colonial boundaries should not be revised afterwards and did not impose such a ban on demands of self-determination. However, African countries themselves "criminalized" self-determination, while trying to institutionalize the colonial boundaries, from which the local elites benefited the most.[10]

As representatives of the African Union declared during interviews, the separate existence of Somaliland has no justification due to the fact that the British and Italian colonies united into one state voluntarily and without any challenge of this act. Therefore, the doctrine of acceptance was applied in this case, which means that when a certain state persists and is not questioned, it comes into validity.[11] According to a former Foreign Minister of Somaliland, however, the act of uniting the British and Italian colonies into one state took place under a manipulated and rigged referendum and, therefore, it is considered to be invalid.[12] The Union of Somaliland and Somalia Law was passed by the Legislative Assembly of Somaliland on 27 June 1960, but it has never been signed by the southern authorities. A similar law, Atto di Unione, was passed in southern Somalia on 30 June 1960. However, this law significantly differed from the one passed in Somaliland and, therefore, it did not come into force (Poor 2009). Dissatisfaction of

---

[7]Interview with the Mission of EU to AU official, Addis Ababa, 29.9.2010.
[8]Interview with the Somaliland's former Minister of Foreign Affairs, Addis Ababa, 15.10.2010.
[9]Interview with the Somaliland's former Minister of Foreign Affairs, Addis Ababa, 15.10.2010.
[10]Interview with the AU Border Programme official, AU Commission, Addis Ababa 18.11.2011.
[11]Interview with the Political Affairs Department official, AU Commission, Addis Ababa, 15.11.2011.
[12]Interview with the Somaliland's former Minister of Foreign Affairs, Addis Ababa, 15.10.2010.

the representatives of northern Somalia led to the boycott of constitutional referendum, and thus, the constitution was approved only due to the high voter turnout in southern Somalia.

Similarly to South Sudan, Somaliland also justifies its independence by the declaration that the right to self-determination of northern clans and their human rights have been violated (Jhazbhay 2003, 44) and, therefore, they should exercise their remedial right to self-determination. Marginalization of the northern Isaaq clan and the dictatorial regime of Siad Barre resulted in a resistance struggle of the local population and the outbreak of civil war, which flared up in the north at first. All these factors led to the overthrow of the regime, and on 18 May 1991, the independence of the State of Somaliland was unilaterally declared. Its independence was confirmed in the "national referendum" held in 2001 (Roethke 2011, 37–38). However, the representatives of the African Union declared during the interviews that an all-Somali referendum is one of the crucial conditions for granting recognition. Moreover, the constitutional referendum held in Somaliland in 2001 is not, in their opinion, perceived as an explicitly expressed referendum on the independence of Somaliland.[13] In the case of South Sudan and Eritrea, however, the referendums held solely in the regions that tried to secede from their parent states were enough for the recognition of independence.

A relatively successful democratization process and the creation of representative institutions in Somaliland are the key arguments used by the Somaliland's political representatives in order to justify their demands for self-determination and independent existence.[14] At this time, Somalia is still a failed state and the internationally recognized Somali government does not have adequate capacities to provide internal self-determination. In this context, the right to unilateral remedial secession of Somaliland can be seen as justifiable. Secession and independent existence would contribute to economic and political development of the country, and it could possibly positively affect the development of entire region.[15] Although the international organizations have been recognizing the successes achieved by Somaliland's government, especially in contrast to the development in southern Somalia, the successful peace process in Somaliland is perceived by them more as motivation for southern Somalia, but not a strong argument for international recognition.[16]

The AU fact-finding mission was sent to Somaliland between 30 April and 4 May 2005 under the leadership of a deputy chairman of the AU Patrick Mazimhaka. This mission found that Somaliland fulfils many aspects of statehood and positive developments have been achieved. It is expressed in the report, prepared on the

---

[13]Interview with the Peace and Security Council official, AU Commission, Addis Ababa, 7.10.2010.

[14]Interview with the Somaliland's former Minister of Foreign Affairs, Addis Ababa, 15.10.2010.

[15]Interview with the Somaliland's former Minister of Foreign Affairs, Addis Ababa, 15.10.2010.

[16]Interview with the Peace and Security Council official, AU Commission, Addis Ababa, 7.10.2010.

basis of this mission, that the case of Somaliland deserves special consideration and may not be viewed as opening of the "Pandora box". Consequently, the African Union should try to find a way how to deal with Somaliland without international recognition.[17] Another AU Mission sent to Somaliland between 12 and 14 September 2008 came to similar conclusions. At the summit of the Foreign Ministers of the AU in Accra, in the same year, however, the case of Somaliland was sidelined. Subsequently, in 2010, the Peace and Security Council of the AU recommended the Chairperson of the AU Commission to approach the cases of Somaliland and Puntland as parts of an overall effort to achieve peace and stability in Somalia (Clapham et al. 2011, 11). Somaliland applied for membership in the African Union in 2005. However, since it has not been internationally recognized, it may not be accepted as a member and, moreover, the African Union does not recognize observatory status.[18] On account of this fact, the political representation of Somaliland has been trying to establish unofficial political and economic relations with influential states, both in Africa and Europe. For example, Somaliland has opened its liaison offices in Great Britain, USA, Ethiopia, Norway and other countries. It establishes international relations by means of its ministry of foreign affairs. Its political representation pays regular visits to European and African countries and USA as well and, on the contrary, it welcomes delegations from all over the world. The most important political and economic partner of Somaliland in the region is undoubtedly Ethiopia, which has signed a number of bilateral agreements with Somaliland, for example the agreement on the use of the port of Berbera on the Somaliland coast in 2006 or on the provisions of customs offices along the common border (Farley 2010, 789).

A problematic issue of the situation in Somaliland seems to be the fact that no agreement has been reached with the internationally recognized Somali Federal Government, which controls the southern parts of Somalia, and its predecessor, Transition Federal Government. In addition, some of Somaliland's politicians have been steadfastly refusing any negotiations. The interviews, conducted at the African Union, however, indicated that an agreement with the Somali government is seen as a crucial point to recognize the independence of Somaliland from the African Union.[19] In this context, the talks between Somaliland and Somalia started in 2012 in the UK and continued by the negotiations mediated by Turkey in 2013. It was the first time Somaliland politicians met with their Somali counterparts and talks continued in Dubai, London, Djibouti and mainly in Turkey since then. However, the talks were not successful at the end because of mutual distrust and blame and the negotiations scheduled for 2015 in Turkey were postponed (Gamute 2015).

---

[17]Interview with the Peace and Security Council official, AU Commission, Addis Ababa, 7.10.2010.

[18]Interview with the Political Affairs Department official, AU Commission, Addis Ababa 15.11.2011.

[19]Interview with the Peace and Security Council official, AU Commission, Addis Ababa, 7.10.2010.

The issue of international recognition of Somaliland is affected by the regional geopolitics, since each of the regional powers has its own interests in this area. The African Union perceives the Somali government as the representative of the entire Somalia; a similar view is held by Egypt, since it supports a strong Somali state as a counter-balancing force to Ethiopia. Ethiopia has developed political and economic relations with Somaliland. On the other hand, it does not support the international recognition of Somaliland, since it worries that recognized independent existence of Somaliland could cause insurgencies among the Somali population in the Ethiopian region of Ogaden. The Western states have adopted an attitude of non-interference in the African affairs in the case of international recognition of Somaliland, and they have been waiting for African states to recognize Somaliland first (Lalos 2011, 811–813). The problem of Somaliland, according to the representatives of the Legal Counsel of the AU, is that it is "too successful" and, therefore, does not attract much attention of the international community.[20] In a similar fashion, Prof. Jhazbhay identifies as a problem of Somaliland its small size and importance. For this reason, Somaliland needs a patron state, which would contribute to its reconstruction and help it to achieve international recognition.[21]

Additionally, Somaliland's ability to achieve international recognition is largely influenced by the interests and policies of regional powers, especially Ethiopia. It also occupies a prominent position within the regional organizations, such as IGAD and the African Union. However, due to its position, Ethiopia, although it has developed a broad spectrum of unofficial relations with Somaliland, is not willing to be a proponent of international recognition of Somaliland since it fears to be accused of fragmentation of Somalia (Shinn 2002, 3).

5 Conclusion: Possibilities of Border Revisions? South Sudan and Somaliland Compared

As the two analysed case studies have shown, referring to a separate colonial past is an important legitimization factor in the African context. Member states of the OAU and later the AU have committed themselves to respect the territorial integrity of African states and the existence of borders inherited from the colonial past. These principles were enshrined in the OAU Charter, Resolution 16 (1) adopted in 1964 and the Constitutional Act of AU. For this reason, both South Sudan and Somaliland referred to the distinct historical and political development during the colonial era, in order to legitimize their claims to independence.

The interviews conducted have revealed that an important requirement for justifiable secession in Africa is negotiations with the parent state and the conclusion

---

[20]Interview with the AU Director of the Office of the Legal Counsel, AU Commission, Addis Ababa, 17.11.2011.

[21]Interview with Prof. Iqbal Jhazbhay, Addis Ababa, 18.11.2011.

of an agreement under which the referendum on independence would be held. Based on this requirement, the independence of Eritrea and South Sudan was recognized by the international community. In the case of Eritrea, EPLF succeeded together with the EPRDF in removing the Mengistu Haile Mariam's regime by military means. Subsequently, EPLF was able to negotiate the holding of the referendum, under which the independence of Eritrea was recognized. Although SPLM was unable to defeat the Sudanese regime militarily, the result of diplomatic negotiations supported from abroad was the conclusion of the CPA. Under this agreement, a referendum was held and vast majority of South Sudanese population voted for the independence of South Sudan, which was recognized by the international community immediately after the declaration of an independent South Sudanese State. In the case of Somaliland, however, the situation is complicated by the fact that Somalia has been a failed state since the outbreak of civil war in 1991. Despite international support for the peace process and many efforts to create a representative and credible government in southern Somalia, for a long time there has not been any credible partner who Somaliland would be willing to negotiate the future of its state with.

The right to self-determination of nations prevailed over the principle of uti possidetis in the case of South Sudan, since identity of the South was formed during a long period of British colonial rule. South Sudan has managed to achieve independence and international recognition without any doubt because its political representatives managed to gain the support of the international community. Although the case of South Sudan showed more signs of secession than Somaliland, in this case it was acceptable for the African Union to recognize its independence, because there was a long civil war going on that resulted in a humanitarian crisis. The protracted civil war led to the devastation of both the south Sudanese land and local population, which provoked outrage around the world. For the African Union, in this situation, it seemed more acceptable to acknowledge the emergence of a new state in southern Sudan, which could lead to a greater degree of stability in the region. In this case, the question whether recognition of Somaliland could also contribute to solving long-term Somali civil war arises. Somaliland paradoxically does not enjoy much attention of the international community, because there is relative peace, institutions have been created there and certain success has been achieved in the area of democratization. Moreover, people of Somaliland are still considered to be part of the Somali nation, and thus, the right to self-determination is being challenged in their case. As it is evident from the presented case studies, the right to self-determination of peoples and the principle of uti possidetis are used ambivalently, and in the African politics and international law, they are still very vague terms. Each case is being treated differently, and the emphasis is also put on the perception of the state abroad and on the approach of the international community. For Somaliland, in order to achieve international recognition, the only option is to try to turn the attention of international community to its case and gain the political support from the African states in particular. Only African states can raise the issue of international recognition at the Assembly of African Union. Due to the fact that Somaliland has been marginalized in international politics and more attention has been paid to the southern regions of Somalia, it will continue to be interesting to observe whether political representation of Somaliland will be successful in its efforts.

References

Addo, M. (1988). Political self-determination within the context of the African charter on human and peoples' rights. *Journal of African Law, 32*(2), 182–193.
African Commission on Human and People's Rights. (1995). *Katangese Peoples' Congress v Zaire*. Communication 75/92., 8th Annual Activity Report of ACHPR. ACHPR Com. 75/92 1995.
African Union. (2000). *Constitutive act*. http://www.peaceau.org/uploads/au-act-en.pdf
Bradbury, M., Abokor, A. Y., & Yusuf, H. A. (2003). Somaliland: Choosing politics over violence. *Review of African Political Economy, 30*(97), 455–478.
Bryden, M. (2003). The "banana test": Is Somaliland ready for recognition? *Annales d'Ethiopie, 19*, 341–364.
Clapham, C. et al. (2011). *African game changer? The consequences of Somaliland's international (non) recognition*. Discussion Paper 2011/05. The Brenthurst Foundation. http://www.thebrenthurstfoundation.org/Files/Brenthurst_Commisioned_Reports/BD-1105_Consequences-of-Somalilands-International-Recognition.pdf. Accessed October 27, 2016.
Collins, R. O. (2008). *A history of modern Sudan*. Cambridge: Cambridge University Press.
Deng, F. (1995). *War of visions. Conflict of identities in the Sudan*. Washington, DC: The Brookings Institution Press.
Deng, F. (Ed.). (2010). *New Sudan in the making? Essays on a nation in painful search of itself*. Asmara: The Red Sea Press.
Dersso, S. (2012). The African human rights system and the issue of minorities in Africa. *African Journal of International and Comparative Law, 20*(1), 42–69.
El-Tigani, M. (2001). Solving the crisis of Sudan: The right of self-determination versus state torture. *Arab Studies Quarterly, 23*(2), 41–59.
Farley, B. (2010). Calling a state a state: Somaliland and international recognition. *Emory International Law Review, 24*(2), 777–820.
Gamute, H. (2015). The deadlock of Somaliland and Somalia talks. Center for Policy Analysis. http://centerforpolicy.net/the-deadlock-of-somaliland-and-somalia-talks-2/. Accessed October 27, 2016.
George, A. L., & Bennett, A. (2005). *Case studies and theory development in the social sciences*. Cambridge: The MIT Press.
Gittleman, R. (1982). The African charter on human and peoples' rights: A legal analysis. *Virginia Journal of International Law, 22*(4), 667–714.
Griffiths, I. (1986). The scramble for Africa: Inherited political boundaries. *The Geographical Journal, 152*(2), 204–216.
Herbst, J. (1989). The creation of national boundaries in Africa. *International Organization, 43*(4), 673–692.
Hoch, T., & Rudincová, K. (2015). Legitimization of statehood in de facto states: A case study of Somaliland. *AUC Geographica, 50*(1), 37–49.
Idris, A. (2004). The Racialized and Islamicised sudanese state and the question of Southern Sudan. In A. Jalata (Ed.), *State crises, globalisation and national movements in North-East Africa* (pp. 30–44). London and New York: Routledge.
Illés, Z. (2011). Towards an independent Southern Sudan. In I. Tarrósy, L. Szabó, & G. Hyden (Eds.), *The African state in a changing global context. Breakdowns and transformations* (pp. 101–115). Berlin: LIT Verlag.

International Crisis Group. (2010). *Sudan: Regional perspectives on the prospect of southern independence*. Africa Report No. 159. http://www.crisisgroup.org/en/regions/africa/horn-of-africa/sudan/159-sudan-regional-perspectives-on-the-prospect-of-southern-independence.aspx. Accessed September 29, 2015.
Jhazbhay, I. (2003). Somaliland: Africa's best kept secret. A challenge to the international community? *African Security Review, 12*(4), 77–82.
Kalpakian, J. (2006). War over identity: The case of Sudan. In C. Clapham, J. Herbst, & G. Mills (Eds.), *Big African states* (pp. 39–61). Johannesburg: Wits University Press.
Kolstø, P. (2006). The sustainability and future of unrecognized quasi-states. *Journal of Peace Research, 43*(6), 723–740.
Lalos, D. (2011). Between statehood and Somalia: Reflections of Somaliland statehood. *Washington University Global Studies Law Review, 10*, 789–812.
Lijphart, A. (1971). Comparative politics and a comparative method. *The American Political Science Review, 65*(3), 682–693.
Organization of African Unity. (1963). *OAU charter*. http://www.au2002.gov.za/docs/key_oau/oau_charter.pdf
Organization of African Unity. (1964). *Resolution on border disputes among African states*. OAU Document AHG/Res. 16(I).
Organization of African Unity. (1981). *African [Banjul] charter on human and peoples' rights*, OAU Doc. CAB/LEG/67/3.
Pegg, S. (1998). *International society and the de facto state*. Aldershot: Ashgate.
Piknerová, L. (2009). Deviantní podoby státnosti—příklad kvazistátů. *Acta FF ZČU, 3*, 259–273.
Poor, B. (2009). Somaliland: shackled to a failed state. *Stanford Journal of International Law, 117* (45), 117–150.
Prunier, G., & Gisselquist, R. (2003). The Sudan: A successfully failed state. In R. Rotberg (Ed.), *State failure and state weakness in a time of terror* (pp. 101–127). Washington, DC: Brookings Institution Press.
Republic of Somaliland. (2001). *Constitution of the Republic of Somaliland*. http://www.somalilandlaw.com/Somaliland_Constitution_Text_only_Eng_IJSLL.pdf
Riegl, M. (2010). Terminologie kvazistátů. *Acta Politologica, 2*(1), 57–71.
Riegl, M., & Doboš, B. (2014). Secession in post-modern world: Cases of South Sudan and Somaliland. *Acta Geographica Universitatis Comenianae, 58*(2), 173–192.
Roethke, P. (2011). The right to secede under international law: The case of Somaliland. *Journal of International Service, 20*(2), 35–47.
Rudincová, K. (2015). When colonial borders still matter. The emergence of South Sudan. *Journal of African History, Politics and Society, 1*(1), 85–115.
Shinn, D. H. (2002). *Somaliland: The little country that could. Africa notes* (Vol. 9, pp. 1–7). Washington, DC: Centre for Strategic and International Studies.
Southern Sudan Referendum Commission. (2011). *Results for the referendum of Southern Sudan*. http://southernsudan2011.com/. Accessed October 27, 2016.
Tekle, T.-A. (2011). African Union accepts South Sudan as new member state. *Sudan Tribune*. http://www.sudantribune.com/spip.php?article39670. Accessed October 26, 2016.
Touval, S. (1972). *The boundary politics of independent Africa*. Cambridge: Harvard University Press.
UN General Assembly. (1960). *Resolution 1514 (XV). declaration on the granting of independence to colonial countries and peoples*. A/RES/1514(XV).
United Nations. (1966a). *International covenant on civil and political rights*. A/RES/2200A(XXI).
United Nations. (1966b). *International covenant on economic, social and cultural rights*. A/RES/2200A(XXI).
Ženka, J., & Kofroň, J. (2012). Metodologie výzkumu v sociální geografii—případové studie. Ostravská univerzita.

Author Biography

Kateřina Rudincová is an Assistant professor at the Department of Geography, Faculty of Sciences, Humanities and Education, Technical University of Liberec. She is dealing with the international relations, politics and border issues in Africa and, in recent years, has published in this field. Her main research interest is the territorial fragmentation of Somalia with special focus on the emergence of Somaliland studied in comparison with the fragmentation of Sudan. She conducted three researches at the Commission of African Union in Addis Ababa in the years 2010, 2011 and 2015.

Long Way to Recognition: Challenges Facing the European "Newborn" from the 2015 Perspective

Jan Bečka

Two very different images would provide, at least in the opinion of the author, the best scene-setter for this contribution.

17 February 2008: the Kosovo Assembly, despite the boycott of all its 11 Serb minority members, unilaterally declared independence. In Kosovo's capital, Pristina, people gathered in front of the newly unveiled "Newborn monument" and in other popular places and celebrated the news. The unpopular UN interim administration (United Nations Mission in Kosovo, UNMIK) came to an end. The jubilant mood of the Albanian majority population persisted as several leading world and European powers, such as the United States, the United Kingdom, France or Germany recognized Kosovo's independence in the matter of days after its declaration.[1] While some problems with Pristina's international standing were to be expected, such as the negative attitude of Russia and China, and the complicated relationship with Serbia, overall the future looked quite bright. Despite the end of international administration, the new state would still be assisted in its political and economic development by a host of international organizations such as the UN, the EU, OSCE and others. NATO KFOR mission would remain in the country to maintain safe and secure environment, even though its numbers would gradually be reduced.

This chapter is dedicated to the Charles University Research Development Schemes, programme PROGRES Q18—Social sciences: from multidisciplinary to interdisciplinary.

---

[1]France, the United States and the United Kingdom recognized Kosovo already on 18 February, Germany on 20 February. For the full list of countries that have recognized Kosovo, see Who Recognized Kosovo as an Independent State?, http://www.kosovothanksyou.com/. Accessed 29 November 2015.

J. Bečka (✉)
Faculty of Social Sciences, Institute of International Studies,
Charles University, Prague, Czech Republic
e-mail: jan.becka@gmail.com

© Springer International Publishing AG 2017
M. Riegl and B. Doboš (eds.), *Unrecognized States and Secession in the 21st Century*, DOI 10.1007/978-3-319-56913-0_12

23 October 2015: the session of the Kosovo Assembly had to be suspended twice as the opposition law-makers interrupted an ongoing debate on adopting agreements with Serbia and Montenegro by throwing canisters with tear gas into the main assembly hall. It was just another incident of this kind within the last 2 or 3 months and more were to follow. Outside the building, government supporters and protesters violently clashed, forcing the Kosovo Police to disperse them (The Balkan Insight 2015). The incidents in the Assembly followed a protracted political crisis which had already started in 2014 and which the Assembly elections in June of that year only further exacerbated. The opposition attacks and protests, while in this case motivated by unpopular "rapprochement" with Serbia, had in fact been a reflection of a growing frustration with the political and economic situation in Kosovo and disappointment with the slow pace of its Euro-Atlantic integration. Seven years after the declaration of independence, it again became clear that there is a long way ahead.

1 Becoming Truly Independent: Is It Easy to Start a New Country?

In the wake of Kosovo's declaration of independence, Joshua Keating published a short article in *Foreign Policy* in which he, in a somewhat relaxed fashion, provided a manual for creating a new state. In particular, using the example of Kosovo, he listed four necessary steps for accomplishing this goal: (1) make sure you are eligible; (2) declare independence; (3) get recognized; (4) join the club (meaning the UN) (Keating 2008). Despite the nature of the article, which is not meant to be taken completely seriously, the points that Keating is listing as preconditions for "starting a new country" are essentially applicable, of course to a degree. In analyzing the reasons behind the challenges that Kosovo has been and will be facing in the coming years, many of issues closely related to international recognition, membership in the UN (and other international organizations), creating a national identity and a functioning state apparatus, will come to the fore. The author will be basing his research and arguments mainly on primary documents, especially those prepared and made public by the international institutions active in Kosovo. In addition, scholarship by academics and experts dealing with various aspects of Kosovo's statehood and national identity will also be made use of.

2 International Recognition

As already mentioned, some of the important supporters of Kosovo have granted recognition to the new entity almost immediately after it was declared. While this was definitely an encouragement for the Kosovo government, it was clear that it would be much more difficult to obtain such recognition from others. Almost 8 years after the declaration was made, Kosovo has received 112 diplomatic recognitions. 108[2] UN member states recognize it as an independent state, as do 23 out of 28 EU member states.[3] While the numbers do seem impressive, it has to be kept in mind that in the recent years the new recognitions have come from the countries which are not major players on the world scene—for example the Solomon Islands or Lesotho.

The states that refuse to recognize Kosovo have various reasons for their stance. Countries like Spain, Slovakia or Romania fear that accepting the existence of independent Kosovo would bolster the claims of their minorities for independence (as in the case of Catalonia) or at least for much greater autonomy (as in the case of Hungarian minorities in Slovakia and Romania). For Cyprus, there are self-evident parallels with the occupation of the northern part of the island by Turkey in 1974 and the establishment of the Turkish Republic of Northern Cyprus, recognized only by Ankara. Greece, the last of the five EU states which have not recognized Kosovo, feels obliged to support the position of Cyprus and is also very concerned about the future of the Eastern Orthodox monasteries in Kosovo after independence. Despite the fact that in recent years especially Greece, and to some very limited degree Slovakia, have shown willingness to modify their stance, so far no major progress has been reached on establishing regular diplomatic relations.[4] This might have serious implications in the future with regards to Kosovo's aspirations to join the EU. The European Parliament has urged the five non-recognizers on several occasions[5] to proceed with the recognition, but it has no authority to order them to do so.

While the position of the EU members might eventually change, the refusal of Russia to recognize Kosovo would be a much more difficult hurdle to overcome. Since the beginning of the Kosovo crisis in 1999, Russia has taken a very clear stance in support of Serbia and the deployment of its forces to the Pristina Airport in June 1999 almost led to an open conflict with NATO. From Moscow's point of view, Kosovo remains a part of Serbia, temporarily administered by the UN based on the UN Resolution 1244. Even after the International Court of Justice delivered its advisory opinion on the Kosovo's declaration of independence on 22 July 2010 (International Court of Justice 2010), in which it stated that it did not violate international law, Russia's stance remained unchanged. The often repeated argument that the acceptance of the unilateral declaration would open the "Pandora's box" for other separatist movements and groups, however, became rather weak after Russia had endorsed and directly supported similar actions in South Ossetia,

---

[2]The four non UN members are the Cook Islands, Niue, Republic of China (Taiwan), and Sovereign Military Order of Malta.

[3]Available at http://www.mfa-ks.net/?page=2,33. Accessed 10 January 2016.

[4]Three of these countries—Greece, Romania and Slovakia—are represented in Pristina on the level of a liaison office. Spain and Cyprus are not represented.

[5]For example in 2015, as a part of a yearly resolution dealing with the progress made by the states in the Western Balkans towards EU accession (European Parliament 2015).

Abkhazia, and more recently, in Crimea (the case of Eastern Ukraine being rather more complicated in this regard). While it would be easy to criticize Russia for its hypocrisy on this matter, and it has been done on a number of occasions, Moscow could counter these accusations by saying that it has only done what the Western countries have previously done in Kosovo. In any case, Russia is extremely unlikely to recognize Kosovo in the current situation unless granted a concession in other disputed issues.

Finally, the relationship with Serbia still remains fraught with complications. Since 2008, the situation has somewhat improved as Belgrade and Pristina have agreed to hold both high-level and technical talks together, mediated by the European Union. The talks under the so-called "Brussels Agreement"[6] started in Brussels in the spring of 2013 and have continued since, although with a varying frequency. From the outset, it was clear that while certain issues, such as an agreement on collecting car insurance, integration of police forces in northern Kosovo into the Kosovo Police force, or issues related to energy and telecommunication services will ultimately be resolved, there are things where Pristina and Belgrade will repeatedly clash. For example, the agreement envisioned the establishment of the "Association/Community of Serb Majority Municipalities" in Kosovo, which was to have "a full overview of the areas of economic development, education, health, urban and rural planning" (RTS 2013). The text of the agreement, however, is very vague on details and the interpretation of the authority and competencies given to the Association/Community was left open to interpretation of either side. Thus, while Pristina viewed the entity more as a loosely organized association of the municipalities where the Serbs form the majority or a significant part of population, Belgrade presented it as a fully autonomous unit funded partially from the Kosovo budget and partially by Belgrade.[7] Even the perception of the international community of the benefits of establishing such an entity varied. While the supporters of the idea of "Association/Community" pointed out that it will help to ensure further economic and social development of the municipalities with significant Serbian population and guarantee the protection of the Serbian cultural heritage, some observers worried that it might in fact become "a state within the state" (something like Republika Srpska in Bosnia and Herzegovina), thus threatening the territorial integrity of Kosovo. The negotiations about the practical implementation of the agreement were extremely difficult and as a result, the Association/Community was only established in August 2015 (Kelmendi 2015). Its practical impact thus still remains to be seen but even the signing of the agreement

---

[6]The agreement on the principles of future relations and on the main issues to be tackled within the framework of Belgrade-Pristina negotiations was reached after the talks between the Prime Minister of Serbia Ivica Dacic and Prime Minister of Kosovo Hashim Thaci. For the original text of the agreement, see (RTS 2013).

[7]This disagreement was present from the beginning and is reflected already in the fact that in the English text of the agreement, both "Association" and "Community" are used in the name of the entity. "Association" reflects the point of view of Pristina, while "Community" is closer to the view taken by Belgrade.

was already met with strong criticism from the opposition in the Kosovo Assembly, while the Serbian politicians in Kosovo celebrated it as their victory.

The process of European integration could be, and has already been, an important factor in solving these outstanding issues between Belgrade and Pristina. Serbia is, of course, in a much later stage of the EU accession process than Kosovo. The EU has made it clear that the relationship with Kosovo must be resolved before Serbia is accepted—the negotiation framework adopted by the European Council in December 2013 states in article 12: "The Negotiating Framework also takes account of Serbia's continued engagement and steps towards a visible and sustainable improvement in relations with Kosovo. This process shall ensure that both can continue on their respective European paths, while avoiding that either can block the other in these efforts and should gradually lead to the comprehensive normalization of relations between Serbia and Kosovo, in the form of a legally binding agreement by the end of Serbia's accession negotiations, with the prospect of both being able to fully exercise their rights and fulfil their responsibilities" (European Council 2014, p. 5). While the document talks about a "legally binding agreement" and "comprehensive normalization of relations", it does not explicitly mention a mutual recognition, which is still unacceptable to Serbia. On several occasions in the past, the EU has denied that diplomatic recognition of Kosovo is a precondition for Serbia to be accepted into the EU.[8] At the same time, since Serbia is well ahead of Kosovo in its accession negotiations, there has been some anxiety on the part of Kosovar authorities that in the future, Serbia as a full member of the EU might block Kosovo's accession. It would be impossible for Kosovo to join the EU if all the member states did not recognize its independence. While the other "non-recognizers" might eventually change their stance (also under growing pressure from the EU), with Serbia this change would be difficult to come by and Belgrade would definitely use such a situation to put pressure on Brussels in other areas where it would feel it might gain something. The anxiety felt by Pristina was very well demonstrated by the words of the previous Kosovar Minister of Foreign Affair Enver Hoxhaj, who stated in 2013 that the EU should admit both Kosovo and Serbia at the same time to deny Belgrade the chance to veto Pristina's accession (Ministry of Foreign Affairs of Kosovo 2013). Given the current state of affairs, however, this is extremely unlikely to happen.

Moreover, it is reasonable to assume that even if Serbia did eventually change its position in the future, it would not have a decisive impact on Russia or China (despite the claims made by some Russian officials). Russia presents itself as the defender of Serbian interests and the Orthodox Church, but in fact it is more concerned about maintaining its position in the Balkans. Even the often publicly presented support for Serbia and cooperation in economic and military affairs is not as substantive as it might seem. Russia's refusal to recognize Kosovo stems from different reasons than concern for Serbia's territorial integrity and Moscow is unlikely to change its stance unless it receives something in return. For China,

---

[8]See, for example The Balkan Insight (2012).

Kosovo is not a major factor—it is geographically distant from the Balkans, has no interests in Kosovo and recognizing its independence would not bring it any particular gain or advantage.

3 Membership in International Organizations

The issue of international recognition is very closely inter-related with a full membership in a wide array of international organizations. Kosovo is well aware of this fact, and also of the fact that the more organizations it participates in,[9] the greater the chance that the number of states that have recognized it will increase even further.

3.1 The European Union

The state of European integration has already been touched upon in the previous part of the article. The problem here lies not so much in the fact that Kosovo is not universally recognized as a state, but, at least from the perspective of Brussels, in the lack of progress that Pristina has made in a number of areas. Already in October 2012, a feasibility study prepared on behalf of the European Commission found that there are no legal obstacles to sign the Stabilisation and Association Agreement (SAA) with Kosovo. The document specifically states: "From a legal point of view, the EU can conclude a Stabilisation and Association Agreement with Kosovo, as per Articles 217 and 218 TFEU. A Stabilisation and Association Agreement between Kosovo and the EU can be concluded in a way that it respects the positions of Member States on the status of Kosovo. On several occasions, the Council has confirmed the European perspective of the Western Balkans. Most recently, the Council confirmed this perspective for Kosovo in December 2011. Kosovo's European ambitions enjoy strong support from the general public in Kosovo (European Commission 2012, p. 12)." Yet, despite these rather optimistic words, the Stabilisation and Association Agreement with Kosovo was only signed on 27 October 2015,[10] 3 years after the study had been conducted, and entered into force on 1 April 2016. In a comprehensive progress report on Kosovo for 2015, the EU criticizes Kosovo for delaying key reforms, for increasing polarization of the political spectrum, for absence of a truly independent control mechanism and regulatory institutions and many other issues. It recognizes that some progress has been achieved, but at the same time it points out that overall, Kosovo is still at an

---

[9]In this respect we can mention Kosovo's membership in some influential sport organizations like FIFA or the International Olympic Committee.

[10]For the full text of the agreement, see European Commission (2015a).

early stage of alignment with European standards (European Commission 2015b, pp. 5–6). While the Kosovo government remains confident that the accession process is on the right track, the EU is becoming increasingly worried about the slow pace of reform. Lack of progress in the individual areas, rather than the opposition of non-recognizers or of Serbia, is at the moment the key issue that Pristina must tackle.

Two other international organizations which should be definitely mentioned here with regards to the Kosovar aspirations are the North Atlantic Treaty Organization (NATO) and the United Nations. Obtaining a full membership in these two bodies could be even more challenging than the EU accession process, although in each of the two cases for different reasons.

3.2 NATO

Kosovo, since the end of the 1999 war, has been hosting a NATO mission, the NATO Kosovo Force, on its territory, even though over the years the numerical size of KFOR and the scope of its activities have been greatly reduced.[11] The character of the mission has also been gradually changing. The initial mission statement is still based on the text of the UN Security Council Resolution 1244, which gives NATO in Kosovo the following key tasks:

- "Deterring renewed hostilities, maintaining and where necessary enforcing a ceasefire, and ensuring the withdrawal and preventing the return into Kosovo of Federal and Republic military, police and paramilitary forces, except as provided in point 6 of annex 2;
- Demilitarizing the Kosovo Liberation Army (KLA) and other armed Kosovo Albanian groups as required in paragraph 15 below;
- Establishing a secure environment in which refugees and displaced persons can return home in safety, the international civil presence can operate, a transitional administration can be established, and humanitarian aid can be delivered;
- Ensuring public safety and order until the international civil presence can take responsibility for this task;
- Supervising demining until the international civil presence can, as appropriate, take over responsibility for this task;
- Supporting, as appropriate, and coordinating closely with the work of the international civil presence;
- Conducting border monitoring duties as required;

---

[11]When KFOR was at its strongest, it had approx. 50,000 soldiers who were stationed in the camps all over the Kosovo territory. By 2016, the force numbers came down to fewer than 5000 troops from 31 troop-contributing nations, with many of the previously used camps and military facilities closed or turned over to Kosovo authorities. Further reductions are planned, based on the security situation in Kosovo. For the recent numbers and force posture of KFOR, see (NATO KFOR 2016).

- Ensuring the protection and freedom of movement of itself, the international civil presence, and other international organizations (United Nations Security Council 1999, p. 3)."

Just by looking at the tasks mentioned in the previous paragraph and at the current security situation, we can clearly observe that some of the mission objectives have largely been met (such as the disarmament of the Kosovo Liberation Army, which is no longer in existence) or have become rather outdated and highly unlikely to occur (such as the possible return of the Yugoslav, now Serbian, military and paramilitary forces to the area of operation). The number of inter-ethnic incidents involving violent clashes between the two main ethnic groups, Kosovo Albanians and Kosovo Serbs, has decreased[12] and the Kosovo Police, with the support of the European Union EULEX mission, is largely able to handle the situation without military intervention. In fact, out of the specially designed cultural heritage sites of the Serbian Orthodox Church in Kosovo that KFOR used to guard in the past, only the monastery in Visoki Decani still has any permanent KFOR presence.

In this context, it is possible to ask several questions. The first one would logically be what the main role of NATO and KFOR in Kosovo is now and whether the mission should not be gradually terminated. In this regard, it needs to be pointed out that in addition to KFOR, NATO also has the NATO Advisory Team (NAT) and NATO Liaison and Advisory Team (NLAT) in Kosovo. Their core task, unlike KFOR, is to liaise, assist and support the Kosovo Security Force (KSF) and the Ministry for Kosovo Security Force (MKSF). And, once more, here we come to the issue of recognition and full state sovereignty.

The Kosovo Albanian politicians have on a number of occasions expressed their aspiration for Kosovo to join NATO as a full member. Yet, there are several obstacles to this end. First, Kosovo at the moment does not have a regular army in the proper sense of the word. The KSF, mentioned above, is more a paramilitary force of a limited size and with only certain capabilities. The makers of the Kosovo constitution, under pressure from the international community, deliberately avoided the term "armed forces", as the creation of Kosovo Army would be opposed not only by Serbia, but likely also by certain NATO member states, especially those that do not recognize Kosovo. In addition, the Law on the Kosovo Security Force, which the constitution directly refers to, gives the KSF only limited responsibilities: "(a) to participate in crisis response operations, including peace support operations. This will include operations outside the territory of the Republic of Kosovo where invited to do so; (b) to assist civil authorities in responding to natural and other

---

[12]According to the OSCE Office in Pristina, in the reporting period from 1 July 2014 to 30 June 2015, there were in total 479 incidents which were likely motivated by inter-ethnic issues and which had potential implications for the security perception of their victims. Out of these 479 incidents, most (310) affected the Kosovo Serbs, often those who came as religious pilgrims to visit the Serb Orthodox Church sites or those who have returned to Kosovo as a part of the repatriation program. See OSCE Mission in Kosovo (2015, p. 9).

disasters and emergencies, including as part of a regional or international response effort; (c) to conduct explosive ordnance disposal; (d) to assist civil authorities through civil protection operations (Kosovo Assembly 2008, p. 5)." In practice, this means that the KSF's main tasks are primarily in the area of civil defence, such as assisting the population during natural disasters or with explosive ordnance disposal (EOD). It does not possess heavy military equipment or air force of its own and for most of its existence has been limited to 5000 active service members and approx. 2000 reservists.

The deliberate limitation of the national sovereignty of Kosovo in the area of national defence, which is one of the key areas where any state demonstrates its full sovereignty and authority, has never been fully accepted by the Kosovo Albanian politicians. What makes the situation even more humiliating from Pristina's point of view is the fact that the KSF is at the moment not allowed to operate in the four northern municipalities of Kosovo (Mitrovica North, Leposavic, Zubin Potok and Zvecan) populated almost exclusively by the Serbian minority. Under the current arrangement, the tasks assigned to KSF in the rest of Kosovo are carried out by KFOR north of the Ibar River. This is an extremely sensitive issue for both Belgrade and Pristina and also for the international community. There have been attempts to change the attitude of the Serbian population in the north towards KSF, but so far not much progress has been achieved.[13]

The Pristina authorities are thus caught in a difficult situation. Their NATO membership aspirations would be likely strengthened if the KSF was transformed into a regular armed force. At the same time, such a change would require a change of the constitutional law on KSF, which, based on the Kosovo political system, would require the support of Serbian members of the Assembly. There were already several attempts in the past to reach a compromise with the Serbian politicians, offering them concessions in other areas, but so far these attempts have not been successful. In addition, Pristina at the moment does not have sufficient funds to cover the expenses associated with expanding the KSF in terms of personnel and equipment, as it already now heavily relies on foreign support (countries such as the US, the UK and Turkey are bilaterally supporting the KSF in the areas, such as training and mentoring).

In conclusion, as some of the Kosovo security experts also state, the NATO membership is likely to be a long process, involving the necessary reforms of KSF, launching of a formal dialogue with NATO, the need to convince the

---

[13]Every small step in the "right direction" is presented in the media as a sign of progress. For example, in 2014, the Serbian mayor of Zubin Potok specifically requested the KSF divers to come to the assistance of the local police after a boat had capsized on one of the lakes in the municipality. While this event was showcased by the media in Pristina and by NATO, it did not really mean any significant breakthrough. See for example KFOR (2014, pp. 4–5).

"non-recognizers" to recognize Kosovo (which is the same problem as in case of the EU accession), training of the KSF according to NATO standards and procedures, and securing the necessary funds for the medium to long-term period.[14]

3.3 The United Nations

Finally, the issue of the full membership of the United Nations will be addressed. In this forum, unlike in the EU or NATO, Russia as the staunchest supporter of Serbia is directly present and, as a member of the Security Council, is likely to block any attempts directed at the full membership of Kosovo.

The Pristina authorities are quite aware of this problem. On the other hand, the UN membership is to a degree even more important with regards to international recognition than the membership in NATO or the EU. As David I. Efevwerhan correctly points out in his article on this topic, "...Although the UN does not recognize States, admission of an entity into its membership signifies that that entity has been accepted as a State by all its members... there is no known independent sovereign State today that is not a member of the UN (Efevwerhan 2012, pp. 95–96)." In other words, according to the interpretation of some experts on international law, unless and until Kosovo has been accepted into the UN, it cannot be considered a fully sovereign, independent state.

Yet, due to the opposition of Russia (and to a degree, also China), the chances of an outright approval of Kosovo's membership if it submits an application are extremely limited. As mentioned above, Kosovo has already received 108 recognitions from the UN member states, and on several occasions in the past various UN representatives have expressed their support for Kosovo's eventual acceptance into the organization.[15] This, however, would not in itself be enough to change the current situation. In response to this, Kosovo has adopted what could be called an incremental approach, trying to attain membership in various organizations under the umbrella of the UN or somewhat related to it, as well as institutions which provide financial support, loans and grants, where the opposition is likely to be less determined. To a degree, this approach has been successful so far. For example, already in 2009, Kosovo joined the International Monetary Fund and the World Bank after applying for membership in 2008.[16] In December 2012, Kosovo joined

---

[14]See for example a very informative and well-structured paper on the Kosovo's NATO future (Avdiu 2015).

[15]See for example Office of the President of the Republic of Kosovo (2012).

[16]In this regard, however, it has been suggested that Serbia deliberately allowed Kosovo to join the World Bank without much of a protest because it would mean that Kosovo would take on itself the obligation to pay a part of the Yugoslav debt, which amounted in case of Pristina to USD 231 million. See Kasapolli (2009).

the European Bank for Reconstruction and Development (EBRD).[17] In June 2014 Kosovo was officially accepted into the Venice Commission.

However, there are also serious setbacks associated with the incremental approach. For example, in 2015 Kosovo attempted to become a full member of UNESCO. This attempt has been strongly criticized by Serbia from the very beginning, accusing Pristina of not doing enough to protect the Serbian cultural heritage in Kosovo. Both sides had lobbied heavily for their cause in the months and weeks leading to the decisive vote. While Pristina initially achieved victory when the UNESCO Executive Board voted in October 2015 in favour of Kosovo's bid, the ultimate vote by the member states held in November 2015 failed to pass the necessary majority threshold of 95 votes.[18] In the reaction to the vote, the Serbian nationalist president Tomislav Nikolic hailed the result as a "justified and moral victory in almost impossible conditions" and again stated that Serbia "will not give up southern province (Collaku 2015)".

The failure of the Kosovo's UNESCO bid, despite being a close one, could well forebode how the proceedings would go with the full UN membership. It is very likely that a similar, but even stronger, anti-Kosovo campaign would be launched by Serbia, Russia and possibly also other non-recognizers. If this is the case, what are the options for Pristina to join the UN?

As mentioned above, even the ongoing Brussels Dialogue between Serbia and Kosovo will not necessarily lead to a full mutual recognition, but rather just to a comprehensive normalization of relations. Thus, even the accession of Belgrade into the EU would not in itself solve the problem. In addition, Russia's stance is not conditioned just by its support for Serbia, but, and perhaps primarily, by its own interests and concerns. Any solution within the UN Security Council would thus have to be a compromise between the West and Russia, which would definitely involve mutual concessions. At the current moment, when the relationship between Moscow and the western states is extremely strained, this is not likely to happen, given also the fact that the Kosovo question no longer attracts so much attention in the international affairs and would probably not generate enough interest on either side to be discussed and eventually resolved just by itself. It would be perhaps more feasible to include it in a more comprehensive negotiation package with Russia, where it would be "just" one of the contentious issues for discussion. In any case, the Kosovo UN membership is still a long-distance goal for Pristina, despite its symbolic significance, and this will not change anytime soon.

---

[17]This opened the door for the investments of the EBRD in Kosovo. By May 2016, the Bank invested EUR 180 million in cumulative EBRD investments and EUR 82 million in cumulative disbursements. There are 46 ongoing EBRD projects in Kosovo (EBRD 2016).

[18]It is, however, necessary to keep in mind that the final tally was indeed a very close one. The Kosovo bid attracted 92 votes (thus just three votes short of the threshold), with 50 states voting against and 29 abstaining (Collaku 2015).

4 National Identity and Identification with State and Symbols

In the final part of this paper, the focus will be placed on the Kosovo statehood, national identity and the challenges associated with these concepts. Identification of the population with the state entity, at least to a degree, can also be seen as one of the signs of a sovereign state and of its long-term viability.

In the moment when Kosovo declared independence in 2008, most of its inhabitants, including the top political leaders, would agree that there was no such thing as a "Kosovo national identity". The society was deeply divided among ethnic lines, with Kosovo Albanians and Kosovo Serbs being the two dominant ethnic groups. Even Hashim Thaci, who emerged as one of the leaders of the new country following the Kosovo War, bluntly stated in December 2007: "A Kosovo identity does not exist (Bilefsky 2007)". Albin Kurti, in 2007 a young political activist and Albanian nationalist living in Pristina, who later became the head of the radical Vetevendosje! (Self-Determination) party, argued that the fact that many Kosovars had accepted the Albanian identity during the war was more than anything else an act of defiance against the Milosevic regime (Bilefsky 2007). The political representation of the new entity realized, however, that such a situation is not tenable for the future and that an attempt must be made to endow the Kosovars with an identity of their own.

In his article on this topic, Bujar Aruqaj describes the process of creating the Kosovo identity. At a certain point, he describes Kosovo as an "imagined community" with an "invented identity (Aruqaj 2013, p. 13)". It is true that the state symbols—the Kosovo flag, seal and anthem—do not have a connection with the history of Kosovo. The flag and seal were designed with the purpose to give the population a sense of unity and of belonging to one place shared by various ethnic groups.[19] On the other hand, the anthem of Kosovo–Europa—has been chosen not only to demonstrate the Euro-Atlantic orientation of the new state but also because, as Aruqaj points out, it does not have lyrics and is thus more easily acceptable for all the ethnic groups speaking their own languages (Aruqaj 2013, p. 16).

More than 8 years after the independence was declared, it is perhaps not too early to offer at least a preliminary evaluation of whether the new identity has been taking root with the Kosovo population. The author of this study had the opportunity to spend 1 year in Kosovo and was, therefore, able to make at least limited first-hand observations. While the Kosovar flag and seal can be seen in Pristina and in other places, they are usually only on official buildings, such as ministries and other governmental offices, seats of municipalities, police stations and such. On the other hand, the people themselves often prefer to place the flags associated with their ethnic identity on their homes. Albanian flags in the south (except for the Serb

---

[19]The individual ethnicities are each represented by a star. Thus, there are six stars for each of the official recognized nationalities—Albanians, Serbs, Turks, Roma, Bosnjaks and Gorans.

enclaves) and Serb flags north of Ibar are omnipresent. At a first glance, there is little sentiment of Kosovar nationalism—it is not absolutely non-existent, but it is definitely weaker than the identification with one's own primary ethnicity. Jano Dorian in his article about Kosovo correctly talks about multi-layered identity, where the first-order identity is ethnicity-based (i.e. Albanian, Serbian, Bosnjak, etc.), the second-order identity is Kosovar (related to the place of residence or, in some cases, of origin) and the third-order identity is European (Kosovo as part of the wide European community of nations) (Dorian 2013, p. 37).

It could perhaps be argued that given the historical enmity between the various ethnicities and especially given the fact that the war, during which both sides of the conflict committed numerous atrocities, only ended in 1999, it is too early to expect that such an identity would form already. This is indeed true and such a process would likely take years in other countries as well. On the other hand, there are certain prerequisites which need to exist for the process of planting and growing a new identity to be successful.

One of the key factors in forging a new national identity in the Kosovo context is to promote inter-cultural and inter-ethnicity dialogue between the ethnic groups, mainly the Kosovo Albanians and Kosovo Serbs. While there are some attempts exactly in this direction, so far they have not been as successful as they could have been. The OSCE Mission in Kosovo, which monitors, among other things, the state of intercultural dialogue and the rights of communities, states in its report for 2014–2015: "At the central level, the main achievement to date is the establishment of the Working Group on Dealing with the Past and Reconciliation, chaired by the Office of the Prime Minister and with membership from a range of ministries and civil society organizations. Although formally established by the government in June 2012, the working group has failed to meet regularly and made minimal progress in developing a Strategy on Transitional Justice, as well as struggling with very limited communities' representation (Kosovo Serb participation has generally been limited to one participant). As of 30 June 2015, the Working Group had failed to agree on the timeframe the Strategy would cover despite the substantial support and encouragement provided by a United Nations Development Programme (UNDP) project tailored to support the working group (OSCE Mission in Kosovo 2015, p. 6)." On the community level, there are also very few efforts at bringing the various ethnicities together and the media remain polarized along ethnic lines. Another problem, which can have major implications for the future, is the fact that the educational system remains essentially separated, with young Serbs not being taught Albanian and vice versa. This could in the future drive the two communities even further apart.

Another important aspect of forging a national identity is the identification with the state institutions and the level of confidence that the public places in them. In this regard, situation is getting worse in Kosovo year by year. In September 2015, for example, only 17.3% of the population trusted the government. The level of trust in other state institutions and representatives was also very low—prime minister 14.6%, Assembly 19.9%, speaker of the Assembly 19.8%, courts 13.9%, prosecutors 12.8%. The only slightly better value of public trust was for the president—30.4%. Yet, even in the case of the presidential office, the public trust has slumped by more than 20% in comparison to 2007 (UNDP Office Kosovo 2015, p. 3). In general, the public is more inclined to trust the KSF and the Kosovo Police—69% for KSF and 56% for the police respectively. It is telling, however, that 17 years after the end of the Kosovo War, KFOR with 65% is the second most trusted institution in Kosovo (Kosovo Centre for Security Studies/National Endowment for Democracy 2015, p. 10).

The trends described above are not only worrying because they show the extremely low level of trust of the population in its own state. They are also worrying because the negative perception of the performance of Kosovo institutions is, along with the unsatisfactory economic situation and lack of opportunities, among the key push factors for migration. In January and February 2015 alone, it is estimated that 50,000 people left Kosovo and applied for asylum in the EU (Alexander 2015). While the EU policy is to grant no more asylums to the citizens of Kosovo (as well as other countries in the Western Balkans), the exodus from Kosovo, along with the fact that its territory also functions as transit area for refugees and asylum seekers from other countries and that the government is unable to stem the illegal migration, are a major hurdle on the way towards the EU visa liberalization that Kosovo has been seeking for a number of years.

The polarized political scene, corrupt and inefficient public institutions, weak sense of national identity and related phenomena lead not only to migration from Kosovo, but also to radicalization of certain segments of society. While there are still some that tend to become more nationalistic, the far greater danger at the moment are the activities of Islamist networks and organizations. Kosovo is one of the countries from which the highest number of foreign fighters who joined the Islamic State in Syria and Iraq originate. It is estimated that there are 100–150 foreign fighters from Kosovo, i.e. approximately 83 fighters per 1 million of Kosovar citizens (RFE/RL 2016). In addition to the security concerns that this issue raises not only in Kosovo, but also in Europe in general, it is another welcome argument for non-recognizers who use it to point out that Kosovo is not able to effectively function as a state and to carry out its sovereignty and basic tasks of a state on its territory.

5 Conclusion

Kosovo's emergence on the political map of Europe as a self-proclaimed independent state has aroused a lot of controversy from the very beginning. It has been used as a negative precedent by its opponents, portrayed as a breach of international law (despite the opinion of the International Court of Justice), and has been denied full recognition by the international community ever since.

While there has been some progress achieved in a number of areas, there is still a lot of work to be done. The optimism which in general accompanied the declaration of independence in 2008 (at least among the Kosovo Albanian population) has proved to be largely unjustified. Seventeen years after the end of the war and 8 years after the declaration of independence, Kosovo is still far from becoming a member of the UN, the EU or NATO. The political scene is polarized and thus paralyzed; the divides between the various ethnic groups have not only persisted, but in some cases have even become more rigid; the national identity is still hazy and has not taken deeper roots.

The issue of international recognition and of the domestic functioning of a state is, according to the opinion of the author, deeply intermingled and intertwined. While Pristina cannot influence by itself the stance of such countries as Russia and China, which is primarily determined by their own concerns and interests, it can try to improve the overall political climate in Kosovo and to address the main problems and grievances in a more effective fashion. If the central and local institutions as well as the society were strengthened, it could well be that Kosovo could eventually grow into a state rather than being "just" recognized as one.

References

Alexander, H. (2015, February 21). Exodus from Kosovo: Why thousands have left the Balkans. *The Telegraph.* http://www.telegraph.co.uk/news/worldnews/europe/kosovo/11426805/Exodus-from-Kosovo-Why-thousands-have-left-the-Balkans.html. Accessed November 15, 2016.

Aruqaj, B. (2013, Fall). Construction of nationalism in the Republic of Kosovo. *The politics of deeply divided societies.* https://www.academia.edu/7418143/Construction_of_National_Identity_in_the_Republic_of_Kosovo. Accessed May 10, 2016.

Avdiu, P. (2015, May). *Destination NATO: Kosovo's alternatives toward NATO membership.* Kosovo Center for Security Studies Policy Paper 05/2015. http://www.qkss.org/repository/docs/Destination_NATO_Kosovos_Alternatives_towards_NATO_Membership_556716.pdf. Accessed May 10, 2016.

Bilefsky, D. (2007, December 9). A difficult question for Kosovars: Who are we? *The New York Times.* http://www.nytimes.com/2007/12/09/world/europe/09iht-kosovo.4.8660025.html?pagewanted=all&_r=0. Accessed June 1, 2016.

Collaku, P. (2015, November 9). Kosovo's UNESCO membership bid fails. *Balkan Insight.* http://www.balkaninsight.com/en/article/kosovo-unesco-membership-vote-11-09-2015. Accessed November 29, 2015.

Dorian, J. (2013). Kosovar multi-layer identity: What is the same, different and in common with Albanian identity. *Journal of European and International Affairs, 1*(1), 27–40.

EBRD. (2016, May 1). *Kosovo data.* http://www.ebrd.com/kosovo-data.html. Accessed May 28, 2016.

Efevwerhan, D. I. (2012). Kosovo's chances of UN membership: A prognosis. *Goettingen Journal of International Law, 4*(1), 93–130.

European Commission. (2012, October 10). *Communication from the commission to the European Parliament and Council on a feasibility study for a stabilisation and association agreement between the European Union and Kosovo.* http://ec.europa.eu/enlargement/pdf/key_documents/2012/package/ks_feasibility_2012_en.pdf. Accessed February 15, 2016.

European Commission. (2015a, October 27). *Stabilisation and association agreement between the European Union and the European Atomic Energy Community of the one part, and Kosovo*, of the other part.* http://ec.europa.eu/enlargement/news_corner/news/news-files/20150430_saa.pdf. Accessed December 17, 2015.

European Commission. (2015b, November 10). *Commission staff working document: Kosovo* 2015 progress report*. http://ec.europa.eu/enlargement/pdf/key_documents/2015/20151110_ report_kosovo.pdf. Accessed April 14, 2016.

European Council. (2014, January 21). Accession document. *Subject: General EU position ministerial meeting opening the intergovernmental conference on the accession of Serbia to the European Union*, Brussels. http://register.consilium.europa.eu/doc/srv?l=EN&t=PDF&gc= true&sc=false&f=AD%201%202014%20INIT. Accessed February 16, 2016.

European Parliament. (2015, March 2). *B8-0214/2015*. http://www.europarl.europa.eu/sides/ getDoc.do?type=MOTION&reference=B8-2015-0214&language=EN. Accessed December 10, 2015.

International Court of Justice. (2010, July 22). *Accordance with the international law of the unilateral declaration of independence in respect of Kosovo*. http://www.webcitation.org/ 5rRB9e3bz. Accessed January 10, 2016.

Kasapolli, V. (2009, July 20). Kosovo's costly World Bank membership. *Osservatorio balcani e caucaso*. http://www.balcanicaucaso.org/eng/Areas/Kosovo/Kosovo-s-costly-World-Bank-membership-46297. Accessed February 16, 2016.

Keating, J. (2008, February 26). How to start your own country in four easy steps. *Foreign Policy*. http://foreignpolicy.com/2008/02/26/how-to-start-your-own-country-in-four-easy-steps/. Accessed January 10, 2016.

Kelmendi, V. H. (2015, September 2). Kosovo: The Association of Serb municipalities. *Osservatorio balcani e caucaso*. http://www.balcanicaucaso.org/eng/Regions-and-countries/ Kosovo/Kosovo-the-Association-of-Serb-Municipalities-163867. Accessed February 3, 2016.

KFOR. (2014, July). *KFOR chronicle*. https://www.google.cz/url?sa=t&rct=j&q=&esrc= s&source=web&cd=1&ved=0ahUKEwj4h8rP8IjNAhUEahoKHUVGATUQFggeMAA&url= https%3A%2F%2Fjfcnaples.nato.int%2Fsystems%2Ffile_download.ashx%3Fpg%3D3266% 26ver%3D1&usg=AFQjCNEkcT-v1h5w4RYRG14ZH34yDxcC_g&bvm=bv.123664746,d. d2s. Accessed November 17, 2015.

Kosovo Assembly. (2008, March 13). *Law no. 03/L-046 Law on the Kosovo security force*. http:// www.mksf-ks.org/repository/docs/Law%20on%20the%20KSF.pdf. Accessed February 10, 2016.

Kosovo Centre for Security Studies/National Endowment for Democracy. (2015, December). *Kosovo security barometer*. http://www.qkss.org/repository/docs/Kosovo_Security_ Barometer_-_Fifth_Edition_523670.pdf. Accessed June 1, 2016.

Ministry of Foreign Affairs of Kosovo. (2013, November 20). *Hoxhaj: 2013, vit i suksesshëm i politikës së jashtme*. http://www.mfa-ks.net/?page=1,4,1958&offset=5. Accessed February 10, 2016.

NATO KFOR. (2016, May). *Kosovo force: Key facts and figures*. http://www.nato.int/nato_static_ fl2014/assets/pdf/pdf_2016_05/20160511_2016-05-KFOR-Placemat.pdf. Accessed June 1, 2016.

Office of the President of the Republic of Kosovo. (2012, January 17). *President Atifete Jahjaga met with the chairman of the UN General Assembly, Nassir Abdulaziz Al Nasser*. http://www. president-ksgov.net/?page=2,6,2139#.V0_5wcsVi70. Accessed March 11, 2016.

OSCE Mission in Kosovo. (2015, November). *Community rights assessment report* (4th ed.). http://www.osce.org/kosovo/209956?download=true. Accessed May 5, 2016.

RFE/RL. (2016, June 2). *Foreign fighters in Iraq and Syria: Where do they come from?* Radio Free Europe/Radio Liberty. http://www.rferl.org/contentinfographics/foreign-fighters-syria-iraq-is-isis-isil-infographic/26584940.html. Accessed June 2, 2016.

RTS. (2013, April 19). *First agreement of principles governing normalization of relations*. http:// www.rts.rs/upload/storyBoxFileData/2013/04/20/3224318/Originalni%20tekst%20Predloga% 20sporazuma.pdf. Accessed January 28, 2016.

The Balkan Insight. (2012, September 5). *EU: Serbia does not have to recognize Kosovo*. http:// www.balkaninsight.com/en/article/eu-does-not-request-serbia-to-recognize-kosovo. Accessed February 15, 2016.

The Balkan Insight. (2015, October 24). *Kosovo parliament hit by more tear gas, protests*. http://www.balkaninsight.com/en/article/kosovo-parliament-hit-by-more-teargas-protests-10-24-2015. Accessed December 15, 2015.

UNDP Office Kosovo. (2015, October). *Public pulse X*. http://www.ks.undp.org/content/dam/kosovo/docs/PublicPulse/pp10/ENG%20version%20Public%20Pulse%20X.pdf?download. Accessed June 1, 2016.

United Nations Security Council. (1999, June 10). *United Nations Security Council resolution 1244: S/RES/1244/1999*. https://documents-dds-ny.un.org/doc/UNDOC/GEN/N99/172/89/PDF/N9917289.pdf?OpenElement. Accessed February 12, 2016.

Author Biography

Jan Bečka, Ph.D. is a part-time assistant professor at the Institute of International Studies, Faculty of Social Sciences, Charles University. He works at the Defence Policy and Strategy Division, Ministry of Defence of the Czech Republic. His main research interests include the US foreign and security policy, US relations with the countries of the Middle East, East Asia, South Asia and Southeast Asia (since 1945 and in the current perspective) and the mutual cultural perceptions and their impact on foreign relations.

Conclusion: Future of International Recognition?

Martin Riegl and Bohumil Doboš

Secession, recognition and presence of entities irregular within the framework of the Westphalian international order is an issue likely to influence the international politics for the years to come. These issues are relevant for all levels of international politics' analysis irrespective of the scale or of the theoretical and methodological approach. Regardless whether we perceive the unrecognized entities as deviations within the system and secession only as a way to establish new state entities, or whether we understand the changes in the post-Cold War international relations as systemic, secession and (non-)recognition remain key research objectives.

De facto states can be found all around the globe from the Western Sahara to Taiwan, from Abkhazia to Somaliland and from Kosovo to Palestine. The effort to comprehend these entities is a crucial step to engage them and to increase the possibility to resolve the conflicts, which are in fact the underlying reason for their existence. As pointed out by Nina Caspersen in the first chapter, the level of understanding of the de facto states is increasing but has yet to reach maturity. We still need to understand reasons for their appearance and more-or-less effective existence. While Urban Jakša and Mikulas Fabry pointed out the fact that we cannot understand secession and de facto existence without understanding the context of identity, other factors clearly present themselves as well. One of the important and often overlooked issues is the problem of referendum question wording. Any effort to follow the will of the people may be hampered simply by manipulating the final question presented to the voters at the ballot box. Přemysl Rosůlek emphasized this issue and presented several advices for the future referenda. If the ultimate goal of the international community is democratization of the global polity, the implementation of these recommendations is necessary in order to give the people a clear choice.

M. Riegl · B. Doboš (✉)
Faculty of Social Sciences, Institute of Political Studies,
Charles University, Prague, Czech Republic
e-mail: bohumil.dobos@gmail.com

Analysis of secession must also take into account geopolitical interests of great powers and the local political and economic context. It is not only important to understand the role of great powers as pointed out by the book editors in general, or as shown on the particular case of Kurdistan. If the entity is not in the sphere of interest of the great powers, regional actors hold their stakes and reflect them in the policies influencing the secession and recognition outcome as is the case of Somaliland or Bougainville as explained by Kateřina Rudincová and Vladimír Baar. All these cases illustrate the important exogenous factors influencing the outcomes of secession (recognition) processes.

Moreover, it is crucial to understand the internal functioning of these entities which, as pointed out by Vincenc Kopeček, is more complex than a simple black box, thinking that appeared in some of the previously published literature. De facto states may indeed establish their own complex political institutions mirroring their internal and external context. The importance of this context was also presented by Jan Bečka on case of Kosovo or by Robert Czulda on case of Iranian separatist entities.

Taken together, the articles presented in this book emphasize and focus on the major dynamics that need to be further unravelled in order to get a better grasp of the entire issue in question. The volume broadly identified three major research fields that can be subsequently divided into more clearly defined research papers and that stand at the beginning of the research of the de facto states and secession. These three broad categories of questions include regional dynamics; international context; and issues related to identity and self-determination. No matter whether research focuses on macro- or micro-level, takes into consideration more theoretical or empirical approach, or attempts to explain concrete cases or make wider generalizations, the scope and volume of research to be done is still wide indeed. This book intends to fill some of the existing gaps and to open new topics for discussion.

It is clear that the number of issues and cases related to the research of secession and de facto states are enormous and this volume does in no way pretend to cover them all. Nevertheless, the views and the research presented in the previous chapters should be a stimulating and inspirational reading for researchers and practitioners alike. The questions raised throughout the book are far from being solved, yet every attempt to move the understanding of secession and de facto statehood forward enhances our ability to engage them and to provide a proper advice on the appropriate reaction.

Author Biographies

Martin Riegl was born in 1980. He currently lectures at the Institute of Political Studies of Faculty of Social Sciences, Charles University. He graduated in 2010 at Faculty of Social Sciences, Charles University (program Political Science), where successfully finished doctoral studies in the field of Political Geography. Since 2008, he has been lecturing at the Department of Political Science (FSS, UK). His academic research is focused on the institution of the sovereign state, geopolitics of political disintegration, secession, unrecognized states and state failure. Actively participated at scientific conferences and workshops in the Czech Republic, Slovakia, Germany, Belgium, Poland, UK, Taiwan etc.

Bohumil Doboš is a PhD student at the Institute of Political Studies, Faculty of Social Sciences, Charles University. His research interest lies in areas of post-Westphalian geopolitics, New Middle Age theory, geopolitical anomalies, geopolitics of violent non-state actors and astropolitics. He is also a Coordinator of the Geopolitical Studies Research Centre at the same institute and Employee at the Ministry of Defence of the Czech republic—Defence Policy and Strategy Division.

Lightning Source UK Ltd.
Milton Keynes UK
UKHW02n1622061217
313992UK00003B/131/P